To: Doug Miller

All the best in your
efforts to take
venture philanthropy
to the next level
and info Asia

Wallidy

8 October 2008

Doing Good Well

What does (and does not) make sense
in the nonprofit world

Doing Good Well

What does (and does not) make sense
in the nonprofit world

Willie Cheng

JOSSEY-BASS™
An Imprint of
WILEY

Jossey-Bass

This edition is published in 2009 by John Wiley & Sons (Asia) Pte. Ltd., 2 Clementi Loop, #02-01, Singapore 129809 on behalf of Jossey-Bass, A Wiley Imprint.
989 Market Street, San Francisco, CA 94103-1741–www.josseybass.com

Jossey-Bass books and products are available through most bookstores. To contact Jossey-Bass directly call our Customer Care Department within the U.S. at 800-956-7739, outside the U.S. at 317-572-3986, or fax 317-572-4002.

Jossey-Bass also publishes its books in a variety of electronic formats. Some content that appears in print may not be available in electronic books.

Library of Congress Cataloging-in-Publication Data

ISBN: 978-0-470-82389-7

Typeset in 10/13 point, Palatino Light by Superskill Graphics Pte. Ltd.
Printed in Singapore by Saik Wah Press Pte. Ltd.
10 9 8 7 6 5 4 3 2 1

To Julie

Contents

Acknowledgments

This book took many years in the making, and I had much help getting here.

To a large extent, it began in 2002 with my stint at the National Volunteer & Philanthropy Center (NVPC) in Singapore. I owe much to Lim Soo Hoon for inviting me to chair it, and its then CEO Tan Chee Koon and her team for Nonprofit 101 and the research and support for my articles in NVPC's *SALT* magazine.

We had started *SALT* in January 2004 to fill a gap in the Singapore nonprofit scene. I contributed my first article on the nonprofit "marketplace" in the second issue and over the next two years, wrote the occasional piece. When I left NVPC at the end of 2005, Chee Koon asked me to write a regular column for *SALT* which led to much of the material in this book.

I do want to thank the various editors of *SALT*—Monica Gwee, Suzanne Lim and Daven Wu—who have had to put up with my first drafts which were not always pretty. Thanks also go to Edmund Wee of Epigram and his team (Cynthia Tay and Lee Boon Kian) who produce *SALT* and whose illustrations and design layouts make the articles and magazine so inviting to read. Along the way, several of my articles have also been published in *The Straits Times*, and for this, Andy Ho has done his share to reshape my work.

It was in mid-2006 that Lee Poh Wah of the Lien Foundation suggested that I compile the articles I had written into a book. I had first met Poh Wah in 2003 when he was working at the Ministry for Community Development, Youth and Sports. He and Gerard Ee, a Governor at the Lien Foundation had been a great sounding board for many of the ideas shared in this book and they got me involved with the Lien Center for Social Innovation.

Getting a book published has not been as easy as I had initially envisaged. I would like to thank CJ Hwu, Janis Soo and Joel Balbin of John Wiley & Sons for taking me on and putting up with my many questions on contract terms, writing styles and layouts. My gratitude also to Vivienne Lim for helping me navigate through the book contract.

As the deadline for the book approached (thank you CJ for extending the deadline before we signed the final contract), I got desperate. I had forgotten a fundamental tenet of project management from my consulting days: the last 10 percent of a project takes more than 10 percent of the effort. Along came an angel by the name of Cheryl Tang. A manager with Accenture, she came to catch up with me as she was on leave for three months. She ended up spending much of that time helping me review, critique, research and edit the manuscript.

I spent my working life in Accenture. My consulting experience provided the foundation for the critical thinking and the framing of problems and solutions that have helped in writing this book. More significantly, many of us retired partners continue to feel part of the Accenture family. Several of my former colleagues have been catalysts for some of the "heretical" ideas on the nonprofit sector (some of them are mentioned in the book). I am particularly grateful to Bill Green, Chairman and CEO of Accenture who always inspires everyone, especially when he talks about charity work being "Accenture on its best day," for agreeing to provide the foreword, and to Jayme Silverstone for coordinating the Accenture support.

It now remains for me to thank three other groups of people who have been involved with the minutiae of writing any book: the researchers, the reviewers and the designers.

Many people have helped me with the much-needed research over the years. The team from NVPC includes Kevin Lee, Lui Siut Cheng, Halimah Chew, Terence Leong and Tan Tze Hoong. At the Lien Center, I thank Gabriel Lim and Sharifah Maisharah Binte Mohamed. I am especially grateful to Tze Hoong and Gabriel who continued to provide research support even after they had both left their respective jobs.

In the course of producing the *SALT* articles and the chapters of this book, I passed specific drafts to various people to preview: my thanks to all even though I have not named each of you. In addition, Robert Chew, Joyce Koh, Jerry Ow, Pang Siu Yuin, Gerard Tan and Wong Heng Chew gave this whole book a once-over and their comments. I would also like to thank Gerard Ee, Bill Drayton, Fang Ai Liang, Paulette Maehara, Maximilian Martin and Tan Chee Koon for their reviews and their endorsements.

For the cover design, Kuek Sue Anne, Leslie Lung, Henry Sim and Alicia Tan have done much to provide their creative input. To view the several alternate covers that they came up with, check out www.doinggoodwell.net. I also want to thank Kok Tien Nee and her team for putting up the book website.

Much of the content of this book has been made possible because of the experience and knowledge obtained from the many organizations—commercial, governmental and nonprofit—that I have been involved with. Several of them are mentioned in this book. I would like to acknowledge them specifically here as well as to provide proper disclosure of my relationship with them:

Member of governing body (board of directors or equivalent):
– Accenture
– Accounting Regulatory Authority of Singapore
– Archdiocesan Crisis Coordination Team*
– Council for the Governance of IPCs
– Lien Center for Social Innovation*
– National Volunteer & Philanthropy Center
– NTUC Fairprice* and NTUC Fairprice Foundation*
– Singapore Press Holdings*
– Social Enterprise Fund

Other involvement
– Ashoka Support Network (member)*
– World Toilet Organization (advisor)*

*Current involvement at the time of publication of this book

Of course, the opinions expressed in this book are personal and do not necessarily represent the views of any of these organizations, unless such views are specifically attributed to them.

Foreword

by William D. Green

It came as no surprise to me that Willie Cheng would write a book about shaping the charity sector for the better.

I have known Willie for many years, and have always admired his integrity, strong work ethic, commitment to the people around him—and above all, his commitment to "doing good."

So much has changed in the world of charitable giving and corporate citizenship since the days when Willie and I worked together at what was then known as Andersen Consulting—now Accenture. As partners of the firm at that time, we were expected to contribute to charities, or the firm would deduct money from our pay and donate on our behalf. Despite how that may sound, the intention was well-founded: To instill the value of personal stewardship in making a lasting, positive contribution to the communities around us.

Willie embodies the power of stewardship and giving back. After immersing himself in charity work upon retiring from Accenture, Willie recognized the need for an innovative and thoughtful approach to the dynamics of nonprofit organizations. He set out to combine his understanding of business paradigms from his 26 years as a management consultant with his experience working with many charitable organizations.

The result is a strategic, conceptual and highly readable book, in which he presents a new paradigm for improving the effectiveness and overall performance of nonprofits.

As a business leader, I found Willie's observations timely and relevant, especially as we see businesses and nonprofits collaborating more frequently. With this book, Willie gives both business and nonprofit executives a fresh perspective. He addresses a number of important issues and shares unique insights about topics ranging from the current status of businesses and nonprofits, accountability and governance in the nonprofit sector, the dynamics of giving to how social entrepreneurs and business entrepreneurs can, and must, co-exist to bring about large-scale social change.

One chapter that caught my attention as a CEO is the one on the role of business. At Accenture, we believe corporate citizenship should evolve from the core capabilities of an organization to deliver mutual benefit and create sustainable livings for individuals, their families and their communities. As Willie points out, there will always be differing points of view on the role that companies should play in this area, yet many companies have found that their corporate citizenship programs help energize and inspire their employees, enhance their image and, most important, make a lasting impact on the world.

The culmination of Willie's insights is his proposal for a new framework—what he calls the charity ecosystem. He describes a new era of "doing good well," as more and more charities adopt management concepts and themselves focus on outcomes and high performance. At the end of the day, this is about developing a more holistic and integrated approach to change in the nonprofit sector.

Willie has done a masterful job in keeping the content fresh and intriguing, and infusing the book with his unique style of humor. His ideas are thought provoking and accessible, even to those with no prior business or nonprofit experience. They will provide relevant insights for any individual or organization seeking to better understand the charity landscape and view it in a new way.

It is Willie's belief that "the way we see the world can change the world." His book is a powerful reminder that at the individual level, we can make a lasting contribution to society and do good well.

William D. Green
September 1, 2008

Bill Green is Chairman & CEO of Accenture, a global management consulting, technology services and outsourcing company.

Chapter 0

Introduction

Of Paradigms and Doing Good

The way we see the world can change the world. Such is the power of paradigms.

Paradigms are mental models of how we view various aspects of life. Since paradigms frame our view of reality, they influence how we behave in relation to those aspects of reality.

The importance of paradigms in the business world was popularized by Joel Barker,[1] author and futurist. He defines a paradigm as a set of rules and regulations that first, establishes or defines the boundaries; and secondly, tells us how to behave inside the boundaries in order to be successful.

Barker cites the example of the watch industry to illustrate the impact paradigms have on our decisions and actions. In 1968, the Swiss dominated the watch industry with a worldwide market share of 65 percent. By 1980, their market share had collapsed to less than 10 percent. What happened in between was the entry of the Japanese and others with the electronic quartz watch.

The irony, as Barker points out, is that it was the Swiss themselves who first invented the electronic quartz watch. But Swiss manufacturers rejected the idea from their own researchers because it did not fit their paradigm of what a watch should look like. At the time, watches were mechanical instruments. Hence the idea of an electronic watch devoid of mainsprings, bearings and gears moving in unison, was an anomaly. Electronic watches represented what Barker calls a "paradigm shift." Seiko, a Japanese company, saw the electronic watch on display at the World Watch Congress in 1967, and the rest was history.

Nonprofit Paradigms

I spent 26 years in the commercial world operating with business paradigms, sometimes seeking to understand when and where paradigm shifts might occur.

After I retired from the corporate treadmill in 2003, I became heavily involved with nonprofit work. It felt good to be "doing good." In the charity sector, I came across many who inspire with the purity of heart that should characterize such kind of work.

Coming from a highly organized and structured corporate environment, I found the contrast between the charity world and the commercial world quite stark and startling. I realized that I was trying to make sense of the nonprofit reality by applying corporate paradigms. My nonprofit colleagues likewise struggled to make sense of the alternatives that I presented and oftentimes I met with the common refrain, "That's just not the way we do things here."

As I grappled with the social realities, I began to understand not just the "hows" but also the "whys" that operate within the nonprofit sector. But sometimes the "hows" and the "whys" did not always compute. In time, I became convinced that how we "see" this world and how nonprofits "see" themselves need to change.

One of the nonprofit organizations that I became involved with, early in my retirement, was the National Volunteer & Philanthropy Center (NVPC)[2] in Singapore. As these nonprofit paradigms and paradoxes struck me, I shared some of them in articles that were published in *SALT*,[3] NVPC's magazine, and later in other publications.[4]

What This Book is About

This book pulls together my observations of various charity paradigms, their rationales and implications, and how the respective models can perhaps be different.

This book is not about the "how to," the nuts and bolts of nonprofit management, volunteerism or giving. Instead my focus is on concepts, principles and the thinking behind what works and what does not work in the nonprofit sector, why this is so, and how things can, perhaps, be done better.

Most of the chapters are based on previously published articles; for this book, they have been adapted and updated, in particular for international relevance. Each chapter describes one or more significant aspects of nonprofit reality. Most of the chapters can also be read as stand-alones if the reader's interest is only on a specific topic.

There are twenty chapters. For easy reading, I have grouped them into the following five broad categories:

- *Sector Structure & Governance.* This section looks at the macro aspects of how the charity sector is structured differently from the commercial sector, and the implications for governance and regulation.

- *Nonprofit Management.* This section deals with key questions facing nonprofit organizations, specifically organization growth, fundraising, reserves and staff compensation.

- *Giving.* This covers the various aspects of philanthropic giving and volunteerism from both a corporate and individual standpoint.

- *Social Innovation.* This section covers two new social models: social entrepreneurship and social enterprise. I have also included here the current philanthropic revolution since the chapter highlights innovations in philanthropic giving (though, of course, it could also have been included in the *Giving* section).

- *Doing Good Well?* This is, in a sense, a miscellaneous section of four chapters. There are two chapters on quirks in the charity sector. A case study on the National Kidney Foundation applies the respective paradigms in the context of the largest charity in Singapore. The last chapter wraps this book up by bringing the various paradigms together in a holistic framework and describes how the charity ecosystem is shaping up to do good better.

This book is meant for two groups of people. First, my colleagues in the nonprofit sector. Hopefully, this book can lend some fresh perspectives to their environment and charity work.

Secondly, my colleagues in the business world. My goal is to help explain why some of the assumptions we take for granted in business may or may not be applicable in the nonprofit sector.

For both sets of readers, I hope that any insights gleaned here will help us work together to shape the charity sector for the better. I strongly believe that "heart work" can be made so much more effective and meaningful if it is also led by our heads.

One of my passions is science fiction and comic books. Those of you who have watched the television series, *Heroes*, will recall the tag line: "Save the cheerleader, save the world!"[5] Well, I can imagine my hero of paradigms, Joel Barker, rephrasing that to: "Change the paradigm, change the world!" Changing the world is certainly what charity is about.

Happy reading!

Endnotes:

1   Joel Arthur Barker is author of *Paradigms: The Business of Discovering The Future* (Harper Business, 1992). The book is also published as *Future Edge: Discovering the New Paradigms of Success* (William Morrow and Company, 1992). The story of the watch making industry is found in its first chapter.

2   The National Volunteer & Philanthropy Center was set up in July 1999 as the National Volunteer Center, initially to promote volunteerism in Singapore across all sectors and all levels of society. In 2004, its mission and name was extended to include philanthropy.

3   *SALT* started as a bimonthly publication of the National Volunteer & Philanthropy Center. It targets those who give and those who receive. Launched in January 2004, it carries news on happenings among nonprofits and givers, and covers issues of interest to the nonprofits, volunteers and donors.

4   Other publications include *The Straits Times*, *The Business Times*, *The Social Service Journal* and *Social Space*.

5   That was the tagline for the first season of *Heroes*, which debuted on NBC in the U.S. in September 2006.

Sector Structure & Governance

Chapter 1

The Nonprofit Marketplace

The Missing Hand of Adam Smith

Charities deliver services to beneficiaries who often pay little or nothing. This contrasts with commercial customers who have to pay full value. To fund the difference, charities seek donations. However, donors do not always give based on the value that the charity delivers to the beneficiaries. Rather, they donate based on generosity, connections and the appeal of the fundraising campaign.

To bridge this structural disconnect between revenue and expenses, can the "invisible hand" of Adam Smith be replaced by the visible hand of the donor and the iron fist of governance and regulation?

March to May 2003 was a remarkable but scary period in Singapore's history. The unknown and deadly Severe Respiratory Syndrome (SARS) virus threatened the nation, but the government moved swiftly to contain the situation. Singapore's success in doing so is now a textbook example of an effective national response for handling and arresting a potential pandemic.[1]

Amidst the fear and uncertainty of the damage the virus could wreak, the Courage Fund was launched by several organizations with the full backing of the government in April 2003.[2] The objective was to raise funds to provide relief to SARS victims and healthcare workers. The fund was so named to honor healthcare workers, in particular, those who died or suffered in the fight against the virus.[3]

SARS and the Courage Fund galvanized the nation. Donations poured in. Dr. Lim Suet Wun, Chairman of the Courage Fund's Working Committee remarked that he was pleasantly surprised, sometimes after the event, by the many spontaneous fundraising events that sprouted up around the country and which they had not been previously notified of.[4]

The Courage Fund collected more than S$32 million (US$21 million).[5] At that time, it was arguably the most breathtaking fundraising ever seen in Singapore in terms of the speed at which the money came in, the quantum raised and the broad base of people reached.

In the wake of its runaway success, the Courage Fund invited controversy. Did it raise more money than it really needed? Did it inadvertently divert funds from other more needy charities? What was the excess cash going to be used for? Should fundraising have stopped when it looked like the collections were more than enough for the Fund's needs? The organizers sought to answer these questions[6] and many of them are discussed later in the book.[7]

Beyond these immediate fundraising related questions, the phenomenon of the Courage Fund, in my view, highlights a more fundamental and structural issue in the nonprofit world—the dichotomy between revenue and expenses.

Commercial Reality

In the commercial world, organizations are primarily driven by profits.[8] In the main, companies produce goods and services which they sell to their customers at prices that, hopefully, recover their costs and produce a tidy profit.

Companies live and die by their profits. Those that make losses will eventually close down, reducing supply in the market. If existing companies in a market space make too much profit, competitors will jump into the fray, thus increasing supply and bringing prices and profits down.

Adam Smith, the father of modern economics and the first proponent of laissez-faire, calls this the "invisible hand" that keeps the market in equilibrium. In the long term, the invisible hand continually moves the market towards this steady state, ensuring that there are just enough companies competing to make money, each making just sufficient profits (not too much and not too little) with goods and services priced at reasonable levels (not too high and not too low).

The Nonprofit Difference

Charities are nonprofit organizations that also produce goods and services, but these are not delivered to customers. Rather, they are delivered to beneficiaries who often pay nothing or a nominal charge that is less than the actual cost of producing the goods and services.

To make up for the difference between the actual cost of goods and services produced and what can be recovered from their beneficiaries, charities rely on grants, donations and volunteer time from the government and the community.

However, the fundraising efforts may bear little relation to the nature and value of the goods and services delivered to the beneficiaries. The success of fundraising is often more dependent on connections, marketing and the appeal of various "feel good" or "heart-tugging" approaches.

Consider the popular fundraising shows on television. They tend to feature performances by personalities, stunts, lucky draws and audience responses to challenges. The shows' content usually bears little relation to the charitable causes.

In Singapore, one of the most popular and successful fundraising events is the Ren Ci Charity Show. Since the first show, Venerable Shi Ming Yi,[9] the charismatic monk and then chief executive officer of Ren Ci Hospital and Medicare Center had consistently captured the imagination of television viewers by putting himself at risk. His stunts were the most anticipated part of the show and tended to generate the highest traffic of called-in donations. His abseiling down a 55-story building in 2003; immersion in 1,000 kilograms of ice for half an hour in 2004; balancing on a one-foot square plank on the roof of a building for two hours in 2005; walking across 20m-long, 15cm-wide parallel beams suspended 66 storeys above the ground in 2006; and pulling himself up 17 stories with a rope and pulley in 2007 helped raised over S$35 million (US$24 million) over the course of those five shows.

The Jerry Lewis MDA Telethon[10] held every Labor Day to benefit the Muscular Dystrophy Association of America is carried by 190 stations in America. In 2007, it raised more than US$63 million. Since the start of the show in 1952, it has raised more than US$1.4 billion. The success of the telethons lies, almost without question, in the pulling power of Jerry Lewis, the famous comedian and his celebrity guests, rather than the cause. However, the telethons have greatly helped to promote awareness and support of the cause of muscular dystrophy.

Global charity concerts like Band Aid, Live Aid and 8 Aid have been tremendously successful in raising funds for their respective causes. But it is well recognized that the donations were triggered more because of the singers and personalities on stage performing specific heart-warming favorites such as "We are the World," rather than their adopted causes of famine in Ethiopia and world poverty.

Clinching the right benefactors or supporters can make a big difference in making ends meet. The Courage Fund had the benefit of full media and governmental backing and indeed, the entire country rooting for it. The Tent, a welfare shelter for troubled teenage girls struggled with fundraising until it found a benefactor who auctioned some of her treasured family memorabilia to support its cause.[11] The charity auction in 2003 raised over S$2 million (US$1.4 million). With its 2003 expenditure of S$350,000 (US$240,000), the Tent was then able to focus on long-term plans.

Of course, in the course of raising funds and in acknowledging the donors, the charity's cause and beneficiaries are usually highlighted or at least mentioned. However, it is debatable whether the cause itself is the cause of donations, or if it is the cleverness of the campaign that makes people give.

Just check out any of the fundraising help materials. They are all oriented towards improving the "power of the ask," many of which seem to have little to do with the actual causes or beneficiaries. For example, fundraisers.com's list of the top ten fundraising tips[12] includes "use basic sales technique, chose the right incentive prize, motivate team work, reward the early bird" and so on. nfpSynergy's most important idea to engage the modern donor is to simplify the complexities of life by offering "oven-ready, bite-size, fundraising niches."[13]

A study in contrast would be the National Kidney Foundation (NKF) and the Kidney Dialysis Foundation (KDF) of Singapore. These two charities have essentially the same cause—their mainstay is kidney dialysis, but their financial performances are dramatically different. The situation of both charities in 2002 is shown in Table 1.1.[14]

Table 1.1 KDF versus NKF Fundraising Impact

	KDF	NKF
Funds raised for the year	$1.0 million	$46.6 million
Reserves at year end	$0.18 million	$130.34 million
No. of dialysis patients	174	2,200
Donations per patient	$5,700	$21,182
Reserves per patient	$1,034	$59,245
Note: All $ amounts refer to US$		

Clearly, NKF is the larger charity; it is also more established and better branded. While it does have other programs such as organ donation advocacy, preventive healthcare and clinical research, it is kidney dialysis that the public and donors recognize as its core competency and focus. Yet donors differentiate between the two organizations though they cover largely the same cause. So if it is not the cause, what is it? Well, it is the power of NKF's strategic and innovative fundraising approaches, controversial as they may have been.[15]

Market Failure?

So, there can be little connection between what a nonprofit actually does and how successful it is at raising money to support its causes. There is no invisible hand of Adam Smith to ensure that a nonprofit raises just enough money to deliver an optimal level of services to its beneficiaries.

It is therefore possible to have over-funded nonprofit organizations with more money than they need, and which can end up being splurged on peripherals unrelated to the beneficiaries as in the case of the NKF[16] and other charities.

In a Canadian case, it was reported that most of the money raised did not go to the intended cause.[17] The Organ Donation and Transplant Association of Canada was set up in 2004 by a professional fundraiser to promote and raise funds for research into organ donation and transplant. It raised about US$4 million in its first three years but only 10 percent of it went to transplant research. The bulk of the money was spent on telemarketing expenses to Xentel Incorporated, a commercial entity. The report pointed out conflicts of interest in the boards of Xentel and Organ Donation, misleading claims by telemarketers in their solicitations and Organ Donation taking credit for entire multimillion projects when it only contributed a small portion of the effort.

On the other hand, we have many cases of charities that are serving critical community needs which are unable to find funding to continue their work. Humanity & Golden Kids, a nonprofit center run by Cancerstory.com which offered complementary cancer treatments, closed because its funding ran out after it exhausted the capital donated by the founder.[18]

Not long ago, Amazing Kidz, another charitable organization serving over 100 families with children suffering from brain injuries, had to close after only two years because it continually struggled to raise sufficient funds for its operations.[19]

A recent analysis in the *Stanford Social Innovation Review* concluded that "there is little relationship between how much donors give and how many people need help."[20] The author studied funding for sudden emergencies such as disasters versus funding for chronic health conditions. Private donors, for example, had spent about US$1,839 for each person affected by Hurricane Katrina. In contrast, they had only given US$10 for each person diagnosed with AIDS, or US$3 for each person struck by malaria.

Bridging the Disconnect

The structural differences between the commercial and the charity sector are illustrated in Figure 1.2.

In the charity world, there is a distinct disconnect between the value of services delivered and the source of funding for those services. In the commercial world, the function of aligning value and funding is performed by one party—the customer. With charities, the customer is replaced by two parties—the donor and the beneficiary.

Figure 1.2 Structural Disconnect

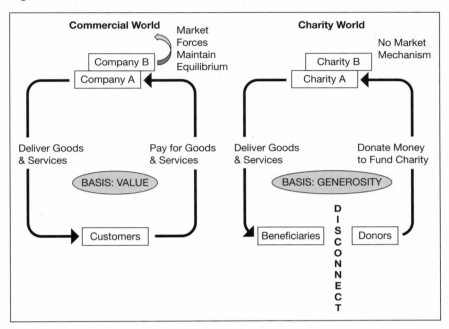

The beneficiary undertakes the function of consumption performed by the customer and the donor takes on the function of payment also performed by the customer. However, the donor has not made the payment on the basis of value as the customer would; rather, he does it for reasons other than value—you could say mainly generosity because that is how many of us choose to view it. Since the donor's decision to pay is not necessarily based on how the charity performs its function, the loop is not closed. Hence, the disconnect.

With this structural disconnect between revenues and expenses in charities, the market forces that might otherwise ensure equilibrium in the charity marketplace are unable to work. Adam Smith's hand is not just invisible, it is absent.

What is the solution? The first possible answer is to get the donor to do what the customer would do—pay on the basis of outcomes and value delivered to the beneficiaries. In charity parlance, this is called "informed giving." It is asking donors to give on an informed basis, knowing what, why and how the charity is doing what it is supposed to do. In other words, replace the invisible hand of Adam Smith with the visible hand of the donor. This subject of informed giving will be explored further in the next chapter.

Informed giving is not the complete solution since it is unlikely that there will be an absolute alignment of donors with the beneficiaries' interests. The fallback answer—derived from the commercial world—would be to back up the donors' visible hand with the iron fist of governance and regulations. However, there are significant differences between charity governance and governance in the commercial world. These will be discussed in greater detail in Chapter 3, "Who governs a nonprofit, really?"

Meanwhile, we may just have to accept that the nonprofit marketplace will never really be, or even trend towards, a "perfect marketplace" as Adam Smith envisaged in his laissez-faire economy.

Endnotes:

Adapted from: "The missing hand of Adam Smith," *SALT*, March-April 2004; and "Charity: Donors should pay more heed to the cause," *The Straits Times*, April 8, 2004.

1   The story of the SARS outbreak is documented in Chua Mui Hoong, *A Defining Moment—How Singapore beat SARS* (Singapore Institute of Policy Studies, 2004).

2   www.couragefund.com.sg. According to a Singapore Medical Association newsletter article ("Book Review of *A Defining Moment*," *SMA News*, December 2004, Vol. 36, No. 12), the Courage Fund was originally started by a couple of young medical officers, then adopted by the Singapore Medical Association and the Singapore Nurses Association, after which it was taken over by the two government-run health groups (the National Health Group and Singapore Health) and renamed The Courage Fund.

3   Andrea Tan, "Courage Fund for SARS victims," *The Business Times*, April 12, 2003.

4   "When is Enough, Enough?, Interview with Dr. Lee Suet Wun, Chairman of the Courage Fund Working Committee," *SALT*, January-February 2004.

5   All amounts are converted to US$ in this book. Exchange rate used are: S$1.45 = US$1, £1 = US$2.

6   "When is Enough, Enough?, Interview with Dr. Lee Suet Wun, Chairman of the Courage Fund Working Committee," *SALT*, January-February 2004.

7   Chapter 6, "The problem of plenty" deals with the questions raised here in relation to excesses from fundraising.

8   This creates a different set of issues which will be discussed in Chapter 8, "Is the business of business just business?"

9   In February 2008, Venerable Shi Ming Yi went on a leave of absence pending investigations by the Commercial Affairs Department into financial transactions made by Ren Ci Hospital under his watch. On July 15, 2008, Venerable Ming Yi was charged for forgery, misappropriation of funds and conspiracy to give false information to the Commissioner

of Charities. At time of publication of this book, the court case is pending. At the time of his arrest, Venerable Ming Yi stepped down from all his positions regarding charities. A new chief executive officer was appointed for the charity, Ren Ci Hospital. During the investigations, the charity lost its status as an Institution of Public Character (IPC), which allows it to issue tax exempt receipts to donors. When the investigations were over and after Venerable Ming Yi was charged, the IPC status was restored. However, thanks to its many years of successful fundraising, the hospital has S$33.5 million (US$23 million) in reserves—sufficient to last it six years.

10   www.mda.org/telethon

11   www.thetent.org.sg; Wong Sher Maine, "Small charities fight for bite of the pie," *The Straits Times*, April 7, 2004.

12   www.fundraisers.com/ideas/topten.html

13   Joe Saxton, Michele Madden, Chris Greenwood & Brian Garvey, *The 21st Century Donor*, nfpSynergy, September 2007), available at www.nfpsynergy.net. nfpSynergy is a specialist research consultancy for not-for-profit organizations.

14   While I have put the figures into a tabular form for readability, these figures are as stated in the original article of the same name written for *SALT* magazine in March/April 2004. I have not updated them for a more recent year or for more accurate figures of 2002 that emerged in the NKF court case and KPMG investigation (the more accurate figures would make NKF look worse) given the change in the situation with NKF today and the significance of the original article in the NKF saga (see Chapter 19).

15   See Chapter 19, "NKF: The saga and its paradigms."

16   Ibid.

17   David Bruser, "Charity's ploy 'horrifying'," *The Toronto Star*, August 4, 2007 at www.thestar.com/Investigation/article/243162; The charity's website is www.organdonations.ca.

18   Wong Sher Maine, "Small charities fight for bite of the pie," *The Straits Times*, April 7, 2004; www.cancerstory.com.

19   www.amazingkidz.org

20   Keith Epstein, "Crisis Mentality," *Stanford Social Innovation Review*, Spring 2006.

Chapter 2

Informed Giving

The Visible Hand of the Donor

Informed giving is designed to ensure that donations are aligned with the interests of beneficiaries. Specifically, donors are asked to be more discerning, discriminating and demanding of their charities so that there is proper accountability of funds used.

Informed giving is difficult to achieve as most individual donors don't really care to do the due diligence needed for charity effectiveness.

 Part of the solution may lie in developing a generation of grantmakers who have the resources and focus to ensure proper funds allocation and usage. What's more, community foundations have evolved to fill the gap for mid-tier donors.

As the name suggests, informed giving refers to donors making properly-informed decisions before they give to a charity.

In the aftermath of a charity scandal, the idea of informed giving usually receives strong and broad-based support from both the authorities and the charities themselves. Rather than see such calls for more diligent giving as merely throwing the ball back into the donors' court, informed giving should be viewed as an everyday part of charity donations and recognized as crucial to the functioning of an effective charity ecosystem.

As we saw in the last chapter, there is a crucial difference between the marketplace for nonprofits and that for profit-based organizations. The nonprofit world lacks what Adam Smith calls the "invisible hand" of the commercial marketplace which helps to regulate and maintain market equilibrium. So, for the nonprofit "market" to work, donors have to take over the functions typically performed by customers. They have to ensure that the nonprofits deliver full value to their beneficiaries. These days, there certainly is a push especially by major donors for their hand to be more visible than just in the handouts. If donors are able to ensure full accountability of charities, then the invisible hand of Adam Smith may be replaced by the visible hand of the donor.

Discerning, Discriminating and Demanding Donors

Informed giving is asking donors to go beyond being just generous. It means asking donors to be more discerning of the charities and causes they give to, to discriminate between deserving and non-deserving charities, and finally to be more demanding of those charities for accountability of the donations they received.

Informed giving seeks to get the donor to understand that he has certain rights before he parts with his money. This is best summarized in *The Donor Bill of Rights*[1] (see Figure 2.1) which was developed by several U.S.-based charity support organizations.

In turn, various organizations have developed guidelines on how donors can and should exercise these rights. The National Volunteer & Philanthropy Center sets out four major indicators in its *Informed Giving Guidelines*:[2]

- Purpose: Clarify the organization's mission and vision so that one can understand its reason for existence and where it is going better.

- People: Look at the people (board and staff) running the show, the process by which they are selected, and trends such as turnover.

- Programs: Check how the organization intends to use the funds and run its programs. Follow up after the event. Look at the financial statements to understand how their funds are used and managed.

- Publicity: Find out external information about the charity. Let the organization tell its side of the story in the event of negative publicity.

Figure 2.1 The Donor Bill of Rights

 The Donor Bill of Rights

Philanthropy is based on voluntary action for the common good. It is a tradition of giving and sharing that is primary to the quality of life. To ensure that philanthropy merits the respect and trust of the general public, and that donors and prospective donors can have full confidence in the nonprofit organizations and causes they are asked to support, we declare that all donors have these rights:

I.   To be informed of the organization's mission, of the way the organization intends to use donated resources, and of its capacity to use donations effectively for their intended purposes.

II. To be informed of the identity of those serving on the organization's governing board, and to expect the board to exercise prudent judgment in its stewardship responsibilities.

III. To have access to the organization's most recent financial statements.

IV. To be assured their gifts will be used for the purposes for which they are given.

V.   To receive appropriate acknowledgement and recognition.

VI. To be assured that information about their donation is handled with respect and with confidentiality to the extent provided by law.

VII. To expect that all relationships with individuals representing organizations of interest to the donor will be professional in nature.

VIII. To be informed whether those seeking donations are volunteers, employees of the organization or hired solicitors.

IX. To have the opportunity for their names to be deleted from mailing lists that an organization may intend to share.

X.   To feel free to ask questions when making a donation and to receive prompt, truthful and forthright answers.

The Donor Bill of Rights was created by the Association of Fundraising Professionals, the Association for Healthcare Philanthropy, the Council for Advancement and Support of Education, and the Giving Institute: Leading Consultants to Non-Profits. It has been endorsed by numerous organizations.

But entrenching the idea of informed giving is not as simple as reading the Donors' Bill of Rights to potential givers and giving them guidelines. Even if donors understand the general concept, they may be hard-pressed to execute it. It is a big challenge to wade through the sea of charities no matter how narrow the locality a person may be living in. Within a small country like Singapore, there are 1,800 registered charities. In Washington D.C, the number is 5,000, while California has more than 153,000.

Navigation tools are thus useful. There are several nonprofit databases that allow donors to search for nonprofits by different categories and that provide important financial and non-financial information about the organizations in question.

These databases are typically provided by charity watchers that evaluate charities, rate them and even make recommendations. Examples of organizations that do this for U.S.-based charities are GuideStar, Charity Navigator, the Better Business Bureau Wise Giving Alliance and the American Institute of Philanthropy's Charity Watch.[3]

They cover the market segments in different ways. Charity Navigator rates charities on a set of organizational capacity and efficiency indicators, using a four-star ranking system. Charity Watch rates charities using financial ratios and analysis of their financial statements, assigning them a grade from "A" to "F". The Better Business Bureau Wise Giving Alliance has a "pass-fail" approach based on a comprehensive analysis of both quantitative and qualitative information. Guidestar does not rate charities but provides its basic financial data for free and, for a fee, in-depth reports of how the given charity performs compared to other charities with similar missions.

GuideStar's database is probably the largest as it contains information on more than 1.7 million tax-exempt nonprofits registered with the U.S. Internal Revenue Service, unlike the more limited numbers by the others: 500 for Charity Watch, 1,000 for BBB Wise Giving Alliance, and 5,000 for Charity Navigator.

Donor Reality

Despite the various information sources available to donors, the reality may be that most people do not care sufficiently to be informed givers.[4]

Based on empirical evidence from various studies on givers' motivation, Professor Lise Vesterlund of the University of Pittsburg[5] concluded that most people give primarily for private benefits rather than public benefits.

Private benefits such as feeling good and recognition are enjoyed only by the individuals contributing. Public benefits refer to the well-being of the charity and does not affect individual donors' benefits. If donors do not care about the public benefits, it is not likely that they will be informed givers.

A narrower study in Australia to evaluate whether donors "care" about increased accountability for charitable organizations concluded that "it would appear that donors do not care about the usage of funds."[6] It found that increased regulation and accountability will not necessarily increase donations. Donors are generally satisfied by the act of giving, rather than learning about how the funds are used.

Even if donors do care, the reality is that most people have neither the time nor inclination to follow through with what informed giving entails: "You mean to give away a few dollars, I have to do all this work?"

Donors may be upset if they find out that their money has been misused, but typically they do not want to be part of the policing system. For most, philanthropy is simply about generosity. Asking them to use their head with their hearts is, well, asking for too much.

As it is going to be near impossible to persuade the whole population of potential donors[7] to be informed givers, what alternatives are we left with?

Applying Pareto's 80/20 rule[8] may help us address this gap. What if we rely on the 20 percent of givers who have the interest and the means to truly effect informed giving? What if we can funnel most of the donations of the remaining 80 percent through this 20 percent of donors?

The Grantmakers

There is a class of donors called grantmakers. They amass donations, generate income, and channel the funds to specific charities. When they channel the funds, they generally do it with due diligence—rigorously evaluating the charity and its needs, and following up to ensure that the money given achieves the appropriate outcomes.

There are various types of grantmakers, from the different kinds of foundations to various community funds. Foundations are generally institutions established by individuals, families or corporations with endowments. There are more than 71,000 foundations in the U.S. today, with names such as the Rockefeller Foundation and the Ford Foundation being among the better known.

Community funds may be set up by umbrella organizations or community groups. Among the earliest of such funds are the Community Chests established in many countries around the world. These are fundraising organizations that collect money from the local community and distribute it to community projects. Those in the U.S. and Canada have experienced name changes and are now called The United Way.[9] Those funds which are owned by an umbrella organization such as the National Council of Social Service[10] or the United Way are essentially fundraising mechanisms of these bodies as the money collected goes to their member charities. Other funds are set up by a community group to provide for certain types of causes, such as Mainly I Love Kids[11] for disadvantaged children.

Foundations tend to go for the big money donation, while community funds will take in small and large sums. The former also tend to have qualified professionals who proactively craft programs, evaluate grant applications, and monitor grants and programs. In the U.S., grantmakers typically spend about 10 percent of their annual grants on managing the foundation and the grantmaking process. Community funds are more variable and the smaller ones tend to work more with volunteers.

From a donor's standpoint, a major disadvantage about making gifts through a traditional foundation or a community fund is that he loses the recognition from the charity and the flexibility of stipulating how and when the donation is to be applied.

To fill the gap for medium-sized donations, a vehicle known as the community foundation has evolved in the U.S. and other more developed countries. Through what is known as donor-advised funds, the donor gets immediate tax and other benefits of giving while retaining flexibility on the timing and application of the donation. In addition, the community foundation will help the individual evaluate and allocate his donation, something which he may otherwise not have been able to do by himself.

The first community foundation was set up in Cleveland in 1914. Today, there are more than 700 community foundations in the U.S. and about 1,000 around the world. Singapore is rolling out its first community foundation in 2008.[12]

How the various grantmakers and individual donors may fit together to address donors' needs is illustrated in Figure 2.2.

As can be seen, in order to effect informed giving, the aim should be to move donors from the left (personal giving) to the right (the

Figure 2.2 The Giving Landscape

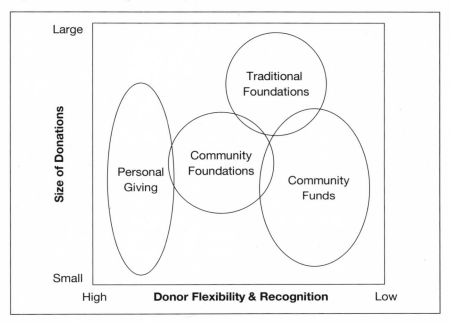

grantmakers). To do so, the grantmaking sector needs to be better developed so that grantmaking is encouraged and supported.

In general, the U.S. has the most developed grantmaking infrastructure with 221 grantmakers per million population. By comparison, the United Kingdom has 128, Canada has 69 and Singapore has 20 grantmakers per million population.[13]

Beyond quantity, grantmakers need to do their job of professionally ensuring accountability as well as being role models of accountability themselves. For just as grantmakers provide the needed due diligence of end-beneficiary charities, there should be appropriate regulations governing grantmakers. In the U.S., private foundations are generally more heavily regulated than public charities.[14] With the increased interest in foundations, law-makers in the U.S. and the U.K. are reviewing existing regulations towards this end.[15]

Meanwhile, many Commonwealth countries such as Singapore do not have a separate set of regulations covering grantmakers, in particular, foundations. Instead, grantmakers are treated like regular charities. However, the requirements for matters such as reserves, expenditure and accounting for grantmakers are quite different and subjecting them to the same rules as end-beneficiary charities may go against the grain of good grantmaking.[16] Such countries should look towards a separate set of rules that govern as well as promote the establishment and functioning of effective grantmakers.

The Charity Exchange

It may be helpful to draw some parallels between the charity sector and the stock exchange. An effective charity sector needs players and mechanisms working in tandem, just like the stock exchange.

In this analogy, charities are similar to the public listed companies. They must be transparent and accountable, but the public gives money to them at their own risk. There must be general awareness by the public of what charity is about—its causes, its programs, its financials, etc. Like stock analysts, there should be a plethora of charity sector watchers that proactively scan, evaluate and rate charities. Grant givers are like the fund managers that collect money from the giving public, and invest them in charities to realize benefits for the community. Unlike shareholders, donors are likely to have less time and motivation to properly "invest their funds." So in many ways, ensuring sufficient and professional grantmakers is more important to the charity sector than fund managers to the commercial markets.

It is time to get a well-functioning "charity exchange" going.

Awareness of informed giving is the first step. While individual donors may continue to give as they currently do, the hope is that we may be able to move from a state of personal giving to giving via grantmakers so that we can better exercise informed giving. In this way, the "invisible hand" of Adam Smith may take the shape and form of the "visible" hand of the informed giver.

Endnotes:

Adapted from: "Helping charity donors make informed choices," *The Straits Times*, April 21, 2006.

1   *The Donor Bill Of Rights* is available at www.afpnet.org/ka/ka-3.cfm?content_item_id=9988.

2   *Informed Giving Guidelines: Improving the way you give*, a flyer by the National Volunteer & Philanthropy Center.

3   For general information on Charity Watchers, go to www.charitywatchdogs.net. For Guidestar, go to www.guidestar.org. For Charity Navigator, go to www.charitynavigator. org. For BBB Wise Giving Alliance, go to www.give.org. For American Institute of Philanthropy, go to www.charitywatch.org.

4   The reasons that people give are covered in other chapters, particularly in Chapter 9, "How charitable are you, truly?"

5   Lise Vesterlund, "Why do People Give?" from *The Nonprofit Sector, A Research Handbook, 2nd edition,* Edited by Water W. Powell and Richard Steinberg, (Yale Press, 2006).

6   Gabrielle Berman and Sinclair Davidson, "Do donors care? Some Australian evidence," *Voluntas: International Journal of Voluntary and Nonprofit Organization,* Vol. 14, No. 4, December 2003.

7   Remarkably, 97% of people in Singapore aged 15 and above are donors, big and small. See endnote 13 for reference.

8   Pareto's principle, also known as the 80/20 rule, or the law of the vital few, states that for many events, 80% of the effects come from 20% of the causes.

9   www.unitedway.org

10   www.ncss.org.sg

11   www.milk.org.sg

12   "Press release: Community Foundation of Singapore, A new initiative to encourage & facilitate philanthropy," Ministry of Community, Youth and Sports, March 5, 2008.

13   *The State of Giving* (National Volunteer & Philanthropy Center, 2005). Data for Canada is 2003; and 2004 for the other countries.

14   Betsy Buchalter Adler, *The Rules of the Road: A guide to the Law of Charities in the United States* (Council on Foundations, 1999).

15   "The birth of philanthrocapitalism," *The Economist,* February 23, 2006. *The Economist* talks about the tough new laws that would dramatically transform the relationship between the federal government and foundations in the U.S. and the review of charity laws in Britain. Regulation is also covered in Chapter 4, "Black box or glass house?"

16   For example, the 80/20 rule for charities in Singapore requires that they spend 80% of their income within two years to qualify for tax exemption. This would work against commitments for multi-year programs which a good foundation should do. Recognizing this, the government removed this 80/20 rule in 2007.

Chapter 3

Nonprofit Governance

Who Governs a Nonprofit, Really?

The theory is that the board of directors governs an organization. In practice, charity boards face greater challenges than commercial boards in ensuring organizational performance, proper board selection and good power dynamics.

In addition, there is one fundamental difference: the definition of owner within the charity context should go beyond the legal owner – to include the volunteers, donors and the community it purports to serve.

In satisfying this public interest aspect of charities, two additional levels of active governance should be applied: regulation and the court of public opinion. In some places around the world, these two additional levels have risen to the fore.

W hen things go awry with a charity, the blame game starts. Donors and the media will ask what happened with corporate governance and why the authorities did not step in earlier.

Part of the reason for this public response is the general assumption that corporate governance should work the same way as it does in the commercial world. It is also assumed that if a regulator has sanctioned a charity, it has essentially done the full due diligence needed.

The actual charity environment is a lot more complex than that. To begin with, the charity sector is not as well-formed as the commercial sector, and its evolution has lagged behind even as the sector and its regulators seek to emulate the workings of the commercial sector— sometimes inappropriately.

Corporate Governance

Definitions of corporate governance abound. It is:

"simply ... the role of the board of directors"[1]

"the relationship among various participants in determining the direction and performance of corporations"[2]

"a set of provisions that enables the stockholders, by exercising voting power, to compel those in operating control of the firm to respect their interests"[3]

Literature on this subject, mostly from the commercial world, converges on several key concepts of what constitutes good corporate governance:

– Ensuring organizational performance beyond conformance

– Proper selection and composition of the board of directors

– Clarity of the power structure or relationship between management, the board and owners

– Ultimate accountability to the owners of the organization

Yet, how these concepts should, or should not, play out both in theory and practice in the charity world is not always fully appreciated, as regulators and the public seek to apply their yardstick of good corporate governance to charities.

As we shall see later below, depending upon the constitutions of the nonprofit organizations, there may be different flavors of governing bodies – a board, an elected council, trustees, etc. For commercial organizations, it is simply the board of directors. For convenience, I shall use the board as a generic way to refer to the governing body of both kinds of organizations for the rest of this chapter.

Organizational Performance

The subject of governance has received much prominence and importance in recent years because of high profile corporate abuse cases such as Enron and WorldCom. Thus, the importance of risk management and compliance with the increasing regulatory load has been a focus of governance in many organizations. Along with this, there has been an emphasis on whistle-blowing, the audit process and the roles of the external auditor, the internal auditor and the audit committee.

While conformance to rules and regulations and ethical conduct are basic and necessary, they are, by no means, sufficient. As the dust settles, many governance experts are now pointing out the need for a board of directors to also take up the responsibility of ensuring the performance of the organization.

However, what constitutes performance differs significantly between profit-based and nonprofit organizations. For commercial companies, it boils down to the financial bottom line. This is a straightforward and legitimate measure of success.

In charity work, organizational performance should theoretically be assessed relative to the organization's mission. That is easier said than done. First, it seldom boils down to a single number or factor. Secondly, the factors may not be measurable. Seeking to get the board and management to agree on the key indicators of success and performance measures can go against the grain of the culture of the charity environment. This makes governance difficult for nonprofit organizations.

The values that are emphasized in the commercial world are economic performance, results and delivery. In the charity world, it is forgiveness and generosity; the passion is for "doing good." Therefore, instead of the disciplined and hard-headed pace that is an expected given by corporate leaders, the pace for charities is slower and clarity of outcomes is less important.

When clear goals are not defined upfront, there is the tendency to declare success with whatever has been achieved after the event. This approach is however changing somewhat with the emphasis on outcome-based funding by major donors and umbrella bodies.

Carrying over a corporate mentality about what constitutes success into the charity world may not always be applicable. In the commercial world, we are dazzled by the mantra of growth. But a charity exists for a cause. Success must be measured by how far the charity has moved towards accomplishing its mission. Ultimate success could therefore mean the total achievement of the societal change it seeks, which in effect is the extinction of the organization.[4] This is a hard concept for corporate leaders who step into the charity world to grasp because for them, liquidation often means commercial failure.

Board Selection

For most commercial boards, there is a fairly rigorous and formal process in place for the selection of board members. One cannot simply get onto a commercial board. Typically, a nomination committee comprising a subset of the board is set up to identify, evaluate and recommend board members. These recommendations have to be approved by the shareholders. That is the theory, of course. In many cases, it is still a bit of an Old Boy's Club, but at least there is a process in place with some degree of checks and balances.

In most nonprofits, there is usually no clear process for selecting board members. It could be based on who the chairperson, founder and other board members know and feel like inviting to join the board. Of course, it is not easy to find good people to serve without pay (while still be exposed to personal liability) on a charity board. Often, nonprofit boards perpetuate themselves, unless there are tenure rules within their constitutions. Sometimes, they may take turns to assume different positions, or come in and out of the boards. Even when there are elections of the governing bodies (such as council members in the case of a society), it can often be a process of selection and rotation by the council members themselves. Also, elections do not necessarily throw up the best skill mix needed for the organizations.

One of the tenets of good corporate governance is the renewal of board members and management. Power corrupts, invariably and eventually. Before it does, complacency would likely have set in. Power is also intoxicating. It would be rare for an incumbent, enlightened as he or she may be, to voluntarily move himself or herself out of a position of power. For that reason, rules that institutionalize tenure and rotation can help deal with the issue without loss of face. However, few nonprofits incorporate such provisions into their constitutions or code of corporate governance, if there is one. Some that do, seem to do so after due reflection upon the departure of long-staying incumbents.

Process and constitutional rules aside, getting the right mix of members for the governing body of a nonprofit can actually be more demanding than for a commercial board. For good governance in either type of organization, you would want a good mix of people with industry content, and largely legal and financial expertise for the fiduciary role. However, for charities, the directors are often expected to perform several more functions: contributing their expertise in the operations of the charity, raising funds, providing linkage to specific communities, and lending their names as a signal to others that the organization is doing good work.

These non-fiduciary responsibilities are not legal requirements of being a director. However, they are so much a part of how nonprofits work that these functions often become the primary roles for which nonprofit directors are appointed. It is fair to say that until the public prosecution of directors of charities for wrongdoings,[5] most directors join charities expecting to help in the "cause" and not so much to govern them. When the work is done by the directors, however, it begs the question of who is governing the work.

The pure governance role is being increasingly emphasized in the wake of charity scandals. It would be advisable for board members to ask who on the board are diligently ensuring good governance because when trouble hits, the board bears collective responsibility.

Power Structure

In commercial companies, the lines of reporting and accountability are fairly clear and hierarchical. The board governs, sets policies and approves the strategic plan. Management and staff get the job done. The board is accountable to the shareholders for the results, the management and staff are responsible for the performance required to achieve those results.

The power structure of a nonprofit is much more diffused. It seems that everyone has a say in how every little thing gets done. For a commercial company, everything moves in a straight line to the shareholders. In the case of a nonprofit, there is a broad spectrum of stakeholders, all of whom want to partake in telling the poor executive director and the staff what they should be doing.

The board obviously has its say, but the nature of nonprofits is such there will be board and committee members who will get more involved in the operational aspects of the organization.

There are also donors and volunteers who expect and want to have their say as well since they are giving their valuable time or money for free. Add to this, beneficiaries, or more likely the relatives of beneficiaries, often have strong views on how things ought to be run.

A key reason for this phenomenon lies in the bare bones staffing and often low compensation levels at nonprofit organizations. Given the limited capacity and capability, what could be regular executive work can only be done if board members and volunteers chip in. Hence, nonprofit boards tend to be more hands-on, with volunteers supplementing staff being the norm. Consequently, if volunteers are doing what executives should be doing, should they not be accorded that similar level of authority and say?

Ownership

Corporate governance literature emphasizes the primacy of accountability to the legal owner of the organization, namely the shareholders. The board's authority emanates from the legal owners who appoint the board. In other words, there are two levels of checks and balances in the establishment of a commercial organization to ensure that it functions as intended.

This should be clearly laid out in the constitution of the company and the corporate laws under which the company is incorporated. In the case of the U.K. and many Commonwealth countries, the relevant legislation would be the Companies Act. In the U.S., it would be the laws of the particular state in which the company is incorporated.

Being a charity, on the other hand, is mainly a tax status. As such, charities need to have a constitutional form. In many cases, a charity may be incorporated as a special type of company under corporate laws. Alternatively, a charity could first be constituted as a society or a trust. There will be separate legislation governing each organizational form.

The implications on ownership and governance of the different organizational forms are briefly covered in the box, "Legal Organizational Forms for a Charity" using the case of Singapore, which should be similar to most other Commonwealth countries.

Legal Organizational Forms for a Charity

In Singapore, a charity is usually constituted either as a society (under the Societies Act) or as a company limited by guarantee (under the Companies Act). About 58 percent of charities are legally registered societies while 18 percent are companies. The rest are either set up by specific statutes or constituted as trusts.

Traditionally, charities were constituted as societies, but increasingly, newly registered charities have taken the company route. From a founder's standpoint, incorporation as a company is easier for control and administration. No elections are needed. Members (essentially shareholders without shares) of the company—which can be as few as two individuals—appoint the board. In fact, the members (the legal owners) and the board are often the same individuals, removing yet another intended level of checks and balances in the organization.

In recent years, some charities previously incorporated as societies have reconstituted themselves as companies. The rationale as explained to me by one charity is that "it makes it easier to get things done." Yet another charity which considered switching from a society to a company for that reason eventually decided not to because it felt that "it would be less transparent."

However, constituting as a society may not necessarily result in better governance. To start with, in a society, there is no longer the two tier structure of ownership and governance. The governors are elected from among the members—the owners of the organization. In addition, even though in theory, the governing council is elected, there is often an inner club of selected members. It is common for elections of a society's office bearers to be uncontested.

In fact, it can be a challenge for some societies to get a quorum at the annual general meeting (AGM). But that's not a real problem either as the constitution of the society invariably incorporates a clause to the effect that if there is no quorum present at the specified time, the meeting is adjourned for half an hour and "the members then present shall be a quorum." In effect, the AGM simply starts half an hour later, and organizers, indeed, often plan for it.

The control and functioning of a company limited by guarantee is generally easier than for a society. However, the duties and liabilities of directors are typically more onerous than that of the elected officials of a society.

A third organizational form which has found favor, particularly for funds, is to set up as charitable trusts through trust documents under the Trustees Act. A trust provides for administrative convenience, but not the flexibility in the change of trustees.

A less common organizational form for charities today is their creation by specific statutes of parliament. This applies to charities, such as the Singapore Red Cross, which were established in Singapore's early history.

As can be seen, demarcation between the legal owners and the governing members is not always clear. In fact, both groups can often be the same people. In addition, the rules and practices are such that there is a high risk of the perpetuation of the same group of people in control of a charity for a long time.

Moral Owners

We should always be uncomfortable with the corporate governance notion that respecting the interests of the owners is paramount for a charity. This discomfort should hold notwithstanding any safeguards built into an institution's constitution or its Code of Corporate Governance for renewal of governing board members. The fact is, the legal owners of a charity usually come down to a select few individuals or organizations. Inevitably, some owners and their appointees will have narrower interests that would not sit well with an objective view of what the charity should be doing.

A commercial organization has a simple objective—maximizing profits for its owners, and it very fairly does so by using the owners' capital. The objective of non-charity nonprofits such as business associations and clubs is also to look after the (narrow) interests of its members. A charity, on the other hand, seeks to achieve societal change and improvements, and draws its resources from the community through volunteers who give of their time and donors who give of their money.

For that reason, beyond legal ownership, there needs to be the concept of moral ownership. Since charities exist for the broader purpose of doing public good, the management and board of a charity need to be accountable not just to the legal owners, but also to the moral owners—the public from whom it gets its funds and the community it purports to serve.

A key means by which this concept of moral ownership is achieved is through external rules and regulations. In a sense, regulation then is the next level of governance for charities.

The Regulatory Framework

A company must follow the corporate laws of the country. In addition, if it is listed, it has to abide by the regulations of the stock exchange on which it is listed. If it is in a regulated industry, such as banking, there are also specific governmental regulations regarding that industry which it has to comply with.

Onerous as these layers of regulations may sound for, say, a bank that is listed on the stock exchange, it can be more complex for a charity. In general, a charity needs to observe four sets of regulations relating to:

1. How the charity is constituted
2. Its charitable tax benefits
3. Relevant umbrella body guidelines, and
4. Activity-based rules, especially fundraising requirements.

Charities have to be constituted as legal organizations in the first place. This can be as a company, a society, a trust or a statutory body as described above. Whichever organizational form the charity takes, it will have to comply with the laws governing that organizational form and of course its own constitution (e.g. memorandum and articles of association or trust deed, etc). The laws governing organizational forms are generally agnostic of any charitable status of the organizations. There are little or no additional provisions requiring an organization to operate for the public benefit.

Secondly, the charity will have to comply with the laws that give it its charity status. It should be noted that in most jurisdictions, a charity in law is primarily a tax status. In the U.S., to qualify for tax-exempt charitable status, an organization must satisfy the requirements of Section 501(c)(3) of the U.S. Internal Revenue Code. In Singapore and similarly in many Commonwealth countries, an organization must be a registered charity (under the Charities Act) for it to be tax-exempt and also be qualified as an Institution of a Public Character (formerly under the Income Tax Act but moved to the Charities Act in 2007) in order for it to issue tax-exempt receipts to donors.

As a charity is not a legal entity, but a tax status, it has to abide by both the rules governing its constitutional form and the tax-benefit regulations. The latter can be specific charity regulations which are overseen by a regulator such as the Commissioner of Charities in Singapore or the Charity Commission in the U.K. In 2006, the U.K. introduced a new legal form—the Charitable Incorporated Organization—which gives charities the benefits of incorporation (limited liability and legal personality) as well as tax benefits, all under a single regulator, the Charity Commission for England and Wales.

Most charity safeguards are to be found in these tax-benefit regulations (charity legislation and/or tax regulations). However, it should be noted that the benefit of being a registered charity goes beyond just the tax benefits. The public image of being officially recognized as a charity helps an organization reach out to the community for volunteers, donations, and other support.

Thirdly, there are umbrella body guidelines. Charities come together with other like-minded charities for synergy and effectiveness. Some of these are associations, such as the Council on Foundations[6] in the U.S. and the National Council for Voluntary Organizations[7] in the U.K.; while others are government or statutory bodies such as the National Council of Social Service[8] in Singapore. These umbrella bodies may issue guidelines to its members. The guidelines are more akin to best practices if the bodies are privately led. The guidelines would have more teeth if they are quasi-regulatory as in the case of the National Council of Social Service.

A final set of regulations that charities (and non-charities) may have to observe are those pertaining to certain activities, especially fundraising. For these activities, they have to apply for licenses or permits and comply with the related regulations. For example in Singapore, charities must obtain a permit from the police for certain solicitations of donations from the public under the House to House and Street Collections Act. Permits granted have certain requirements attached.

Overall, the regulations covering charities seem more disparate and less granular than those that regulate commercial companies. Most charities tend to be small and hence do not have the resources to ensure full and proper compliance. Hence, the reluctance of many good people to join the governing boards of charities when they understand the implications of their liability and diligence needed as directors.

Despite the array of regulations, matters do sometimes go off course. When this happens, the result is a renewed call for legislative review and changes to be made. In the last few years, this is precisely what has occurred with the charity regulations in the U.S. and Singapore.[9]

There are times when more drastic actions may be needed for individual cases. An example was the Singapore government's grave concerns in 1987 about the Singapore Turf Club running a thriving horse racing and gaming operation. It was then a private members' club constituted under the Societies Act. One concern was the large reserves accumulated from the gambling operation which could theoretically be distributed to its members if the club was dissolved. Although the money was earned legally under a governmental license, the argument was that it was made from the gambling public and could be used for private benefit.

To deal with the situation, the government passed a new law to enable the Singapore Turf Club assets, worth several hundreds of million dollars, to be unilaterally transferred to a new statutory body called the Singapore Totalisator Board (commonly known as the Tote Board). The Tote Board then set up a proprietary club, the Bukit Turf Club, to run the horse racing operations. Left with not much else to do, the old Singapore Turf Club (the private members club) folded and deregistered itself. Several years later, the Bukit Turf Club renamed itself the Singapore Turf Club.

The good news is that the Tote Board donated S$55 million (US$38 million) a year to charities in the immediate years following the changeover, which was five times more than the old Singapore Turf Club's donations in the immediate years preceding the takeover. Today, with more than S$300 million (US$207 million) in annual grants, the Singapore Tote Board is by far, the largest grantmaker in Singapore.[10]

Public Opinion

History has shown that the law has always tended to play catch-up with social and technological developments. What then is the fallback to external regulations in the oversight of corporate governance in charities?

Well, where the court of law falters, the court of public opinion may step in.

It was public opinion that forced the American Red Cross to reverse its decision to spend donations collected in the aftermath of September 11 on projects that did not benefit the people directly affected by the attacks. The public controversy also led to the resignation of the body's then president.[11]

Even in reticent Singapore, furor greeted the court revelations of the misdeeds of the National Kidney Foundation in its civil suit against Singapore Press Holdings. While there was no judgment handed down by the courts as the case was withdrawn, it was the public fury that led to the resignation of the chief executive officer and the board of directors, and the subsequent criminal investigations and legal actions.[12]

Unfortunately, public opinion of the explosive kind as witnessed in the National Kidney Foundation and American Red Cross cases occurs only when the perceived wrongdoing is massive and visible. The situation is obviously very unhealthy by the time it gets to that stage. In such a context, public opinion would be the ultimate level of governance when the first two levels of governance (corporate governance and regulation) have failed.

But public opinion should be more than just the final brake in the governance chain. Public opinion or rather public confidence should cast a wider net of both threat and support to charities in their functioning. It should manifest in continual public interest in what charities are doing, and in the public's individual choices of which charities they support. It is a manifestation of the concept of informed giving (covered in the previous chapter). Only when donors, volunteers and the community are discerning, demanding and discriminating of the money, time and support they give to individual charities, will there be a greater interest by charities to pay attention to their own corporate governance.

Charities need to realize that beyond the resources that they receive from the community to do their work, it is the relevance and legitimacy that the community bestows on them which allow them to exist and thrive in the first place. That public opinion is akin to another level of governance that ranks equally with rules and regulations to keep charities focused on their mission and effectiveness.

Levels of Governance

In conclusion, if we go back to the original question of who really governs a charity, the answer must be the three levels of governance (see Figure 3.1).

The first level is akin to the corporate governance that exists for a commercial organization. However, to be effective, there must be a good understanding of the nuances and peculiarities of the charity environment by the members of the governing body. At the same time, the charity should also have a greater willingness to incorporate good governance practices such as renewal, accountability and clarity of roles.

The second level is the active regulation that should focus more on the public interest aspect of charities. Regulations have to go beyond protecting the legal owner, which is sometimes not important when it comes to charities as the legal owner may be the same as the governing body. Rather, active regulation ensures accountability to the moral owners, namely, the community.

Finally, the community must take an active part itself in ensuring that the public interest is met. The last level of governance, public opinion,

Figure 3.1 Three Levels of Charity Governance

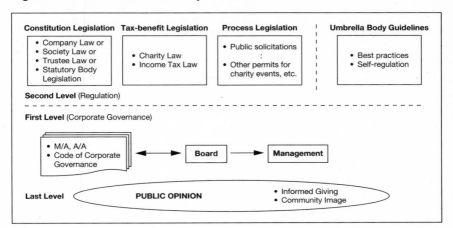

should not kick in only when things go haywire. Rather, it should be exercised on an ongoing basis through informed giving and continual feedback and support. This will prevent charities from going astray at all.

Endnotes:

Adapted from: "Who governs a nonprofit, really?" *SALT*, January-February 2006; "Who governs charities, really?" *The Straits Times*, January 11, 2006; and "Governance: profits vs. nonprofits," *The Social Service Journal*, Vol. 24, September 2007.

1   John Carver with Caroline Oliver, *Corporate Boards That Create Value* (Jossey-Bass, John Wiley & Sons, 2002).

2   Geoffrey Kiel and Gavin Nicholson, *Boards That Work* (The McGraw-Hill Companies Inc, 2003).

3   Peter Wallace and John Zinkin, *Mastering Business in Asia: Corporate Governance* (John Wiley & Sons (Asia) Pte. Ltd., 2005).

4   This subject of nonprofit success is explored in Chapter 5, "End Game: Extinction."

5   As happened in the NKF case. See Chapter 19, "NKF: The Saga and its Paradigms."

6   www.cof.org

7   www.ncvo-vol.org.uk

8   www.ncss.org.sg

9   The impetus for charity reform is discussed in Chapter 4, "Black box or glass house."

10   The grant amounts are drawn from following sources: Tan Tai Siong, "Cut the naivete, plead instead for wider use of gamblers' dollar," *The Straits Times*, May 18, 1991; Tan Siok Sun, "A second wind," *The Straits Times*, July 7, 2007; *The State of Giving* (National Volunteer & Philanthropy Center, 2005).

11   The Red Cross case is described in Chapter 6, "The problem of plenty."

12   See Chapter 19, "NKF: The saga and its paradigms."

Chapter 4

Regulation

Black Box or Glass House?

Regulators may position charities as trusted institutions with the government's seal of approval (the black box model) or as organizations that need to be transparent in a *caveat emptor* or "buyer-beware" marketplace (the glass house model).

The aim of regulation is to ensure compliance with charity laws—and the spirit in which those laws were conceived. In essence, these laws should promote the health of the charity sector by ensuring public trust and confidence, as well as provide charities and the sector with every opportunity to achieve their potential.

In that spirit, the glass house model is likely the better choice. In the wake of charity scandals, increasing regulatory restraints and powers essentially moves towards a black box model and paradoxically could take the charity sector a step backwards.

The role of the charity regulator is to ensure compliance with charity laws. Across various jurisdictions around the world, charity laws are being reviewed and revised:

- In England and Wales, the first major reform of charity law for 400 years was passed into legislation with the Charities Act 2006. The changes include an updated list of charitable purposes, a clear link between charitable status and public benefit, and the establishment of an independent Charity Appeal Tribunal.

– The Scottish Executive passed the Charity and Trustee Investment (Scotland) Act in 2005, its first major reform of charity law in 50 years. The Act includes a list of charitable purposes, a charity test and new fundraising regulations while setting out the functions of the regulator.

– In Singapore, changes to the regulation of charities were passed into legislation in March 2007. It streamlined the regulatory framework, adding more teeth for the regulator while raising the bar on minimum standards of governance, fundraising practices and financial reporting.

– The Australian government decided to abandon the draft Charities Bill 2003. However, there is now a move by several nonprofit bodies seeking to clarify certain definitions of charities and charitable activities, and to overhaul the legal framework and regulatory environment.[1]

– In the U.S., the Senate Finance Committee has, especially since 2004, been proposing major charity reforms. Many of these have been rebuffed by the charity sector but some of the less controversial ones have been passed in various bills. The process is ongoing for many of these charity reforms.

The previous chapter looked at the role of regulation in the overall charity governance framework from the perspective of the charities. In this chapter, we will examine, mainly from a regulator's viewpoint, the impetus of the charity law reforms and the regulatory approaches available.

Why Charity Law

What is the purpose of charity regulation? Most would answer that it is to ensure public confidence and build trust in the charities. This is vital for charities as they depend on the community for resources and support. Without public confidence, charities—more than any other kind of private organizations—would not have the legitimacy, let alone the resources, to function.

The general expectation is that such public confidence will be maintained only if charities exist for genuine charitable purposes and they function properly. Thus, many of the charity laws have tended to center on qualifications and evaluation for charity registration and continuity, what charities can or cannot do, especially with regards to fundraising, and how they can be held accountable for their actions.

The focus of charity laws is therefore mostly on risk management and compliance. For the regulator and the charities, it is to make sure that the rules are adequate and are followed so that no charity falls by the wayside.

 However, as corporate governance pundits would tell us, there are two sides of the governance coin: conformance and performance. Hence, regulation, which is the second level of governance (after corporate governance) for charities,[2] should also proactively focus on their performance. A parallel objective of charity laws should therefore be to enable and encourage charities to reach their full social and economic potential. This includes minimizing regulatory roadblocks while facilitating their functioning.

This holistic approach to charity regulation reflects an appreciation of the role of the charity sector as an essential third pillar of a society and economy (the other two pillars being the public and the private sectors). In many respects, charities form a bridge between the public and private sectors just as they fill any gaps left behind by the other two. Hence, the charity sector has been described as being about "private action, public benefit."[3]

Impetus for Reform

A good illustration of this enlightened approach to the charity sector is that taken by the British government. Its revamped Charities Act 2006 seeks to make it easier to establish and operate charities through a greater range of available legal forms, clearer and wider rules, and independent, fair and proportionate regulation. The reform was, in fact, a collaborative effort between the government and charities; the latter came together as a federation of nonprofits called the Coalition for a Charities Act.[4]

Revamping the regulatory framework was but one of several initiatives which the British government had collaborated with the charity sector on. Another initiative, the Changeup program, seeks to significantly build the capacity of the charity sector by radically improving the support available.[5]

A vision-driven and collaborative approach like the U.K.'s is ideal. Unfortunately, change is often driven by disruptive forces. For some jurisdictions, charity reforms are triggered by "media accounts of scandals in charities of all sizes, types and pedigrees," notwithstanding that these may be "outliers and concern over them is exaggerated."[6]

In Scotland, the collapse of Moonbeam, a children's cancer charity and investigations into 56 other Scottish charities put pressure on the Scottish Executive to move ahead with its charity reforms.[7]

In recent years, charitable organizations in the U.S. have come under the Congressional microscope as a result of investigative articles in the Boston Globe.[8] The series of articles that started in October 2003 highlighted abuses at several private foundations. For example, the trustee of the Paul and Virginia Cabot Charitable Trust channeled a significant part the foundation's assets to pay his high salary and for his daughter's luxurious wedding.[9]

The articles prompted an investigation and hearings by the Senate Finance Commission in June 2004. Proposals were made for nearly 100 wide-ranging reforms. These included giving the U.S. Internal Revenue Service the power to regulate the size of charity boards and radically broadened legal exposure while imposing stricter liability and compliance requirements similar to public corporations, and accreditation requirements for charities.[10]

The proposed reforms sent "shock waves through the nonprofit sector" which quickly regrouped to moderate the impact.[11] The Independent Sector, the largest advocacy organization for U.S. charities created the Panel on the Nonprofit Sector to discuss and provide its set of recommendations for charity oversight and accountability. In January 2005, the Alliance for Charitable Reform was formed by The Philanthropy Roundtable as an emergency advocacy initiative from the grantmakers' standpoint, to respond to Congress and "to help bring common sense to the charitable reform debate."[12]

Since then, the Senate Finance Committee and the charity sector have sought to find "ways to improve the sector without overwhelming exempt nonprofits with increased regulation." In August 2006, President Bush signed into law a charitable package that is, in many respects, "a watered-down version of provisions that were advanced by the Senate

Finance Committee" and the Panel on the Nonprofit Sector. The package included seven incentives for charitable giving as well as nearly 20 reforms designed to increase regulation of exempt organizations.[13] A year later, the Senate Finance Committee sought to expedite revision of Form 990 (the annual reporting form for federally tax-exempt organizations) to improve transparency and reporting of charities.[14]

In Singapore, the impetus for reform came hot on the heels of the National Kidney Foundation (NKF) debacle and other scandals.[15] Prior to the NKF saga, a committee formed by the government in January 2004, the Council for the Governance of Institutions of a Public Character (IPCs), issued its recommendations on the minimum standards for governance, transparency and fundraising in September 2004. The government accepted the recommendations with some modifications in May 2005, with implementation scheduled from January 2007.

However, while this was awaiting implementation, the NKF case erupted in July 2005. In response, the government formed another committee, the Inter-Ministry Committee on the Regulation of Charities and IPCs in October 2005 to overhaul the charity sector. The Committee made its recommendations within three months. After public consultation, the government accepted the recommendations three months later. Implementation kicked in within another three months, from July 2006.[16]

Although the Inter-Ministry Committee built upon the recommendations of the preceding Council of Governance of IPCs, the record time and fast forwarding of the implementation of the reforms illustrate the urgency with which the government felt it had to respond to the situation created by the NKF episode. The first Council took three years from formation to the scheduled start of implementation. The Inter-Ministry Committee took nine months.

Most reforms, whatever their impetus, will likely be couched in positive terms. The authorities want to improve the sector, increase its capacity and move charities forward—and they really do. However, those reforms that are triggered by accountability concerns such as those arising from charity scandals or the influence of the Sarbanes-Oxley Act,[17] naturally tend to focus on the compliance and risk management aspects of charities. It is natural to want to increase the list of restrictions on charities, to increase the powers of the regulator, and to have more punitive measures to prevent, discourage and penalize wrongful behavior. It is then left to the charity sector to push back and moderate any excessive measures.

Black Box versus Glass House

Regardless of the catalyst for change, it may be useful for regulators to think in terms of two contrasting approaches to regulation.

Does the regulator want the public to view a charity as a black box[18]—a trusted institution with the government's seal of approval? Or does it want the public to see a charity as transparent as a glass house? In the latter case, the charity sector operates in a *caveat emptor* ("buyer beware"—or in this case, "donor beware") environment.

Figure 4.1 contrasts the differences between these two approaches.

Figure 4.1 Black Box versus Glass House

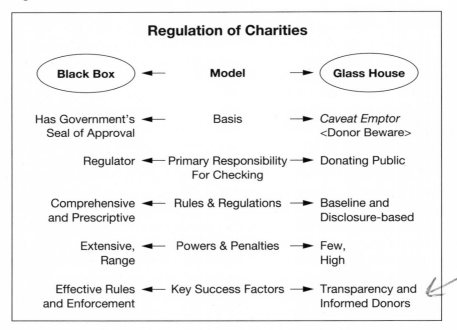

In the black box model, the primary responsibility for ensuring the integrity and soundness of a charity rests with the regulator. For the regulator to be effective, the rules and regulations which a charity must comply with must be both comprehensive and prescriptive. The attendant powers available to the regulator to investigate and enforce those rules have to be extensive.

In the glass house model, the primary responsibility rests with the public. It decides which charities to support and donate to. The glass house model supports self-regulation by the sector. There is still a need for rules and regulations, but these are minimal, sufficient only to ensure a certain level of soundness and stability on the part of the charities. More importantly, most of the rules are about transparency. For this model to work, disclosure rules have to be mandatory and extensive.

Disclosure serves two objectives. First, it allows the public to make informed decisions and take responsibility for those decisions, as to which charities they prefer to support. Secondly, visibility has the remarkable effect of inducing compliance and discipline on the matters being disclosed. A simple example is the trend of listed corporate boards disclosing board attendance which has had the effect of improving the attendance of directors at board and committee meetings.

I am reminded of a piece of valuable advice my English boss, John Skerritt, gave us when I worked in the U.K. many years ago. He was briefing a group of consultants and responded to a question on the appropriate personal behavior outside office hours. He said that we should simply apply one of two tests: 1. Would the Queen Mother do it? (Apparently, she was very strict), or 2. Could you explain it all on television the next morning?

When organizations complain that disclosure standards are onerous, they do not usually mean that it takes a lot of administrative effort to make the disclosure—how much effort can it take to provide information you already have? What they may mean is that by having to disclose the information, organizations and directors often feel compelled to comply with what may be a good practice—but they really do not wish to.

A glass house environment requires transparency and accountability, not only on the part of the charities, but also on the part of the regulator. It is important that the regulator explains its actions and its findings. The public can then decide whether it wishes to continue to support the charity based on the findings, adverse or otherwise, revealed by the regulators.

An effective glass house model also requires a couple of key ingredients that go beyond mere good faith and conduct on the part of the charities and the regulator.

The first is an educated and informed public. Donors have to understand and practice informed giving. They need to accept that it is a *caveat emptor* environment where they have to do their part in deciding which charities they are supporting.

Secondly, the support infrastructure to facilitate an open and self-regulating environment must be present. It is not always possible for the individuals in the community to independently assess and make sense of the array of charities out there. There must be the adequate intermediaries who provide the analysis, the education and the tools to enable a glass house environment to thrive.

Black Box or Glass House?

So, which environment is more suitable for a specific charity jurisdiction?

Both environments are workable. In the commercial world, one could say that the stock market approximates the glass house approach. On the other hand, the regulation of the banking industry tends towards the black box approach.

Public listed companies have clear disclosure requirements. They are penalized for failing to make timely and full disclosures. If a listed company does not do well or if it goes under, there could be howls of protests and pain, but, by and large, the investing public accepts that as part and parcel of doing business.

In contrast, if a bank goes under, it is a major crisis of confidence that raises questions about the regulators as much as it does about the bank. What were the regulators doing or rather not doing to avert the collapse? To ensure that banks have that seal of approval, the banking authority has an army of regulators to formulate the rules and analyze the massive amounts of data that the banks regularly provide. It also has the powers to ensure that banks stay in line with respect to their reporting and conduct. These measures are, however, not visible to the banking public who mostly operate on the basis that the banking system is sound.

My guess is that most charity regulators in the developed world will say that they support the glass house approach. It is in keeping with modern ideals of democracy and minimal intervention on the part of the state. It seems like a practical approach that allows the regulator to focus on ensuring proper disclosure and transparency at large. If a charity does not work out, that is largely the responsibility of its board and those who support it. The regulator can also divert some of its resources to deal with the performance aspects of the charity sector rather than just the risk management and compliance aspects.

But the glass house model comes under threat when there is a crisis of faith with charities and the regulators. In the aftermath of charity scandals, the pressure is to move towards a black box environment with a focus on greater risk management, compliance and regulatory actions. There will be calls for more controls of charities and more powers for the regulators to catch and punish errant charities. Charity law reforms undertaken in such a climate carry the risk of creating an environment with too high a regulatory hurdle for charities to operate in and the sequestering of draconian powers by the authorities to act on charities.

Would a hybrid system work? My view is that mixing black box controls and powers with an espoused glass house environment would be a mistake in the long term. Hybrid rules send the wrong message of whether the environment is glass house or black box. It also provides greater ammunition for critics of regulatory failure when the next scandal occurs. Too many restraints on charities will cripple their effective functioning. Extreme powers for the regulator that allow it to, say, close or suspend charities willy-nilly without due process and public accountability by the authorities, could lead to abuse in the future by the regulator. It also raises the question of who is watching the watcher?

In short, a balanced perspective is needed in the formulation of reforms. The English reforms, for example, specifically emphasize regulation that is independent from political and other interference; open and not stifling; and proportionate to the size of the organizations it is regulating.

In seeking this balance, it may help to go back to the basics of what a glass house environment is. It is a model based on minimal regulatory constraints while incorporating adequate levels of disclosure so that the public can make informed decisions of the charities they support. The public must be prepared to live with the consequences of their giving decisions. They, and the regulators, must accept that once in a while, there will be fallen angels like the NKF, Moonbeam and the Paul and Virginia Cabot Charitable Trust. Hopefully, with an environment ruled by proper disclosure, the fault-lines will be caught earlier and the ensuing costs will not be as high with these errant charities.

The Spirit of Charity and the Law

The aim of regulation is to ensure compliance with the charity laws—and the spirit in which those laws were conceived. That spirit should be to promote the health of the charity sector through first, increased public trust and confidence and, secondly, through providing charities and the sector with every opportunity to achieve their potential.

In that spirit, the glass house model is likely the better choice but the support infrastructure and an educated and informed public must also be present.

The political pressures following a crisis may push the authorities and the public towards a more comfortable black box model where the authorities basically take care of everything. However, that would be a regression. For the social scene in each locality to progress, the community needs to take responsibility for getting there. Regulations, after all, should only provide a baseline for a charity to get started and to operate from.

Endnotes:

Adapted from: "Charities: Black box or glass house?" *SALT*, March-April 2006; and "Glasshouse better than the black box," *The Straits Times*, March 3, 2006.

1   *Charity Now: Redefining Charity Law for the New Millennium. Discussion Paper and Recommendations for Reform* (Jobs Australia, VCOSS and ACOSS, 2006).

2   See Chapter 3, "Who governs a nonprofit, really?"

3   *Private Action, Public Benefit. A Review of Charities and the Wider Not-For-Profit Sector* (Strategy Unit, Cabinet Office, United Kingdom, September 2002). This is the publication describing the proposals for charity reform in the U.K.

4   This is a group of leading charities and charitable organizations convened by the National Council for Voluntary Organizations (the umbrella body for the voluntary sector in England, with sister councils in the rest of the U.K.). See www.ncvo-vol.org.uk/press/releases/?id=3564&terms=charity%20reform.

5   www.capacitybuilders.org.uk

6   Dana Brakman Reiser and Evelyn Broady, "Chicago-Kent Symposium: Who Guards the Guardians?: Monitoring and Enforcement of Charity Governance," *Chicago-Kent Law Review*, 2005.

7   "Charity reform 'long overdue'," *BBC News*, October 19, 2003.

8   www.acreform.com/who/history.html

9   Beth Healy, Francie Latour, Sacha Pfeiffer, and Michael Rezendes & Walter V. Robinson, "Some officers of charities steer assets to selves," *The Boston Globe*, October 9, 2003.

10   "Charity Oversight and Reform: Keeping Bad Things from Happening to Good Charities," Senate Finance Hearing, White Paper, and Roundtable, *News From The Center*, Center for Nonprofit Advancement, June 2004, http://www.nonprofitadvancement.org/newsletter1852/newsletter_show.htm?doc_id=234486. The Senate Finance Commission was chaired by Senator Chuck Grassley.

11   Kay Sohl, "Charity Reform Debate," *TACS News*, Technical Assistance for Community Services, Summer 2005.

12   www.acreform.com

13 "August 2006 Charity Reform Update: House Approves Charitable Giving Incentives and Reforms," *Guidestar News*, August 2006, www.guidestar.org/DisplayArticle. do?articleId=1039.

14 "Charity Reform Update, June 2007: Senate Finance Committee Leaders Advocate Form 990 Revision," *Guidestar News*, June 2007, www.guidestar.org/DisplayArticle. do?articleId=1134.

15 See Chapter 19, "NKF: The saga and its paradigms." Other scandals and questionable actions of charities following the NKF include the Singapore Association for the Visually Handicapped, Youth Challenge, St. John's Home for Elderly Persons and Ren Ci Hospital and Medicare.

16 "Move toward more transparency. New rules for charity," *The Straits Times*, June 26, 2006. The transfer of the office of the Commissioner of Charities was effected on September 1, 2006, and new legislation was enacted on March 1, 2007.

17 Sarbanes-Oxley is a U.S. federal law enacted in July 2002 in response to corporate and accounting scandals involving Enron, Tyco, Peregrine Systems and Worldcom. The legislation establishes new or enhanced standards, considered onerous by many, for U.S. public listed company boards, management and accounting firms.

18 A black box is a technical term for a device or system or object viewed primarily in terms of input and output characteristics. The inner workings of the box are not visible. Most people will be familiar with its use in aviation where it is a flight data recorder and cockpit voice recorder that records the cockpit communications of an aircraft flight.

Nonprofit Management

Chapter 5

Nonprofit Mission

Endgame: Extinction

The mantra for businesses is growth, growth and more growth. The opposite should apply to nonprofits. Nonprofits are created to achieve societal change. Ultimate success occurs when the nonprofit's mission is achieved and its existence is no longer needed.

Extinction, not growth, should therefore be the endgame for nonprofits. For many reasons, this generally is not the case. After all, it is hard to celebrate the death of an organization, rather than its birth and growth.

However, there are enlightened nonprofit boards and executives of charities—and even foundations—which understand the value of a focused mission, accomplishing it and then closing out.

Across the world, nonprofit organizations are in growth mode, growing in numbers and in variety. The Johns Hopkins Comparative Nonprofit Sector Project, a pioneering study of the nonprofit sector in over 40 countries, calls the phenomenon a "veritable global associational revolution," where there is a "massive upsurge of organized private, voluntary activity in virtually every region of the world—in developed countries of North America, Western Europe and Asia; through Central and Eastern Europe; and in much of the developing world."[1]

In the U.S., the total number of public charities and foundations increased from nearly 600,000 in 1996 to over 1 million in 2006, a growth of over 70 percent in a decade.[2] In the U.K., the number of registered charities rose marginally by 3.5 percent to more than 190,000 in the same period.[3] In Singapore, there were 400 registered charities in 1983. By 2006, the number had increased four and a half times to more than 1,800.[4]

But it is not only the number of charities that has grown; the size of each charitable organization is also growing. While the number of U.S. public charities grew by 68 percent in the decade leading to 2003, expenditure grew by 88 percent and the value of assets held increased even further by 104 percent.[5]

The Growth Mantra

That all sounds great for many of us, especially those from the business world. "Growth, growth and more growth" is a refrain second only to "maximizing shareholders' value." In fact, growth is seen as a key way to increase shareholders' value.

Commercial companies grow by two means. They can do more within their core business i.e. by selling more of their existing products and services to their customers. Most companies initially grow by doing this.

However, when companies hit the limit of what they can do within their core business, they often expand by moving into adjacencies. These are areas away from the original core business, but which are often related in varying degrees so that the company can leverage its core competencies, existing customer relationships, brand, networks and other strengths. Examples of the various ways in which a commercial company can expand beyond its core is illustrated in Figure 5.1.

Nonprofit organizations tend to follow this model. They start off trying to do as much as they can in relation to their cause. As they become successful at what they do, they also tend to look into adjacencies.

For example, one of America's largest and best-known charities, Toys for Tots, is expanding into literacy. The nonprofit started in 1947, and for 61 years, it faithfully delivered Christmas presents to needy children across America. In 2006, it delivered 20 million toys. Then, in 2008, it launched the "Toys for Tots Literacy Program" to collect books and other educational material and distribute these to needy children.[7]

Figure 5.1 Growing Beyond the Core

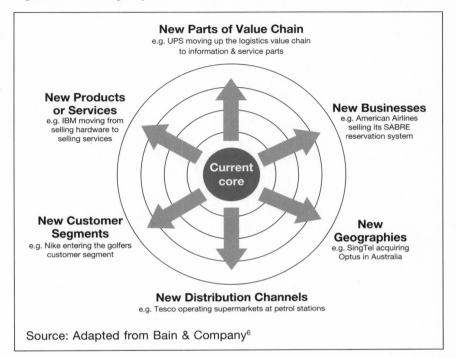

Source: Adapted from Bain & Company[6]

Many other nonprofit examples abound. But the question is this: should charities, in fact, be following the business dictates of growth for growth's sake?

Extinction Agenda

Philosophically, if we go back to the raison d'être for the existence of a charity, we find that it is about causes. Whether that cause is about people (The Children's Society), animals (Society for Prevention of Cruelty to Animals), or toilets for that matter (World Toilet Organization), the purpose is to effect change through advocacy and/or service in all or some parts of society.

Success for a charity, therefore, comes when it has achieved its goal of effecting the societal change that it originally set out to do. In other words, ultimate success must mean that a charity no longer needs to exist! This is the antithesis of the commercial world, where liquidation often means ultimate failure.

Therein lies a key contrast between the two worlds. In the commercial world, you succeed by growing and expanding. In the nonprofit world, you succeed by becoming extinct.

I first became acquainted with this notion in 2005 when I had dinner with Iftekhar Zaman, the executive director of Transparency International (TI) Bangladesh.[8] TI is an international non-governmental organization devoted to combating corruption. Zaman had his work cut out for him as Bangladesh was then ranked at the bottom of the global Corruption Perceptions Index. "My job is to catalyze conditions where we won't be needed anymore," he said. "If corruption can be brought down to a tolerable level and Bangladesh moves up the global rankings, TI-Bangladesh will have its mission accomplished."

Unfortunately, he did not anticipate this happening soon. Such a sentiment is certainly not motivated by any desire to stay on the job forever as he narrated the difficulties of working in an environment where the powers-that-be were against what he was doing.

Perhaps extinction may be easier for Transient Workers Count Too (TWC2).[9] The non-governmental organization was set up by a group of social activists to champion the rights and fair treatment of migrant workers in Singapore. Its founding President, Braema Mathi, said at an awards ceremony honoring the charity that "we aim to disappear, because that means our work is done." Mathi, who started the charity in 2003, has given the group until 2010 to "self-destruct."[10]

Looking for Extinctions

I reckon that if there are any charities that should be extinct in due course, they would likely be those in the healthcare sector. With rapid medical advances, it is likely that charities set up to deal with specific health causes should, in time, become extinct. Let's look at two: leprosy and tuberculosis.

Leprosy was an endemic disease, especially in many tropical countries, in the mid-1900s. The World Health Organization (WHO) had targeted to eliminate leprosy as a public health problem through effective implementation of multi-drug therapy. It has met with much success. WHO estimates that the number of leprosy cases worldwide had decreased from 10 to 12 million in 1985 to about 2.4 million in 1994.[11] The number of new cases worldwide has been declining year on year, with less than 300,000 in 2006.[12]

A number of nonprofit organizations help WHO in its mission of eliminating leprosy. One of them is LEPRA, or the British Empire Leprosy Relief Association.[13] It was set up in 1924 "to rid the Empire of leprosy." While it continues to pursue the cause of leprosy, it has expanded in several ways. Geographically, it has been expanded to cover more countries including many in Africa, Asia and Latin America, even as the British Empire exists in all but name only. It has also gone beyond leprosy to include HIV/AIDS, tuberculosis, eye care and sight-saving surgery, and social rights. In fact, its revised mission statement is "to address unmet health needs of people affected by leprosy, tuberculosis, HIV/AIDS and other health conditions exacerbated by poverty, discrimination and stigma."

In Singapore, leprosy is very much under control. The Singapore Leprosy Relief Association[14] provides a home and care for ex-leprosy victims. The number of residents is declining, and as the Association plans its move to a new home, it intends to expand its coverage to skin diseases beyond leprosy, such as eczema, psoriasis and venous ulcers.

Tuberculosis is a much more deadly disease than leprosy. It was a major killer in Singapore in the 1960s, but it is now under control. Between 1960 to 2004, the number of cases was reduced from 310 to 39 per 100,000 resident population. The Singapore Anti-Tuberculosis Association[15] was set up in 1947 with the aim of combating tuberculosis. By 1972, it had dealt with over 46,000 cases. In recent years, the number of new tuberculosis cases dealt by it has ranged from four to 29 annually.

Despite the few tuberculosis cases, the organization continues strongly with four clinics and a staff of 120. The charity has evolved from a tuberculosis clinic to a healthcare provider, mainly of general medical services such as pre-employment checkups and health screenings. It now goes only by its acronym of "SATA" and its revised mission statement is to "promote lung health and provide health screening to the community."

Extinctions Found

In looking for cases of extinctions, we can, of course, start with the list of those charities that no longer exist. Official reasons for termination are not usually available. A few years back, I did a poll of charities that had closed in Singapore. It appears that almost all did so either to change organizational forms (that is, they were pursuing the same causes under a different umbrella) or they were unable to survive. In the latter cases, it was usually a result of inadequate funding and support from the community.

It is rare to find an organization closed because it has accomplished its mission and disbanded. Such organizations are often those born for a very specific mission and the leaders of the organizations were, and continued to be, clear about the mission and the timelines.

One example of a focused nonprofit is Families Against Casino Threat in Singapore (FACTS). It was set up in 2004 when the political leaders were considering granting casino licenses for the first time in Singapore. FACTS provided a platform for Singaporeans to register their anti-casino views via an online petition to the President of Singapore. It gathered 29,000 signatures and submitted its petition in April 2005. You could debate whether FACTS was successful since the government's decision came down against the petition, but FACTS did perform its stated role and its cause was effectively over when the government made its decision to allow two casinos.

Even though Fong Hoe Fang, founder of FACTS, acknowledged at the time that there was talk among the signatories "to form some kind of an organization to combat the social ills that will befall our land once the casinos come on track," this has not yet happened. The orientation and skills to deal with problem gamblers is different from that of mobilizing an online advocacy group.

Another focused nonprofit is The September 11th Fund.[16] The Fund was set up immediately after the World Trade Center attacks on September 11, 2001 by the New York Community Trust and the United Way of New York. The response was immediate and overwhelming. Within 24 hours, it collected US$15 million. The Fund eventually disbursed US$528 million to the victims, families and communities affected by the attacks. The Fund was then closed in December 2004, just slightly over three years after it was created—a short time to spend half a billion charity dollars.

In the case of The September 11th Fund, its board and chief executive officer (CEO) were very clear of the purpose and tenure of the Fund. Several of the board members had experiences in "specific projects [that] turned into institutions that lasted too long, sometimes in search of a purpose."[17] Yet, "working purposefully towards your own obsolescence" created a lot of challenges, the biggest of which was emotional.[18] It is hard to see death, even of an organization, as a cause for celebration rather than something to be mourned.

Perpetual Causes

But a pertinent question is this: Is extinction a meaningful measure of nonprofit success?

Some would argue that many social causes are effectively perpetual. We can all imagine that global poverty, world peace, climate change, and even cruelty to animals will take a long time to solve, maybe never. So should extinction be a non-issue for such causes?

Granted, some causes will be with us for a long time. But the mission of a nonprofit can be defined more precisely to make it more meaningful and actionable. The *Stanford Social Innovation Review* recently described several key characteristics of a successful nonprofit mission statement.[19] It noted that, above all, the mission statement should be focused—rather than be grand posturing to solve the problems of the world. While mission statements should be inspirational, and even aspirational, they should also be framed in practical terms proportionate to the resources that can be brought to bear. The journal noted that mission statements should be timeless and should only be altered in truly exceptional situations, rather than be changed to accommodate the next flavor-of-the-month activities the board or staff wishes to undertake.

Foundations with endowments are a type of charity that many of us would assume to be perpetual. Here, a philanthropist creates a foundation by leaving a large sum of money behind. The annual income that could be generated by the endowment is used for grants. U.S. federal law requires that five percent of the net investment assets, which is a reasonable long term economic rate of return on monetary assets, are distributed as grants by a private foundation. With this approach, a foundation can effectively be perpetual unless the funds or the foundation is mismanaged.

The rationale for having perpetual foundations is that they allow the preservation of long-term money for solving long-term social problems. This would include having a sufficient pool of money to resolve unanticipated social problems. That may be the argument, but often it may simply be that the donor wants to leave a long-lasting legacy and ensure that a tradition of philanthropic giving continues in the family.

There is a new wave of thinking that runs counter to this. The view is that it is "irresponsible, even immoral, to keep large amounts of tax-advantaged wealth on the sidelines when present needs are so great."[20] Instead, several philanthropists today are establishing limited-term foundations with expressed wishes that the money be spent on specific causes within a fixed period of time.

The first such foundation that I came across was a smallish one in Singapore—the Ian Ferguson Foundation. According to Peony Ferguson, her husband's will stated that the money should be spent within 10 years and as chairperson of the Foundation, she was working towards fulfilling that wish.

A more well-known limited-term foundation is the Aaron Diamond Foundation. Aaron and Irene Diamond had decided on a 10-year lifespan for their foundation and for the allocation of monies to various types of causes. When Aaron Diamond died, his wife did just that. From 1987 to 1996, the foundation gave away US$220 million to more than 700 New York City organizations. One of the projects was the establishment of the Aaron Diamond AIDS Research Center that subsequently pioneered the use of the combination drug therapy that helped reduced by five times the AIDS-related death rate in America and Western Europe.[21]

Other foundations such as the John M. Olin Foundation that closed in 2005 and Atlantic Philanthropies which intends to do so in 2016, have similarly taken this route. Even the Bill & Melinda Gates Foundation which can probably last indefinitely based on the sheer scale of its assets, is setting the pace in this area of foundation governance. It has declared that it would spend its money and go out of business within 50 years of the death of its last trustee, rather than become a permanent institution.[22]

Exiting Graciously

So what does it take to make extinction happen?

To initiate the process of extinction, Carol Kellemann, the CEO of The September 11th Fund offers three lessons:[23]

– A closeout cannot be undertaken without full support from the board and the CEO. Given the difficulties of closing out, including the emotional challenges, Kellemann felt that this was the most important element of the closure.

– Start the closeout process well in advance and give staff, colleagues and partners ample time and compassion so that they can plan, reflect and accept the new reality. This lessens the pain of getting people to work themselves out of a job.

– Start right away to ponder posterity, for example how and what documentation about the life and work of the organization should be saved and shared. This is about capturing history efficiently and wisely.

While the closeout may be painful, it probably takes more discipline not to veer in the other direction of unwarranted expansion. It is easy to be distracted or attracted by other opportunities that are initially at the periphery of a nonprofit's core mission but which, in time, lead the organization further and further away from its core. This is called "mission creep."

A case study of how mission creep can be avoided is the Rural Development Institute (RDI).[24] RDI is a nonprofit organization, comprising attorneys, economists and public policy experts, that helps the rural poor in developing countries obtain legal rights to land. The organization has helped 400 million poor farmers around the world own some 270 million acres of land. It does so with a very lean staff of 23, field offices in various countries and a total annual budget of just US$2 million.

RDI has been effective because it steadfastly makes decisions related to its scope based on its articulated mission "to secure land rights for the world's poorest people, those 3.4 billion chiefly rural people who live on less than $2 a day." The success of the organization has brought tempting opportunities for it to expand into new areas, to aid new populations and to adopt new methods. But it has not yielded to such temptations. For example, despite the lucrative offer of a subcontract to help a fully-funded urban land rights reform program in the former Soviet Union, RDI declined because the program did not deal with its core constituency, the urban poor. It turned out to be a good decision because other opportunities that fitted its niche came along that enabled RDI to do what it wanted in the former Soviet Union. In time, RDI helped allocate about 106 million acres of land to the impoverished in the former Soviet Union.

A closeout is often difficult also because of perceived "waste." If a nonprofit were to close, or just simply scale down its programs in line with the needs of its cause, does this mean that all the expertise, volunteers and value that had been built up is lost? Well, it need not and should not be. The people involved and the capabilities developed can, and should be, harnessed for other causes.

The nonprofit sector is replete with examples of serial social activists and entrepreneurs who move from successfully leading one charity to the next. Prior to founding TWC2, Braema Mathi was instrumental in starting the School Pocket Money Fund[25] that seeks to alleviate the financial burden of education for low-income families. She also initiated the White Ribbon Campaign to end violence against women and children for the Association of Women for Action & Research. Currently, she is the coordinator for MARUAH, a group that is facilitating an ASEAN Human Rights Mechanism.[26] Jeroo Billimoria[27] first started a telephone hotline for children in distress in India, then moved on to a global network of children's helplines, and most recently to another global network to empower poor children through social and financial education. Nicholas France[28] is another serial social entrepreneur, who founded several social enterprises: manufacturing and selling furniture, cutting greenhouse pollution emissions, with the most recent being to cool the globe via rapid, large scale energy efficiency.

It could be argued that this, in a sense, is similar to what some charities are seeking to do, as their original mission is being accomplished. By expanding under the original organizational umbrella, a charity is able to leverage on its infrastructure, capability and brand.

On the other hand, moving to a new cause under a new charity setup avoids having to deal with the confusion over the original cause (often built into the charity name e.g. "Toys," "Tuberculosis," and others). It also avoids the tricky question of donors' intentions on the use of their donations for different purposes.[29] More importantly, having a clear cause and an end goal provides focus and optimizes the use of community resources.

The Road to Extinction—and Growth

Thus, extinction should be the endgame of nonprofits. Nonprofits can get there if they define their mission statements in focused and practical terms, and single-mindedly strive towards achieving their mission in the stipulated timeframe. The challenge is to overcome our natural tendency and business upbringing to pursue organizational growth for growth's sake.

Doing so would make for a more vibrant and effective charity sector. As each charity focuses and accomplishes its mission, the resources are better utilized and can be productively harnessed for new charities and causes. This will grow the sector. The end goal for the individual charities is extinction, but paradoxically, the collective result for the sector would be its growth.

Endnotes:

Adapted from: "Endgame: Extinction," *SALT*, July-August 2005; and "Charities should aim 'to be extinct'," *The Straits Times*, July 23, 2005.

1   Lester M. Salamon, Helmut K. Anheier, Regina List, Stefan Teopler, S. Wojciech Sokolowski and Associates, *Global Civil Society: Dimensions of the Nonprofit Sector* (The Johns Hopkins Comparative Nonprofit Sector Project, Kumarian Press, 1999); Lester M. Salamon, S. Wojciech Sokolowski and Regina List, *Global Civil Society: An Overview* (Center for Civil Society Studies, Institute for Policy Studies, The Johns Hopkins University, 2003).

2   "Number of Nonprofit Organizations in the United States, 1996-2006," National Center for Charitable Statistics, http://nccsdataweb.urban.org/PubApps/profile1.php?state=US.

3   Statistics from: Sarah Brennan, "An up-to-date picture of information held on the register of charities and insight into charities and public service delivery" (paper presented at the National Council for Voluntary Organizations Research Conference, "Measuring the voluntary sector," September 2007), www.ncvo-vol.org.uk/uploadedFiles/NCVO/What_we_do/Research/Research_Events/Brennan_S_PDF.pdf.

4   Statistics from: Wong Sher Maine, "Small charities fight for bit of the pie," *The Straits Times*, April 7, 2004; and *Commissioner of Charities Annual Report for the year ending December 31, 2006* (Singapore: Commissioner of Charities, 2007).

5   The *United States Nonprofit Sector* (National Council of Nonprofit Associations, 2003), www.ncna.org/_uploads/documents/live//us_sector_report_2003.pdf.

6   This diagram is adapted with permission from a slide presentation by Bain & Company, Inc. More information on this concept can be found in Chris Zook, Bain & Company, Inc, *Beyond The Core: Expand your market without abandoning your roots* (Harvard Business School Press, 2004).

7   Philip Rucker, "Toys for Tots to expand mission with children's literacy campaign," *Washington Post*, March 2, 2008. See also www.toysfortots.org and www.toysfortotsliteracy.org.

8   www.ti-bangladesh.org

9   The group was originally called TWC2, named after The Working Committee, an initiative aimed at strengthening civil society in Singapore. See John Gee and Elaine Ho, *Dignity Overdue* (Select Publishing, 2006) and www.twc2.org.sg.

10 Yap Su-Yin, "Group honored for helping foreign workers," *The Straits Times*, November 25, 2005.

11 "Leprosy Statistics," eMedTV, http://diseases.emedtv.cogm/leprosy/leprosy-statistics.html.

12 "Weekly epidemiological record, No. 32, 2006, 81, 309-316, Global leprosy situation, 2006," World Health Organization, August 11, 2006, http://www.who.int/lep/resources/wer8132.pdf.

13 www.lepra.org.uk

14 www.starhub.net.sg/~nc0038/main.html

15 www.sata.com.sg

16 www.september11.org (this site may not be around for too long). Also see www.nycommunitytrust.org/page30798.cfm.

17 Carol Kellemann, "Closing America's largest charity," *Executive Update*, March 2005, www.asaecenter.org/PublicationsResources/EUArticle.cfm?ItemNumber=11501.

18 Ibid.

19 William F. Meehan, "Making missions that won't creep," *Stanford Social Innovation Review*, Winter 2008.

20 Vincent McGee, "Spending out as a philanthropic strategy," in *Philanthropy in the 21st Century* (The Foundation Center, 2006).

21 Allan R. Clyde, "A conversation with Irene Diamond," *Foundation News & Commentary*, Vol. 39, No. 2, March/April 1998.

22 Judith H. Dobrzynski, "Philanthropy Now: Diversity and creativity for changing times," *Carnegie Reporter*, Vol. 4, No. 2, Spring 2007.

23 Carol Kellemann, "Closing America's largest charity," *Executive Update*, March 2005, www.asaecenter.org/PublicationsResources/EUArticle.cfm?ItemNumber=11501.

24 Kim Jonker & William F. Meehan, "Curbing Mission Creep," *Stanford Social Innovation Review*, Winter 2008. See also www.rdiland.org.

25 www.straitstimes.com/School+Pocket+Money+Fund/School+Pocket+Money+Fund.html

26 www.maruahsg.wordpress.com

27 www.schwabfound.org/schwabentrepreneurs.htm?schwabid=341. Jeroo Billimoria is also described in Chapter 15, "Innovating social change."

28 www.schwabfound.org/schwabentrepreneurs.htm?schwabid=486&extended=yes

29 The subject of donors' intent is covered in Chapter 6, "The problem of plenty."

Chapter 6

Reserves

The Problem of Plenty

Many charities struggle to raise funds. The few that are very successful face a different set of problems.

First of all, when is enough, enough in fundraising? Setting fundraising targets sounds simple enough, but it may not be practical in all cases. When fundraising targets are exceeded, should the charity refund the excess donations to donors or divert the surplus monies to other charitable causes?

For the long term, successful charities have to address the question of how much is enough in reserves? Apart from issues of measurements, there is a difference of views about whether there should be a reserves level and what that level should be. Some faith-based groups have set an extreme level of zero for reserves. This approach keeps charities relevant and accountable.

Finally, whatever it does with donors' money, a charity must respect the basis under which the money is given. Charities that have violated donor intent have suffered grave consequences.

The September 11, 2001 attacks on New York's World Trade Center stunned the nation and the world. Almost immediately, the American Red

Cross created the Liberty Disaster Relief Fund (the Liberty Fund).[1] The donations poured in as Americans showed their support for the victims and their country. About half of all donations in the aftermath of 9/11 went to the Red Cross. There was clearly more than enough for immediate disaster relief for items such as food and health services. So the Red Cross made a decision early to spend more than US$250 million of the Liberty Fund on other long-term programs, including preparedness for future terrorist attacks.

However, public outcry on such use of donations led to Congressional hearings. Many donors felt that the money they gave to the Red Cross was meant directly for the victims of 9/11. Several thousand angry emails were sent to the Red Cross during the hearings. On November 14, 2001, the American Red Cross back-pedaled. It publicly pledged that all of the Liberty Fund's proceeds would, henceforth, go exclusively to the people directly affected by the 9/11 attacks and offered refunds to disgruntled donors.

The Singapore Red Cross was faced with a similar situation in the wake of the Asian tsunami that hit on Boxing Day, 2004. In January 2005, it set up the Tidal Waves Asia Fund[2] in response to the tragedy. The initial fundraising target was S$1 million (US$690,000), but this was quickly exceeded. It ended up with S$88 million (US$61 million) in the kitty. As a metaphorical tidal wave of donations swept in during the first few weeks of the appeal, there was disquiet among other volunteer groups and charities that were also responding to the crisis. They felt somewhat deprived of the almost unidirectional flow of funds to the Singapore Red Cross. Prodded by the Singapore government, the Singapore Red Cross set up a coordinating committee to make the money available to other Singaporean organizations helping out with the tsunami reconstruction efforts.[3]

Charities usually keep excess funds whenever they can as reserves for future use. But the disclosure of a high level of reserves (S$189 million or US$130 million) in the National Kidney Foundation in Singapore led to public disquiet and its eventual unraveling.[4]

The experiences of these three organizations highlight what one may call "the problem of plenty" for charities. It may be a happy problem for the charity with the plenty, but it is a controversial matter for donors and other charities.

There are several related questions which the charity sector has been grappling with:

– What is an adequate level of reserves?

– Should every fund communicate a financial target?

– Should charities return excess money to donors or channel the money to other charitable purposes?

– How far should a charity go to respect donor intent and how should this be managed?

Level of Reserves

Saving money for a rainy day is an old-fashioned value. It is how most of us are brought up. In a similar way, the accumulation of some reserves by nonprofit organizations is generally accepted, if not encouraged. Reserves allow a charity to absorb setbacks and take advantage of opportunities as they arise.

Yet too high a level of reserves is frowned upon by some donors and other charities. The thinking is that excessive reserves may deprive other deserving charities of needed funds, assuming that the donor pool is finite.

Rather than question the absolute level of reserves, the right approach is to ask how long the reserves will last a specific charity. In this respect, the industry agrees on a common yardstick of a "reserves ratio"—the number of months or years that the reserves can cover a charity's operations. However, for the moment, there is no common agreement on the components of the reserves ratio or even what an appropriate level of reserves is.

The reserves ratio is simply the total amount of reserves divided by the net operating expenses (what would be required to operate the charity if there were no further fundraising). At the practical level, there are questions of whether the reserves amount should include designated funds locked up for specific purposes and whether one should include or exclude certain operating expenses or income which would bolster or reduce the net operating expense figure.

The key reason for the difficulty in reaching common agreement on these issues is that a conservative approach to accounting rules would yield a lower (that is, a better) ratio compared to a more liberal approach (see box on "Measuring Reserves"). Authorities tend towards a more liberal approach while some charities will push the envelope with a full conservative approach.

Measuring Reserves

The reserves ratio measures the length of time a charity can sustain itself without any further fundraising. It is computed as follows:

$$\text{Reserves Ratio} = \frac{\text{Reserves}}{\text{Annual Net Operating Expenses}}$$

The differences of opinion on how the components should be computed are described below.

Reserves

Reserves are investment assets that belong to a charity which can be expended at the trustees' discretion in furtherance of the charity's objectives. These are usually captured in the balance sheet under categories such as General Fund, Endowments and so on.

Many charities conservatively define reserves to exclude funds which are not "free," that is, funds which have already been committed or designated for a particular purpose. Critics charge that such exclusions are used by some charities to distort perception of the actual amount of reserves that they have. The real test, they say, is whether there are real external restrictions by donors versus internal designations of fund use.

A more encompassing approach is to include all such assets, whether designated or otherwise. A charity could then, as part of its disclosure, be specific about the kind of commitments that had, in fact, already been made on the designated funds. The rule that the American Institute of Philanthropy's Charity Watch follows is that an investment asset is part of the reserves as long as the charity "could choose to spend if it wanted to do so."[5] In Singapore, the National Council of Social Service excludes building funds from the computation of reserves amount.

Annual Net Operating Expenses

This is simply the net cost of operating an organization i.e. regular operating costs less any income or cost items which can be expected not to recur if there is no further fundraising. Which elements of income and expenditure to include in determining this depends on whether you adopt a liberal approach (resulting in higher ratio) or a conservative approach (resulting in a lower ratio):

Income Sources	Liberal Approach	Conservative Approach
1. Donations—one-off	No	No
2. Donations from sustained giving programs	Yes	No
3. Government grants	Yes	Yes
4. Income from provision of services	Yes	Yes
5. Investment income from reserves assets	Yes	No

Expenditure Items	Liberal Approach	Conservative Approach
6. Direct Charitable Expenses	Yes	Yes
7. Fundraising Expenses	No	Yes
8. Administrative Expenses	Yes	Yes

Note: When an Income source is excluded or when an Expenditure item is included, the ratio would be lower (conservative approach). Conversely, when an Income source is included or when an Expenditure item is excluded, the ratio would be higher (liberal approach).

The test for inclusion of an item should be the general certainty that income or expenditure elements will continue into future years. The rationale for including or excluding each item is as follows:

– *Donations—one off*. These are excluded from both approaches because if there is no further fundraising, these donations should no longer be coming in.

– *Donations From Sustained Giving Programs*. More sophisticated nonprofits usually build loyalty donor programs where donors give regularly almost without being asked regularly. Examples are the Community Chest's SHARE Program and the National Kidney Foundation's Lifedrops program. Such donations are unlikely to stop unless there is a major crisis of confidence. So it is argued in the liberal approach that one should assume that such donations are still forthcoming, and would help reduce the annual net operating expenses.

– *Government Grants and Services Income*. Since these should logically continue even if there are no donations, they should be factored in to reduce the annual net operating expenses in both approaches.

– *Investment Income from Reserves Assets*. Since reserves assets do generate income (although it will decline as the capital is eroded), logically, they constitute a source of income that can reduce the annual net operating expenses. The income is thus included in the liberal approach. However, since the year-on-year capital erosion is harder to compute, as a practical matter, many organizations and authorities would take the conservative approach of not factoring in such income to reduce the operating expense.

– *Direct Charitable Expenses & Administrative Expenses*. These two items are part of regular operating expenses and are included in both approaches.

– *Fundraising Expenses*. Strictly, if one is seeking to determine how long a charity could last without further fundraising, the cost of further fundraising should be excluded. This would be the liberal approach. The conservative approach continues to include fundraising expenses on the basis that it is easier to compute reserves ratio without breaking down the total expenditure figure.

The Charity Commission for England and Wales observed that some charities "inappropriately use accounting conventions such as designated funds to distort the presentation of their reserves level."[6] These charities felt the need to hide the true levels of their reserves because their revelation might adversely affect their ability to seek donations or grants. However, the Commission stated that, in most cases, reserves had not been a barrier to attracting funding. In fact, it found that proactive disclosure of reserves and a reserves policy went down well with donors from an accountability standpoint.

Besides the mechanics of measurement, there is even less agreement across the world on whether there is an appropriate level of reserves and, if so, what this should be.

Studies by the Charity Commission for England and Wales[7] showed a wide spectrum of reserves levels, from charities that have no funds in reserves to those that hold substantial amounts. While the average reserves levels of British charities hovered at about 12 months, 75 percent of the total reserves were accounted for by only 7 percent of the British charities. The Commission chose not to recommend a specific reserves level. Instead, it suggested that charities formally adopt and disclose a reserves policy. Consequently, the number of British charities with a reserves policy rose from 27 percent in 2002 to 40 percent in 2006.[8]

In other jurisdictions around the world, there are bodies which do specify acceptable reserves levels.

Charity Watch, the online service of the American Institute of Philanthropy which evaluates and rates U.S-based charities, considers that up to three years of reserves is reasonable.[9] Charities with more than five years of reserves are considered to be "the least needy" and are awarded an "F" Grade (the lowest grade possible, "A" being the highest grade) regardless of other measurements. Similarly, the Better Business Bureau Wise Giving Alliance requires that unrestricted net assets should not exceed three times the current operating budget.[10]

In Singapore, the National Council of Social Service[11] recommends that reserves be limited to no more than five years of annual net operating expenditure. Interestingly, an analysis of Singapore's Institutions of a Public Character with reserves of more than S$10 million (US$ 6.9 million), found that the majority were above the five-year band.[12] This is similar to the British situation where the bulk of the reserves sits with the larger charities.

A more extreme take on the level of reserves puts the figure at zero. On this point, we can look at those faith-based organizations that take vows of poverty. For instance, the concept of reserves does not exist for Mother Teresa's Missionaries of Charity.[13] The sisters live a life that is the poorest of the poor, with each nun possessing no more than three sets of clothes which are often mended until the material is too bare to patch. The Order is completely dependent on divine providence as they serve the most severe poverty-stricken and needy cases.

Without going to the extreme of Mother Teresa's example of a hand-to-mouth existence, I see merit in requiring end-beneficiary charities to continually fundraise only for their current (versus far future) needs. Without large reserves to fall back on, charities are more likely to stay relevant to the needs of the community. As donors give money to specific beneficiaries, they are able to require ongoing accountability of the charities.

Finding a charity with an explicit policy of "no reserves," however, is very difficult. The few that I have encountered are funds such as the Community Chest[14] and the School Pocket Money Fund[15] that have a philosophy of collecting only just enough money needed for the current year's planned allocations.

Fund Targets

It is considered best practice within the charity sector to identify and communicate fundraising targets upfront.

That is well and good if the outcome and costs are ascertainable, such as for a building fund or a fund for an established charity's operating needs, but that may not always be the case.

Setting targets when fundraising for an uncertain need, such as a disaster and crisis, can be dicey in that respect.

During the SARS crisis in Singapore, the government set up the Courage Fund to provide relief to SARS victims and healthcare workers.[16] Initially, no fundraising target was established. As the Courage Fund was established at the onset of SARS, it was not clear then what the extent of the crisis would be. Hence, identifying a target level to deal with SARS-related expenditure was near impossible. In the event, the government, to its credit, was able to contain a potential pandemic very quickly and so, not all the money collected was actually needed for the fight. Currently, about S$15 million (US$10 million) or half of the money raised is kept in reserves for "future infectious disease outbreaks."[17]

But even in more stable situations where the amount of money that is needed should be determinable within reason, the approach of some charities is that there is never enough good one could do with more money. Take the case of the Universities Endowment Fund which was established in 1991 to provide for the joint needs of the National University of Singapore and Nanyang Technological University.

The fund was set up with what was described as a very ambitious target of S\$1 billion (US\$ 690 million).[18] By 1996, reserves stood at S\$620 million (US\$428 million). The fund was subsequently split into two separate funds, one for each of the two universities. Since then, both universities have collected much more than the original target. As of 2007, the National University's reserves (inclusive of the endowment funds) stood at over S\$3.4 billion (US\$2.3 billion), while Nanyang University's was more than SS\$1.6 billion (US\$1.1 billion).[19] Nevertheless, fundraising on the university scene continued unabated.

Both universities have not stated how far they intend to go in their fundraising drives. Chew Kheng Chuan, Director of Development at the National University of Singapore, has said that the university is "vision-driven." They take their cue from the leading U.S. universities which have accumulated staggering endowments, such as Harvard (US\$35 billion), Yale (US\$23 billion) and Stanford (US\$22 billion),[20] and they are all still counting.

Excess Donations

The discipline of stopping donations when you have collected enough is a commendable one. My wife was once asked to help a Catholic shelter for abused spouses and families raise some money for a much-needed van. By the time she did a private collection, the nuns had already received sufficient money from other donors to pay for the van. Pressed to take and use the money for other needs of the organization, the sisters declined on the basis that they did not wish to receive funds for unspecified needs, and she had to return the money to the donors.

A month and a half after the Courage Fund was set up, public donations of nearly S\$10 million (US\$6.9 million) had flowed in, but there was much noise over the level of fund buildup. The fund's trustees then announced that the amounts raised should be adequate and they would be "taking a pause and [would] not be initiating and endorsing new fundraising projects."[21] Nonetheless, it was hard to stop the momentum and the fund ended up with three times more money.

In the same way that corporations are often asked by their shareholders to return excess capital, should charities return excess money to their donors?

Returning excess money can be tricky. The Courage Fund did oblige two donors who asked for their money back—about S$1,000 (US$690) in total. But these refunds happened before the money was committed and spent. Even if it now wished to do so for the other donors, it would not be able to identify and communicate to all 22,000 donors who contributed.

Another suggestion could be to channel excess donations to other charities, but this may not be keeping faith with the donors' intentions.

Donor Intent

An inviolable principle that has developed in the charity sector is adhering to the basis under which a donation is given, or what is known as "donor intent." When a donor gives with a specific intent, that intent must be respected in perpetuity. Defending donor intent has spawned a history of family disputes and litigation.

A classic case is that of the Buck Trust.[22] Beryl Buck, a nurse, who died in 1975, specified that the funds in the Buck Trust were to be used "exclusively … in providing care for the needy in Marin Country, California, and for other nonprofit, charitable, religious or educational purposes in Marin County, California."

It is fair to say that Mrs. Buck did not anticipate that her gift would grow from the original amount of less than US$10 million to nearly US$400 million by the mid-1980s. The San Francisco Foundation, which administered the trust, sought to apply the money to charitable purposes in the entire Bay area surrounding San Francisco where the need was arguably greater than in wealthy Marin County. Representatives from Marin County challenged the move in court. The court ruled that Mrs. Buck's intention to use the money for the benefit of Marin County only was clear, and turned over the administration of the Buck Trust funds in 1986 from the San Francisco Foundation to a newly created Marin Community Foundation. Today, the latter foundation has more than US$1 billion in assets.

The Asian tsunami presented similar dilemmas for many charities. During the initial weeks following the disaster, there was a frenzied donation of clothes, food and other items by Singaporeans. These were piled up high at various collection centers. The bottleneck was in the land, sea and air transport needed to get these items into the hands of those who needed the donations most.

After more than a month of sitting at the collection centers, there were discussions among non-governmental organizations as to whether some of the goods, especially the food perishables, would be best diverted towards local beneficiaries. The goods were clearly donated for the tsunami victims. Using them for other purposes, no matter how noble, did not sit right with many. Identifying the donors and getting their consent to do otherwise was not practical. In the event, the goods were finally shipped, although they sat for another long spell at the Indonesian ports.

Three months after the Asian tsunami, another earthquake struck the Indonesian island of Nias. The resulting tsunami from the first earthquake killed 122 people and rendered hundreds homeless on this island. The second earthquake killed 800 with 2,000 casualties. In this case, many non-governmental organizations had raised a tremendous amount of money for the tsunami and at the time of the second earthquake, a significant part of the collected funds was still uncommitted, and hence, available. Could these funds be transferred to the victims of the second Nias earthquake?

At the time, the Archdiocese Crisis Coordination Team, a Catholic charity that I was involved in, discussed the matter. We had collected S$1.5 million (US$ 1 million) from parishioners for the tsunami. Nias clearly had an immediate need and, coincidentally, had a predominant Christian population. After some debate, we concluded that we had to honor the basis on which the funds were raised as parishioners had clearly donated for the tsunami. Any support we provided would have to be for the original disaster, and a separate fundraising exercise would be needed if we wished to give any money for the second Nias earthquake.

The first lesson in relation to donor intent thus is that once a particular cause is specified, the charity is stuck with it, unless it goes back to the donors and asks for a change. But that would be near nigh impossible with dead donors as in the case of Beryl Buck, and with broad-based public fundraising as in the case of the tsunami.

The second lesson which follows from the first would be that it is useful, if not essential, for a charity to be broad when defining its fund objectives and to proactively identify what it would do with its excess funds.

That, in a sense, was what the Courage Fund did. While the general perception is that the money was meant for SARS, the fact is the fund's objectives specifically included benefiting healthcare workers and the wider Singaporean community affected by widespread infectious diseases. So, the Courage Fund was well within its scope to apply two-thirds of the donations to non-SARS related programs.

Despite this, the Courage Fund continues to face heat from donors and politicians that such expenditure is "not the original intention for which the funds were raised" and hence "not in accordance with the spirit of the Courage Fund."[23] That is largely because the Courage Fund was launched under the umbrella of SARS and no one read the fine print.

So, the third lesson on donor intent is that the upfront and clear communication of the broad objectives of an appeal is as important as defining them. The American Red Cross learned this the hard way. Its president, Dr. Bernadine Healey, had defended the decision on broader usage of the Liberty Fund, saying that "the American Red Cross, to my knowledge, has never described its work as limited only to those people who were lost on 9/11 and their families."[24] She claimed that the Liberty Fund was set up not just for the victims of 9/11 but also "those victims of terrorist attacks yet to come."

However, the TV images of the general appeal for blood and money to the Liberty Fund in the aftermath of 9/11 had left a different impression on many donors, even if the planned use of funds was not specified. Eventually, the Red Cross succumbed to public pressure and Dr. Healey resigned due to pressure from the Red Cross board.[25]

Other than the fact that the Red Cross was technically not prevented from applying the Liberty Fund for purposes beyond the victims of September 11, indeed there were experts who felt that, emotions aside, allowing the large sums raised to go beyond the immediate victims was actually the better approach.[26] By the end of 2004, the Liberty Fund had distributed US$390 million in victim compensation to 3,500 beneficiaries, averaging US$110,000 per person. According to Catherine Spence of the *Stanford Social Innovation Review*: "Never before had a charity distributed so much money per person" and "it was the first time that the Red Cross did not directly tie eligibility for aid to the financial need of the victim."[27]

A further irony is that the American Red Cross may not have had to deal with this organizational crisis in the first place. It already had a general Disaster Relief Fund which is used to help victims of hurricanes, floods and other disasters. Some commentators felt that the Red Cross erred in creating the Liberty Fund as a separate and distinct fund.[28] If it had simply channeled donations to its regular Disaster Relief Fund, it likely would have had more flexibility over the way donations were used, as it had done in the past. This comes back to the earlier lesson of keeping the purposes of a fund sufficiently broad so that the question of donor intent does not arise, even as a perception issue.

Keeping Happy Problems Happy

More charities, big or small, need to think about the issues of reserves. They especially need to be more proactive in establishing a reserves policy, fundraising targets and broad fundraising objectives, as well as communicating these matters clearly to donors. In this way, the problem of plenty may stop being a 'problem' as such and becomes, instead, the boon it should be.

Endnotes:

Adapted from: "The problem of plenty," *SALT*, January-February 2007; and "The problem of plenty," *The Straits Times*, January 29, 2007.

1   www.redcross.org/general/0,1082,0_152_1392,00.html#liberty; Catherine Spence, "At Cross Purposes," *Stanford Social Innovation Review*, Spring 2006; Dr. Marta Dede, "Blood and money: The American Red Cross and the terrorist attacks of September 11, 2001," Case study from Ukeleja Center for Ethical Leadership, California State University Long Beach, Spring 2008, http://csulb.edu/colleges/cba/ucel/educational/documents/martha-dede-2007-2.doc.

2   www.redcross.org.sg/tsunamirelief_faq.htm

3   Susan Long, "Aid united: Government mandates Singapore Red Cross to set up a committee to coordinate tsunami relief efforts by local NGOs," *The Straits Times*, January 15, 2005. The article describes how the Singapore Red Cross set up a Tsunami Reconstruction Facilitation Committee comprising of representatives from various NGOs, Voluntary Welfare Organizations, the Ministry of Community, Youth and Sports to manage the Tidal Waves Asia Fund.

4   Siva Arasu, "How NKF vs. SPH became The People vs. T.T. Durai," *The Sunday Times*, July 17, 2005. The NKF scandal is examined in detail in Chapter 19, "NKF: the saga and its paradigms."

5   "Criteria," American Institute of Philanthropy, www.charitywatch.org/criteria.html.

6   *RS3—Charity Reserves* (Charity Commission for England and Wales, Version March 2003), www.charity-commission.gov.uk/publications/rs3.asp.

7 The studies on charity reserves are published as: *RS3—Charity Reserves* (as per endnote 6); and *RS13—Tell It Like It Is: The extent of charity reserves and reserves policies* (Charity Commission for England and Wales, Version November 2006), www.charity-commission. gov.uk/publications/rs13.asp.

8 *RS13—Tell It Like It Is: The extent of charity reserves and reserves policies* (as per endnote 7).

9 www.charitywatch.org/criteria.html

10 www.give.org/standards//newcbbbstds.asp

11 NCSS is the umbrella body for the social service sector in Singapore. As the largest and most well established umbrella body, its guidelines are also used as benchmarks by non-member charities. www.ncss.org.sg/ncss/index.asp.

12 The table is not reproduced here. It was in the original *SALT* article.

13 The Missionaries of Charity was founded by Mother Teresa in 1950 as a Catholic diocesan congregation. Its mission is to care for (in her own words) "the hungry, the naked, the homeless, the crippled, the blind, the lepers, all those people who feel unwanted, unloved, uncared for throughout society, people that have become a burden to the society and are shunned by everyone." What started as a small order of 12 members in Calcutta now has more than 4,000 nuns worldwide across the six major continents. There are numerous references available on Mother Teresa and her work.

14 The Community Chest (ComChest) was established in 1983 as the fundraising arm of the NCSS. It is an affiliate of United Way International. Donations collected by the ComChest are given out as grants to NCSS member Volunteer Welfare Organizations. Annually, Comchest raises more than S$40 million (US$ 28 million) for the various social service programs. In 2006, it raised S$47 million (US$32 million). www.ncss.org. sg/ncss/donate/comchest_home.asp.

15 The School Pocket Money Fund was initiated in October 2000 by Singapore's leading daily newspaper, *The Straits Times*, to help children from low-income families who were attending school without proper breakfast or pocket money to sustain their day in school. Annually, the fund raises more than S$3 million (US$ 2 million) and benefits about 10,000 school kids. www.straitstimes.com/School+Pocket+Money+Fund/ School+Pocket+Money+Fund.html.

16 Background and information on SARS and the Courage Fund are provided in Chapter 1, "The missing hand of Adam Smith." See also www.couragefund.com.sg.

17 Financial summary and allocations of the Courage Fund is available at www.couragefund. com.sg/finance_summary.htm.

18 Braema Mathi, "NUS, NTU get own endowment funds, with boost from the Tote," *The Straits Times*, December 4, 1996.

19 Figures are from the annual reports for fiscal year ended March 31, 2007 for NUS and NTU.

20 All figures are based on 2007 annual reports.

21 "An open letter to Singaporeans," from Mr. Michael Lim Choo San, Chairman, Board of Trustees, The Courage Fund, May 26, 2003.

22 *San Francisco Foundation v. Superior Court* (1984) 37 C3d 285 [S.F. 24726 California Supreme Court, November 21, 1984].

23 The comment made by Nominated Member of Parliament Loo Choon Yong in the Singapore Parliament about the non-SARS expenditure: "Some people may feel that this is not in accordance with the spirit of the Courage Fund" and while they are worthy causes, they were not viewed as the original intention for which the funds were raised. See Lee Hui Chieh, "Courage Fund misused?" *The Straits Times*, March 10, 2006.

24 "Prepared Witness Testimony by Dr. Bernadine Healy to The Committee on Energy and Commerce on Charitable Contributions for September 11: Protecting against Fraud, Waste and Abuse, Subcommittee on Oversight and Investigations," November 6, 2001.

25 Grant Williams, "Red Cross President resigns under pressure from Board," *The Chronicle of Philanthropy*, October 26, 2001.

26 See Deborah Sontag, "Who brought Bernadine Healy down?" *The New York Times*, December 23, 2001. The article indicated that Red Cross officials had internally considered the concept of the fund to be "just right" and that "it was 'moronic' to use the whole Liberty Fund as an A.T.M. machine for the victims' families."

27 Catherine Spence, "At Cross Purposes," *Stanford Social Innovation Review*, Spring 2006.

28 Grant Williams, "Red Cross President resigns under pressure from Board," *The Chronicle of Philanthropy*, October 26, 2001.

Chapter 7

Executive Compensation

Heart Work, Less Pay

Should executives working in charity be paid more, to keep pace with the market? Actually, they are already paid in line with the market—the capitalistic human resource market.

The significant gap between the charity and the commercial sectors' pay scales is due to two factors: a heart factor reflecting the noble spirit of altruism, and a head factor reflecting the environmental aspects of a slower pace and less demanding expectations.

The call to improve accountability and professionalism in the charity sector should see the raising of charity pay to narrow the head gap, but hopefully, leave the heart factor intact.

Pay, especially when it is funded by the public, tends to be a lightning rod for public scrutiny and media attention.

Usually, it is the big numbers that get the buzz. Headlines trumpet the compensation packages of high-flying chief executive officers (CEOs) of public listed companies, the salaries of government officials and, occasionally, the pay and benefits of charity executives that exceed the money spent on their purported charitable causes.[1]

What is not often in the media spotlight is the low level of pay of the average charity worker. For many, both inside and outside the sector, this is a sore point. Those supporting social workers would say that the remuneration is unfair, that it does not befit the effort and that the sector needs to properly "honor their contribution."[2] Some of these advocates of better charity pay contend that paying charity staff salaries "commensurate with alternative jobs they could hold" will ensure the much-needed professionalism to keep pace with the private sector in terms of efficiency and management.[3]

I have found that this subject can be an emotional one, especially with charity staff. But it also gets to the heart of what charity is, or is not about. It may therefore be beneficial to use our head to objectively deal with this "heart" issue.

A Common Base

Perhaps a good starting point is to determine how charity sector compensation compares to the commercial world—though not much proof may be needed. While the quantum of the differential between the sectors may differ, there seems to be enough anecdotal and empirical evidence to conclude that charity sector workers are generally paid lower than their private and public sector counterparts.

Indeed, most literature on the subject assumes that there is a lag between the public and private sector. This is sometimes borne out by comparative surveys.

A U.S. study published in the *Journal of Human Resources* found that average weekly nonprofit wages are 11 percent lower than for-profit jobs.[4] The authors attribute the difference to nonprofit employment being disproportionately concentrated in lower-paying industries such as hospitals, nursing facilities and social services. In the U.K., it was a point for celebration when the annual salaries of CEOs of large third-sector organizations (nonprofits employing more than 1,000 staff) crossed £100,000 (US$200,000). Yet, this is a far cry from the £6.5 million (US$13 million) annual compensation that CEOs of Britain's 10 largest companies received.[5] In the absence of good data in Singapore, I spoke to two executive compensation firms and they see charity executives being paid 30 to 50 percent lower on average, compared to their commercial counterparts for similar corporate services jobs.

So, is the disparity in wages fair? That is where the divergence of views begins.

A 2004 survey by the U.S. charity watch organization, Guidestar,[6] showed that more than half of its readers (many of whom are from the charity sector) felt that charity workers were not fairly compensated, while only 28 percent said they were. The rest were unsure.

By contrast, a 2005 poll[7] on Singaporean attitudes towards charity found that 60 percent felt that charity organizations should be run by volunteers or staff paid below-market wages. The public perception is that donor dollars should go towards mission and cause, and there is a reluctance to put money into the administrative budget.

Similarly, in the U.K., the traditional view is that charities should be "run by highly motivated but relatively modestly paid people."[8] According to a 2006 poll by the think tank, nfpSynergy, more than 80 percent of the 1,000 people surveyed felt that paying charity chief executives high salaries was a waste of money.[9]

In general, it would seem that while many within the charity sector and some outside the sector think that current pay levels are unfairly low, the general public expects lower salaries to be par for the course, and thus deems the practice to be fair.

What Market?

Those who view current pay levels as unfair call for the sector pay to be leveled up and aligned with the market. By market, they mean the commercial market. The implication is that nonprofit pay is currently not market-based.

I would argue that it already is market-based. The nonprofit market for full-time staff is as capitalistic a market as that for, say, financial services or information technology. As in the commercial world, employees join and stay in nonprofit organizations voluntarily, with full disclosure of pay levels. It is a classic case of willing buyer and willing seller. No one is compelled to do nonprofit work. People choose to work in charities at wage levels that they are apprised of upfront and therefore fully accept.

In fact, the human resource market is one single large capitalistic market made up of different sectors, one of which happens to be the nonprofit sector. Within the nonprofit sector, there would be different market segments.

Each market sector and segment comprises individual organizations that decide how they want to price their executives. The law of supply and demand works to move the players around, over the long run. The fact that we have charity organizations that pay their chief executives annual sums of US$400,000 (pay of the CEO of Daniels Fund)[10] or US$530,000 (pay of the CEO of Goodwill Industries Suncoast Inc)[11]—amounts which are deemed much higher than what many comparable sized commercial companies might pay—is in fact, evidence that the capitalist system for human resources is working. These organizations, however governed, independently decided on their executives' pay as they take into account sectoral and other considerations.

The collective pricing for a particular job by all the organizations in a particular sector of the human resources market results in a narrower band of acceptable compensation levels for that job; this merely reflects prevailing common characteristics of that sector. It also leads to the sector's competitiveness of pay relative to other sectors. Thus, according to market data, the U.S. nonprofit market, minus the outliers like those cited above, would generally pay a CEO a range of US$54,000 to US$290,000 (averaging US$112,000) in annual salary in 2007.[12] In comparison, the median CEO salary of only small businesses (less than 500 employees) in the U.S. is already US$290,000.[13] The pay of CEOs of public listed companies would, of course, tend to be in the multiple millions of dollars.

The Heart Factor

So if the job market works according to natural market forces, why is there a distinct wage differential between the charity sector and the other commercial sectors?

Most observers, inside and outside the sector, cite the noble spirit of altruism as the reason. In other words, the sector is about charity, so workers should also be charitable. Like volunteers who donate 100 percent of their time to do work for the sector, charity staff are asked to also "donate" part of their labor back to the organization by not being paid fully for it.

This is seen as a "discount" given by employees for working in a charity organization. Perhaps a more positive way to express it is as a "premium" that the individual gets for the joy of heart work.

Is the heart factor a good reason though for this supposed premium of charity work? I think so.

In many sectors and organizations, there are intangibles that explain why people would take on jobs for smaller sums than they could command elsewhere. It is what Frederick Herzberg describes as a motivator factor versus a hygiene factor.[14] Motivators increase job satisfaction, while hygiene factors—one of which is pay—only cause dissatisfaction, but their presence has little effect on long-term satisfaction.

Many technology companies rally their employees behind the idea of changing the world. Apple tells its employees that "the best way to predict the future is to invent it." Hewlett-Packard's slogan is simply "Invent." Accenture was launched with the vision of "bringing innovations to improve the way the world works and lives."

A good instance of an organization that motivates some of its employees far beyond pay is Club Med. Guests at a Club Med resort cannot fail to notice and be impressed by the GOs (short for gentil organisateur), live-in staff who provide all frontline services to guests. Not to make too fine a point about it, they make a Club Med stay memorable. What is surprising is that they work under tight work regimens, have little discretionary time and low pay. Club Med has successfully created an environment in which adventure-loving and multi-talented young men and women would willingly sacrifice typical job criteria just to work for six months at a time, "earning a bit, enjoying a lot."[15]

These intangibles often relate to our very human desire for meaning in life. What is unique about charity work is that sense of nobleness, of doing good, of giving back to society as part of one's job.

There are other sectors such as religious vocations and political office, where sacrifices of pay are expected for noble reasons.

Many (although not all) religions require their followers to live a modest life as part of their higher calling. A 2006 survey of religious pay in Singapore[16] showed that many Taoist and Buddhist temples supplement their workers' food and board with only a small allowance. The Hindu Endowment Board pays its priests S$500-1,000 (US$345-690) a month based on their seniority. Catholic priests in Singapore receive $500 (US$345) per month with lodging, far less than what any ordinary person would ever accept as adequate compensation for the 24/7 service they provide.

Even Singapore's public service sector which leads the rest of the world in its pay seeks to factor in a one-third discount for ministers' and top civil servants' compensation from the benchmark pay. Critics, however, question whether the benchmark pay, which is determined using the top eight earners from six professions, is appropriate in the first place.[17]

For sectors driven by a sense of nobleness, the relative disregard for pay levels provides the moral authority intrinsic to the sanctity of the sector that is sometimes very necessary for the incumbents to be effective in doing their work. Revving up their pay to commercial levels could be corrupting that very value of charity.

The Head Factor

Yet, I find it difficult to explain the difference between current charity and commercial pay as entirely due to the sacrifice for nobleness. Other factors are at work.

For one thing, most people who have straddled both charity and commercial sector would attest to the significant differences in work environments between the two. The pace in the nonprofit sector is much slower. Outcomes are less clear—if they are talked or thought about at all. People are also generally much nicer to one another.

Hence, I would say that part of what accounts for the differential between charity and commercial pay are these environmental aspects of lower stress, slower pace, and less demanding expectations. You could say it is the head factor, in contrast to the heart factor.

Differential pay for different environmental factors is a common phenomenon across the capitalistic human resource market. Foreign currency dealers are paid very well because their hours are odd, they face the stress of making instantaneous decisions that can have catastrophic consequences and their tenures are highly insecure and short.

A lawyer in a legal firm who defends clients, works to tight court schedules and bears the risk of personal liability for any shortcomings in his work generally gets paid more than if he were employed as a legal counsel in the more stable, less risky legal department of a large corporation.

This occurs even within a company. Those working on the revenue-generating side are generally better compensated than those who are not. Usually, the demands and uncertainties are higher in the front line. Thus in many organizations, where a market-facing person such as an external auditor in a public accounting firm, decides on a career switch to do similar kind of work in the back office, say internal audit, he or she is often asked to take a pay cut.

The Cost of Head

In tandem with the call to level up charity pay is the call to level up the quality of charity work. Over time, the lower pay of the charity sector has resulted in a work culture and effectiveness that lags far behind the corporate world. Why is this so?

Consider a professional of a certain caliber who is worth/earning $12,000 per month, and who is willing to take a 25 percent pay cut (let us say that this is the value of the heart factor for him) to perform exactly the same job in a charity organization. Assuming the charity organization he is interested in offers only $6,000, there will be two possible scenarios. The first scenario has another commercial candidate of a lower caliber earning a lower pay of $8,000 who takes a 25 percent pay cut (same heart factor) to do the job at $6,000. The second scenario has the first candidate earning $12,000 taking a 50 percent pay cut; the first 25 percent for heart and the second 25 percent for head. That means he assumes that the charity organization he is going to is less demanding and therefore merits a further 25 percent pay cut. Both scenarios mean that the quality of work and outcomes would be less than what it would be in a commercial organization.

Certainly the charity sector has many examples of successful professionals who have given up well-paying jobs in the commercial world and taken large pay cuts to follow their hearts. However, the number of such people is probably not large and if anything, they may create the illusion that the premium for the heart factor is very significant. When it gets to large numbers of workers, the average value of the heart premium would come down. So to populate the many jobs available, the sector has likely attracted staff, who at the margin, may not have been paid much more in the commercial world anyway.

It is the law of supply and demand at work again. Without enough properly qualified people who value a high heart premium, the old adage "pay peanuts and you get monkeys" applies. It does not help in the effectiveness of the charity sector, even if these monkeys come with hearts of gold.

Losing Head and Keeping Heart

So, my take is that the capitalistic job market is alive and well. People are being paid what they are prepared to take for the jobs they do.

In charity, the heart factor is a drawing point and should never be replaced by money. For some time now, the price gap established by charity organizations has seemed too big (for the quality level desired by many) given the large number of charity workers needed. The sector has believed that the price gap is for heart. But over time, in addition to the heart gap, a head gap of lower quality and slower pace has built up.

Going forward, the situation looks poised to change. There are greater demands for accountability and professionalism in the charity sector. These demands will push charities to pay what it takes to bring on appropriate staff, which is more than what they have been paying. With similar arguments being made in some places for rising public service pay scales, not relying purely on nobleness to bridge the pay gap is also becoming more acceptable.

As individual charity organizations raise their pay, this will generally lift charity sector pay. Hopefully, the pay rises will only serve to narrow and even eliminate the head factor, but never reduce or remove the heart factor.

Endnotes:

Adapted from: "Heart work, less pay," *SALT*, May-June 2007; and "Capitalism is alive and kicking," *The Straits Times*, June 20, 2007.

1   For example, see Beth Healy, Francie Latour, Sacha Pfeiffer, and Michael Rezendes & Walter V. Robinson, "Some officers of charities steer assets to selves," *The Boston Globe*, October 9, 2003.

2   Peter Manzo, "The real salary scandal," *Stanford Social Innovation Review*, Winter 2004.

3   See Lim Wei Chean, "Charities must pay to get good people: SM," *The Straits Times*, November 27, 2007.

4   Christopher J. Ruhm & Carey Borkoski, "Compensation in the Nonprofit Sector," *The Journal of Human Resources*, Vol. 38, No. 4, Autumn 2003.

5   See "Charity chief executives break £100k barrier," *ACEVO News*, November 1, 2007, www.acevo.org.uk/index.cfm/display_page/news_press/control_contentType/news_list/display_open/news_1034; and Heather Connon, "It pays to be one of the top 10...," *The Observer*, April 16, 2006.

6   Suzanne E. Coffman, "Are nonprofit executives paid fairly? IRS actions and September question of the month results," *Guidestar Newsletter*, October 2004, www.guidestar.org/DisplayArticle.do?articleId=805.

7   Yap Su-Yin, "S'poreans want below-market wages for charity workers," *The Straits Times*, July 23, 2005.

8   Steve Davies, *Third sector provision of employment-related services: A report for the Public and Commercial Services Union* (Public & Commercial Services Union, June 2006).

9   "High salaries 'a waste of money'," *nfpSynergy Press coverage*, June 14, 2006, www.nfpsynergy.net/pressandmedia/presscoverage/150/?PHPSESSID=3f3f6373808a 57553107aefc0b549a05.

10 Pablo Eisenberg, "Excessive executive compensation needs to be stemmed," *The Chronicle of Philanthropy*, www.eisenhowerfoundation.org/pablo/ChroniclePhilanthropy_ excessive_compensation.html.

11 Emily Steel, "He's the highest-paid charity executive around," *St. Petersburg Times*, August 15, 2005.

12 Mark Hrywna, "Special Report: NPT Salary Survey 2007," *The Nonprofit Times*, February 1, 2007. The range of salaries is based on the size of the charity—or its budget.

13 Jeanne Sahadi, "Small biz can lead to big pay," CNNMoney.com, October 18, 2006.

14 Frederick Hertzberg was a noted psychologist who became Professor of Management at Utah University. He first published his hygiene-motivation theory in *The Motivation to Work* in 1959. For a summary of Herzberg's background and his theory, see www.thefreelibrary.com/Frederick+Hertzberg:+the+hygiene-motivation+theory-a0151189056.

15 www.clubmedjobs.com

16 Melissa Sim, "Religious leaders' pay: How much is enough?" *The Sunday Times*, September 17, 2006. In comparison, Singapore's per capital income is US$29,320.

17 "Narrowing the gap: What's enough?" *The Straits Times*, Insight, March 24, 2007; "Time to temper focus on monetary awards," *The Business Times*, March 27, 2007.

Giving

Chapter 8

Corporate Social Responsibility

Is the Business of Business just Business?

For many organizations, Corporate Social Responsibility (CSR) is a binary question of "to give or not to give." Supporters often cite it as good business. However, that plays to the argument of critics that the business of business is business. In this context, CSR is, in reality, enlightened self-interest rather than corporate altruism.

The correct argument for CSR really is the responsibility of power. Corporations have to recognize their impact and their role in the communities they operate. Until that happens, legislative controls, which have already taken place in the areas of environmental controls, ethical conduct and governance, may be necessary. But it is hard to tame the corporate beast, and the long-term answer may lie in changing its constitution.

I spent my entire working life with one company. In those 26 years with Accenture,[1] a big draw for many of my colleagues and me was the corporate culture, aspects of which included making a difference and having a strong sense of stewardship for the future and the community.

I remember in my early years being rather thrilled to hear my managing partner talk about "giving back to the community." We were encouraged to get involved with nonprofit organizations and no one asked about returns from being a volunteer. Later, when I became a partner, I realized how deeply embedded this "giving back" was in our whole corporate mindset. As partners, we had to specify the contributions and charitable causes we were giving to, otherwise, the firm would simply deduct it from our compensation and donate it on our behalf. Of course, we had a corporate foundation that matched some of our individual philanthropic giving.

Today, Accenture is much less differentiated in its community giving. Not because it is doing less, but because many more companies are jumping on the bandwagon of what is termed "corporate social responsibility," or simply CSR.

As CSR gathers momentum, it is no longer a fringe activity only of leading lights like Accenture, Ben & Jerry's, British Petroleum, General Motors and Vodafone (see box on "Good Corporate Citizens").

Corporate Citizens

CSR is about good corporate citizenship. It is a commitment by businesses to address the economic, environmental, moral and cultural concerns of the communities in which they operate.

This commitment is actioned through a wide variety of "progressive" initiatives, ranging from the basics of enlightened human resource practices, ethical conduct and environmental responsibility, to the more charitable actions of corporate volunteerism and philanthropy.

A comprehensive model for CSR is provided in the United Nations Global Compact.[3] The Compact asks companies to embrace, support and enact, within their sphere of influence, a set of ten core principles in the areas of human rights, labor standards, the environment and anti-corruption.

First announced at the 1999 World Economic Forum, the United Nations Global Compact has grown to become the largest worldwide CSR initiative, bringing together governments, non-governmental organizations (NGOs) and businesses. In 2008, it has almost 5,000 participants, including 3,700 businesses in 120 countries.

Good Citizens, Good Business

In 2006, I attended the Inaugural CSR Conference organized by the Singapore Compact for CSR.[4] Hearing the many who championed

Good Corporate Citizens[2]

Accenture

Accenture is a global management consulting, technology services and outsourcing company with net annual revenues of about US$20 billion.

It utilizes the business expertise of its people to proactively engage with communities and "improve the way the world works and lives." It recognizes that community involvement nurtures employee pride and motivation, influences new potential recruits, and transforms the careers of existing professionals.

Its Corporate Citizenship program focuses on delivering tangible outcomes. Besides giving grants through the Accenture Foundation and local office fundraising initiatives, the program also encompass initiatives such as Accenture Development Partnerships, a structured program that helps Accenture employees take a salary reduction to participate in international projects in developing countries. Additionally, Accenture partners with not-for-profit organizations such as Voluntary Service Overseas and offers pro bono work.

Ben & Jerry's

Started in 1978 by two boys who "hated running, but loved food," Ben & Jerry's is an ice-cream making company with a difference.

Ben Cohen and Jerry Greenfield wanted to run a business that would share its rewards with its employees and with the community. Today, the company is well known for its social enterprise and the myriad activities it conscientiously initiates to make the world a better place to live in. It provides an annual Social and Environmental Assessment Report to highlight how it is performing relative to its social mission.

Ben & Jerry's believes in "using the power of our day-to-day business to drive social change." It seeks to integrate concern for human needs and the environment into its business decisions, choosing to engage with businesses that share its social values. Thus, the company sources with a social conscience. For example, it uses only milk and cream from family farmers who do not treat their cows with the synthetic recombinant Bovine Growth Hormone (rBGH), gets ingredients from Fair Trade Certified sources, and creates organic flavors.

Annually, Ben & Jerry's contributes more than US$1 million through corporate philanthropy that is primarily employee-led. The Ben & Jerry's Foundation offers grants to not-for-profit and grassroots organizations throughout the U.S. to facilitate progressive social change by addressing the underlying conditions of societal and environmental problems.

British Petroleum (BP)

BP is one of the world's largest energy companies, providing fuel for transportation, energy for heat and light, and petrochemical products for everyday items.

BP has a strong focus on the sustainability of business. It lives this philosophy in several ways. First, it operates responsibly, not just by complying with laws and regulations but it sets its own standards beyond legal requirements. Secondly, it actively deals with the issue of climate change by contributing to the policy debate, supporting research and developing new, clear technologies in power and transport. Finally, it seeks to influence positively social and economic development through its contributions of tax, jobs, skills and products, as well as sound governance and contribution to the progress of host communities.

BP publishes an annual Sustainability Report on its performance with respect to these areas.

General Motors (GM)

GM is the world's largest automaker, with 284,000 employees across 33 countries worldwide.

As an automobile manufacturer, GM feels that its corporate responsibility is to ensure energy efficiency and diversity, and to minimize its impact on the environment. A set of GM Environmental Principles applies to its facilities, products and employees worldwide, and guides the conduct of its daily business practices.

Beyond energy and environment, GM seeks to improve on social areas such as education, employee training, employee satisfaction, human rights, safety and diversity. Its plants are among the safest in the industry, and it has one of the most diverse work forces in the global business community.

Vodafone

Vodafone is the world's leading mobile telecommunications company, with an estimated 252 million customers worldwide.

Vodafone states that it does not believe that one can be 'half responsible' or pick and choose the convenient areas to act responsibly. Hence, it set out to become a recognized leader in corporate responsibility, aiming to be one of the most trusted companies in the markets in which it operates.

To do this, Vodafone seeks to embed corporate responsibility at every level in all its local operating companies by creating an organizational culture, where the instinctive course of action is the responsible one.

The company facilitates charitable donations and employee volunteering through the Vodafone Group Foundation and a network of local foundations. Core to its Corporate Responsibility strategy is the extension of access to communications in emerging markets. Its rationale is that this offers the single greatest opportunity to make a strong contribution to society by stimulating economic development. Vodafone also finds other ways to leverage its technology to improve how the world communicates.

the cause tell it, it was clear that CSR has many business benefits for companies.

CSR can help build a company's brand. Marketing studies show that consumers like products from "responsible" corporations. When a company shows its willingness to be part of the fabric of a local community rather than be an exploitative outsider, this goes a long way towards building positive public opinion and customer trust. The Body Shop, for example, benefits from consumer perception of its ethical stand, even though detractors say that its use of ingredients that have been tested on animals are contrary to the company's marketing.[5]

CSR programs can also motivate employees. People look for meaning in their life and their work. CSR builds a "feel-good" atmosphere among staff, particularly when they get involved in fundraising and volunteering efforts. The software industry, for example, depends on high-energy, creative and talented individuals. The war for talent has resulted in high attrition rates in many high-tech companies. Salesforce.com has successfully turned the software industry on its head by being a pioneer of offering "software as a service." Its founder and CEO, Marc Benioff, explains in his best practices book on corporate philanthropy how his 1-1-1 model—1 percent each of equity, employee time and profits for good causes—can be used to attract, retain and motivate the best workers.[6]

Many studies show a correlation between CSR and favorable financial performance—although academics argue about cause and effect. The Foundation for CSR examined 100 empirical studies on this subject and concluded that 68 percent of them point to a positive relationship between corporate social performance and financial performance.[7] An often quoted study is the 1999 Harvard Business School's longitudinal study which found that "stakeholder-balanced" companies had four times the revenue growth, more than 700 times the net income growth, and eight times the employment growth of companies with "shareholder-only" focus.[8]

To the CSR advocates, therefore, companies do well by doing good.

The Business of Business is Business

Although it may not always be politically correct, the critics of CSR can be vocal and have very respectable credentials. They take their gospel text from economist Milton Friedman, who said as far back as 1970 that "there is one and only one social responsibility of business—to use its resources and engage in activities designed to increase its profits so long as it stays within the rules of the game."[9]

The well-respected magazine, *The Economist*, has been a long-time supporter of this point of view. Its January 2005 bumper coverage on "The Good Company" suggests that CSR is nostrum based on a "faulty analysis of the capitalist system."[10] It sees CSR as being hype at best, but at its worst, it is a "delusion" that reduces both profits and social welfare. It even goes so far as to argue that corporate philanthropy is a "morally dubious transaction" because it is "charity with other people's money." Its approach would be simply for management to give the money to its shareholders who can then decide for themselves whether and which charities they want to give to.

In a sense, CSR advocates who proclaim that it is good for business are really singing the tune of these CSR critics. The two arguments are opposite sides of the same coin, anchored on the value that the business of business is, well, business. Thus, CSR becomes a business decision: do it if it makes business sense, do not bother if it does not. In this context, CSR is not so much a triumph of altruism but merely enlightened self-interest.

Hence, in some CSR handbooks, it is a valid strategy for corporations that face public relations problems to engage in high-profile CSR programs to divert attention away from their controversial activities, or subdue resentment. Critics have thus questioned the motivations of tobacco companies, such as British American Tobacco and Philip Morris, when they announce high-profile CSR programs and engage in health and other community initiatives.[11] In 2006, when Samsung in Korea faced public backlash over a string of scandals, its chairman apologized and pledged to make the nation's single largest donation to date—over 800 billion Korean won (US$825 million) to charity.[12]

CSR skeptics point to the low take-up rate of CSR as evidence that business is really about business—and it so happens that most do not find it good business. For example, corporate philanthropic giving across the world has tended to hover around a low one percent of pre-tax profits across countries. American corporations are among the most generous at 1.6 percent in comparison to those from Canada at 1.03 percent, the U.K. at 0.95 percent and Singapore at a low of 0.22 percent.[13]

Corporate Power

The other rationale for CSR, separate from the consideration of business value, centers on the responsibility of power. This, in my view, is the proper and truly compelling basis for CSR.

As Peter Parker, alter-ego of Spiderman would hauntingly say, "With great power comes great responsibility." Parker had learned, the hard way, the consequences of ignoring the accountability that came with his gift of superpowers.[14] That lesson applies not just to superheroes, but also to mortals and organizations in positions of power.

Corporations have plenty of power. There are villages and small towns where one or a few corporations control the livelihood of most of the folks. After Asia Pacific Resources International Holdings Limited, a pulp and paper manufacturer, set up shop in the small Indonesian town of Pangkalan Kerinci, Indonesia, the population grew from 200 people to 60,000.[15]

But this pales in comparison to the impact made by the giant transnational corporations with tentacles all around the globe. Wal-Mart, the world's largest retailer, employs more than 1.9 million people, stocking and retailing goods that more than 179 million consumers across the world need for everyday living.[16]

Some of these transnationals are so big, they dwarf countries. If you compare corporate sales and country Gross Domestic Product (GDP) of the 100 largest "economies" in the world (see Table 8.1), nearly half of them are corporations. To put it in perspective, companies such as Citigroup, Toyota Motors and British Petroleum are each bigger, in terms of economic power, than Singapore. The sales turnover of Wal-Mart is bigger than the combined GDP of the bottom 84 countries in the world, including Nepal, Brunei, Jamaica and Bosnia.

Corporations have put their power to good and not-so-good use. Modern civilization with the unprecedented wealth that is enjoyed across the world is testimony to the success of the capitalist structure, and the production of the estimated 63,000 transnational corporations across the globe.

It is inevitable that some corporations will not be above flexing their muscles in unscrupulous and even illegal ways to achieve their narrow financial aims. CorpWatch[18] is an NGO that seeks to make corporations more accountable through education and activism. It provides an ongoing litany of corporate violations of human rights, environmental crimes, fraud and corruption around the world on its website. Its investigations have led to the exposure of corporate excesses, such as the Nike sweatshops in Vietnam, and profiteering by various companies from the war on terrorism and disaster reconstruction.

Table 8.1 Top 100 Economies of the World[17]

Rk	Economy	Country/Industry	GDP or Sales* (US$b)	Rk	Economy	Country/Industry	GDP or Sales* (US$b)
1	United States		13,202	26	Royal Dutch Shell	Netherlands/ Oil & Gas	319
2	Japan		4,340	27	Norway		311
3	Germany		2,907	28	Saudi Arabia		310
4	China		2,668	29	Denmark		275
5	United Kingdom		2,345	30	BP	U.K./ Oil & Gas	266
6	France		2,230	31	South Africa		255
7	Italy		1,845	32	Greece		245
8	Canada		1,251	33	Iran		223
9	Spain		1,224	34	Ireland		223
10	Brazil		1,068	35	Argentina		214
11	Russian Fed		987	36	Finland		209
12	India		906	37	General Motors	U.S./ Consumer Durables	207
13	South Korea		888	38	Thailand		206
14	Mexico		839	39	Daimler Chrysler	Germany/ Consumer Durables	200
15	Australia		768	40	Chevron	U.S./ Oil & Gas	195
16	Netherlands		658	41	Portugal		193
17	Turkey		403	42	Hong Kong, China		190
18	Belgium		392	43	Venezuela, RB		182
19	Sweden		385	44	Toyota Motor	Japan/ Consumer Durables	179
20	Switzerland		380	45	Total	France/ Oil & Gas	175
21	Indonesia		364	46	Conoco Phillips	U.S./ Oil & Gas	168
22	Wal-Mart Stores	U.S./ Retailing	349	47	General Electric	U.S./ Conglomerates	163
23	Poland		339	48	Ford Motor	U.S./ Consumer Durables	160
24	ExxonMobil	U.S./ Oil & Gas	335	49	ING Group	Netherlands/ Insurance	153
25	Austria		322	50	Malaysia		149

Rk	Economy	Country/Industry	GDP or Sales* (US$b)	Rk	Economy	Country/Industry	GDP or Sales* (US$b)
51	Citigroup	U.S./ Banking	147	76	JPMorgan Chase	U.S./ Banking	99
52	Chile		146	77	Sinopec-China Petroleum	China/ Oil & Gas	99
53	Czech Republic		142	78	AXA Group	France/ Insurance	99
54	Colombia		136	79	Berkshire Hathaway	U.S./ Diversified Financials	99
55	Singapore		132	80	Carrefour Group	France/ Food Markets	98
56	United Arab Emirates		130	81	Dexia	Belgium/ Banking	96
57	Pakistan		129	82	Deutsche Bank	Germany/ Diversified Financials	96
58	Allianz	Germany/ Insurance	125	83	Hewlett-Packard	U.S./ Info Tech	94
59	Israel		123	84	Peru		93
60	Romania		122	85	Valero Energy	U.S./ Oil & Gas	92
61	HSBC Holdings	U.K./ Banking	122	86	McKesson	U.S./ Health Care	92
62	Fortis	Netherlands/ Diversified Financials	121	87	IBM	U.S./ Info Tech	91
63	Philippines		117	88	NTT	Japan/ Telecom Svcs	91
64	Bank of America	U.S./ Banking	117	89	Generali Group	Italy/ Insurance	91
65	Algeria		115	90	Home Depot	U.S./ Retailing	91
66	Nigeria		115	91	BNP Paribas	France/ Banking	89
67	ENI	Italy/ Oil & Gas	114	92	Verizon Communications	U.S./ Telecom Svcs	88
68	American Intl Group	U.S./ Insurance	113	93	Aviva	U.K./ Insurance	87
69	Hungary		113	94	Cardinal Health	U.S./ Health Care	85
70	Volkswagen Group	Germany/ Consumer Durables	113	95	Société Générale Group	France/ Banking	84
71	Siemens	Germany/ Conglomerates	111	96	Honda Motor	Japan/ Consumer Durables	84
72	Egypt		107	97	HBOS	U.K./ Banking	84
73	Ukraine		106	98	Deutsche Telekom	Germany/ Telecom Svcs	81
74	UBS	Switzerland/ Diversified Financials	106	99	Kuwait		81
75	New Zealand		104	100	Nestlé	Switzerland/ Food, Drink & Tobacco	81

Number of Countries: 54
Number of Corporations: 46

* Denotes sales turnover for corporations, or GDP for countries
Based on most recent data available, usually 2006 figures.
Source: Lien Center for Social Innovation analysis

Beyond Voluntary CSR

CSR is viewed by most as a movement of voluntary good corporate citizenship. Companies choose to be socially responsible either because they see business benefits and/or because they subscribe to the philosophy of the responsibility of power. That would exclude companies that subscribe to neither viewpoint or merely pay lip service to CSR.

If (voluntary) CSR is inadequate to balance the excesses of corporate power, should social responsibility then be made mandatory for corporations? Two groups of people—one supporting capitalism, the other fearing the excesses of capitalism—would likely agree.

The first group is the purist supporters of free enterprise. As *The Economist* argues, just as it is the role of corporations to maximize their profits, it is the role of governments to be the proper guardians of the public interest.[19] Therefore, governments are expected to intervene through taxes, public spending and regulation to safeguard the interests of its citizens.

The second group comprises NGOs and regulators who have a morbid fear of unbridled capitalism. Some NGOs see (voluntary) CSR as "greenwash" to avoid taking serious action to improve social and environmental performance and to mask their lobbying activities. They prefer to see regulations imposed on corporations for society's benefit.

Friends of the Earth International, which has the most extensive environmental network in the world, believes that common standards on social and environmental performance need to be achieved through changes in the legal framework so that "those affected by a corporation can control the corporation's operations."[20] Their proposals for corporate accountability include environmental and social duties being placed on directors, and legal rights for local communities to seek compensation when they have suffered as a result of directors failing to uphold those duties.

In the area of environmental protection, some level of regulation already exists in most developed countries to control corporate practices with respect to air and water pollution, land protection, endangered species, hazardous waste, etc. With the increasing effectiveness of the campaign on climate change, these regulations are likely to be strengthened. This will likely be led by the European Union where environmental and product safety standards are deemed to be the strictest.[21]

In the area of business ethics and governance, the U.S. has led the way with its focus on transparency, financial reporting and shareholder protection in its securities market. Meanwhile, international and indigenous NGOs are driving human rights and labor laws, targeted in particular at labor exploitation in the Third World.

Rules and regulations may suit environmental protection and ethical conduct—matters that are more about preventing corporates from doing bad things. But can CSR elements that are about corporations doing good things, such as philanthropy, also be mandated?

Well, in a way, discriminatory taxes and legislated contributions amount to mandatory corporate philanthropy. For example, many countries have payroll levies that generate a pool of funds which is then used by the governments to finance skills training in companies. The World Bank estimates that over 30 countries tax employers 0.5 to 2 percent of payroll, sometimes only of workers earning below a certain amount, with the money going into a "skills development fund" or equivalent. These schemes have had a positive effect on increasing in-service training. However, at the same time, they often unfairly benefit the larger employers relative to smaller companies.[22]

A "skills development fund" would be managed by the government. Less common would be the situation where contributions are mandated to charitable organizations. In Singapore, all employees make a monthly contribution—unless they specifically opt out—of between S$0.50 and S$11 (US$0.35 and US$7.60) to the various community self-help groups. These self-help groups focus on lower-income earners through educational programs, social services and worker training assistance.[23]

Redefining the Corporation

However, legislating good corporate behavior may be just dealing with the symptoms of the problem. The root cause of the issue lies in the nature or constitution of the corporation.

Joel Bakan, a legal scholar and author of *The Corporation: the Pathological Pursuit of Profit and Power*, points out that a corporation is actually a legal person, created to put the interests of its shareholders above all other interests.[24] "So basically the kind of person a corporation is a profoundly self-serving person. As you learn in any introductory psychology class, that is the definition of a psychopath." He notes that a charming and benevolent human psychopath is all the more dangerous. For him, CSR dresses corporations to be charming and benevolent.

How does one reconcile Bakan's view of the corporation as a psychopath with the behavior of corporations like Ben & Jerry's or Accenture, both of which have had a long history and tradition of social responsibility and corporate philanthropy? The answer, I believe, lies in the owners of the organization. Where ownership of a company is in the hands of a homogeneous (often small) group of people who emphasize social responsibility, then CSR is "for real" in that organization. Hence, Ben & Jerry's founders started their business with a view to sharing the rewards with their employees and the community. Accenture was a partnership, and it was a requirement for new partners to subscribe to the principles of stewardship which were already ingrained in the company as everyone grew up with them.

However, the model of the corporation in its pure form is dependent upon serving the narrow interests of its shareholders. In a public company with a large base of shareholders, the focus easily gravitates simply and only to profits and shareholder value.

There already exist models of corporate structures that do not result in a pathological focus on shareholder value. Social enterprises are emerging across the world as a new styled means by which profits are generated specifically for nonprofit use.

Long before CSR became fashionable, cooperatives have existed with inbuilt social missions. One such example is NTUC Fairprice, Singapore's largest retailer with more than 220 stores islandwide.[25] Fairprice was founded as a cooperative of the trade union, with the mission of moderating the cost of living for low-income households in Singapore. It has done so for over 30 years, at times selling essential goods during critical shortages at regular low prices despite the opportunity to profiteer. The cooperative, which has its own corporate foundation, has also been generously giving to the community and is rated one of Singapore's top corporate donors.

Corporation 20/20, an initiative of the Tellus Institute and Business Ethics,[26] seeks to develop a vision of how corporations across-the-board can be redesigned. Its premise is that corporations have extraordinary potential to serve the public good but are prevented from fully doing so by a design that is constrained by short-term returns. It has therefore developed a set of principles (see Figure 8.2) that provides businesses, investors, government, labor and civil society with an overarching framework for building a sustainable future.

We are obviously a far way from achieving the vision of Corporation 20/20, but social enterprises and cooperatives are hopeful harbingers of what is possible.

Figure 8.2 Principles of Corporate Redesign

Corporation 20/20
Principles of Corporate Redesign

1. The purpose of the corporation is to harness private interests to serve the public interest.
2. Corporations shall accrue fair returns for shareholders, but not at the expense of the legitimate interests of other stakeholders.
3. Corporations shall operate sustainably, meeting the needs of the present generation without compromising the ability of future generations to meet their needs.
4. Corporations shall distribute their wealth equitably among those who contribute to its creation.
5. Corporations shall be governed in a manner that is participatory, transparent, ethical, and accountable.
6. Corporations shall not infringe on the right of natural persons to govern themselves, nor infringe on other universal human rights.

Corporate Social Reality

In summary, CSR is about companies being good and doing good. Within corporations, the debate on embracing CSR often boils down to the costs and benefits of doing so.

However, from a macro policy standpoint, the CSR movement should be viewed in the light of two unassailable realities. The first is the growing power of corporations to impact the world, for good and for bad. The second reality is that most corporations are constituted to be primarily, some would say exclusively, accountable to their shareholders.

These two realities mean that companies will be socially responsible only when their business owners accept the responsibility that comes with power (only a few will do so); or when corporations see that the benefits of CSR outweigh the costs (increasingly more, but still far from a majority); or when there are increased rules and regulations to tame the corporate beast (a resource-intensive approach).

The long-term solution lies in getting to the root of, and reshaping, the realities. With increasing globalization and openness of economies, the first reality of growing corporate power is here to stay. The second reality of a corporate structure that lopsidedly focuses on the owners' interests can be changed to a broader respect for the diverse stakeholders of the corporation. There are initiatives underway to redesign the corporation in this direction, and there are early role models (social enterprises and cooperatives) that have led the way.

Until these developments come to pass, the risk is that the CSR movement makes everyone—government, corporations, nonprofits, consumers, and the public—feel good, but it may really be no more than a soothing balm that could distract from the longer term solution.

Endnotes:

Adapted from: "The business of business," *SALT*, September-October 2006; and "Is the business of business just business?" *The Business Times*, October 17, 2006.

1 For history buffs, the name Accenture only came into being in the new millennium. I started with Arthur Andersen & Co in 1977. In 1989, the management information consulting division that I was in, became Andersen Consulting, a business unit within what was known as the Arthur Andersen Worldwide Organization. The other business unit was called Arthur Andersen and did attest (audit) and tax consulting work. In August 2000, Andersen Consulting legally and completely separated from Arthur Andersen and the Arthur Andersen Worldwide Organization, and became Accenture on January 1, 2001 (01.01.01).

2 Information on the five corporate citizens was compiled from various sources including the companies' collaterals. CSR information for these companies are obtainable at these weblinks:

Accenture: www.accenture.com/Global/About_Accenture/Company_Overview/ Corporate_Citizenship/default.htm;
Ben & Jerry's: www.benjerry.com/our_company/about_us/social_mission;
BP: www.bp.com/sectiongenericarticle.do?categoryId=9020009&contentId=7036305;
GM: www.gm.com/corporate/responsibility;
Vodafone: www.vodafone.com/start/responsibility.html.

3 www.unglobalcompact.org

4 Singapore Compact for CSR is a tripartite (employers, union and government) coalition based on the UN Global Compact. It was established in 2005. Its Inaugural CSR Conference was held jointly with the National Volunteer & Philanthropy Conference in 2006. A dozen corporate leaders from UBS, Qian Hu, etc., went on stage to explain to over 500 people why and how they were practicing CSR.

5 www.thebodyshop.com; Matthew Gitsham, "The Body Shop's 2005 Values Report— Cleaner, but not sparkling," *The Ethical Corporation*, December 6, 2005.

6 See Marc Benioff, Karen Southwick, *Compassionate Capitalism: How Corporations Can Make Doing Good an Integral Part of Doing Well* (Career Press, 2004) and www. salesforcefoundation.org/node/49.

7 "Is there really a link between CSR and a company's financial performance?" *Foundation for Corporate Social Responsibility Newsletter,* Vol. 3, No. 28, July 17, 2006.

8   John P. Kotter & James L. Heskett, *Corporate Culture and Performance* (The Free Press, 1992). The authors conducted four studies between 1987 and 1991, from which the conclusions were formed.

9   Milton Friedman, "The Social Responsibility of Business is to increase Profits," *The New York Times Magazine*, September 13, 1970. Friedman died on November 16, 2006. *The Economist* called him the most influential economist of the past half-century.

10 "The Good Company—A Survey of Corporate Social Responsibility," *The Economist*, January 20, 2005. Articles in survey series include "The good company" and "The union of concerned executives."

11 *Tobacco industry and corporate responsibility... an inherent contradiction* (Tobacco Free Initiative, World Health Organization, February 2003); "Press release: Tobacco industry accused of corrupting ideals of corporate social responsibility," London School of Hygiene & Tropical Medicine, University of London, December 1, 2002.

12 Choe Sang-Hun, "A gesture of remorse from head of Samsung," *International Herald Tribune*, February 7, 2006.

13 *The State of Giving* (National Volunteer and Philanthropy Center, Singapore, 2005).

14 Recap for Spiderman fans: When Peter Parker first acquired superpowers, he used it for selfish purposes, to make money. One day, he refused to stop a thief. He later learned that the thief subsequently murdered his guardian, Uncle Ben. In the comic's debut of Spiderman in *Amazing Fantasy#15*, as Peter Parker tearfully reflected on how he could have saved his Uncle Ben, the narration said, "A lean, silent figure slowly fades into the gathering darkness, aware at last that in this world, with great power, there must also come great responsibility." In the 2002 movie, *Spiderman*, Parker recalled that Uncle Ben had once told him: "With great power, comes great responsibility." Excelsior! Recap for history buffs: The notion of power and responsibility is not new. Others who have similarly articulated it include: (1) Winston Churchill, "The price of greatness is responsibility"; (2) Franklin D. Roosevelt, "In a democratic world, as in a democratic nation, power must be linked with responsibility.."; (3) Theodore Roosevelt, "...I believe in power; but I believe that responsibility should go with power..." (4) Jesus Christ, "For unto whomsoever much is given, of him shall be much required," (Gospel of Luke, Chapter 12, Verse 48).

15 www.aprilasia.com

16 www.walmartstores.com/AboutUs/

17 This table was originally prepared by the Lien Center for Social Innovation in 2006 using most recent data then available (2004). Gabriel Lim, researcher from LCSI who had since left, kindly updated it in 2008 using the most recent data available—mostly 2006 figures. Several similar versions of this table have been prepared at various dates by various people. The first such table I came across was by Joshua Karliner, founder of CorpWatch.

18 www.corpwatch.org

19 "The ethics of business," *The Economist*, January 20, 2005.

20 www.foei.org; *Briefing: Corporate Accountability* (Friends of The Earth, April 2005), www.foe.co.uk/resource/briefings/corporate_accountability1.pdf.

21 Gerald Davis, Marina Whitman and Mayer Zald, "The Responsibility Paradox," *Stanford Social Innovation Review*, Winter 2008.

22 Amit Dar, Sudharshan Canagarajah & Paud Murphy, Training *Levies: Rationale and evidence from evaluations* (World Bank, December 2003), http://siteresources.worldbank.org/INTLM/Resources/TrainingLevies.pdf. For example, in Singapore, employers are required to pay a skills development levy of 1% of employees salary for those earning below $2,000 (US$1,400) a month. The money is then used collectively to provide incentives to companies to upgrade the skills of employees. For further info, see www.sdf.gov.sg.

23 See www.app.mcys.gov.sg/web/comm_comminv_communityrelations.asp. The community self-help groups are ethnic-based, and individuals contribute to one of the self-help ethnic groups based on his race as follows: Malay/Muslims—Mosque Building and Mendaki Fund (between S$2-11), Indians—Singapore Indian Development Association Fund (between S$1-7); Chinese—Chinese Development Assistance Fund (S$0.50 to 1); Eurasian—Eurasian Community Fund (S$2-10).

24 "Charming Psychopaths" is a side bar to the article by Deborah Doane, "The Myth of CSR," *Stanford Social Innovation Review*, Fall 2005.

25 www.fairprice.com; the corporate foundation is NTUC Fairprice Foundation Ltd.

26 www.corporation2020.org

Chapter 9

The Charity Quotient

How Charitable are You, Truly?

Does the size of a donation determine the level of generosity of a giver? Posed with this dilemma, I sought to construct a charity quotient framework.

In this framework, there are two dimensions of charitableness. One measures the external manifestation of the giving of money, time and self—relative to the giver's capacity. The internal dimension measures the motivation for giving—whether it is for altruistic or selfish reasons.

Juxtaposing the two dimensions identifies four different kinds of givers: the Little Giver, the Value Giver, the Latent Giver and the Virtuous Giver. Unfortunately, most of the world seems to fit into the "Little Giver" category.

It was on the golf fairway that I made a pitch to Ng Kuo Pin, a partner at my former firm, to support a charity golf tournament. "You realize that many of those who signed up are doing it less out of a sense of charity than for reasons like networking?" he remarked.

Over the next few holes, we discussed Kuo Pin's skepticism of certain philanthropic gestures. He questioned whether charities should be celebrating large donations when those donations are small to the donors (given their wealth and earning power) and come with strings attached. We debated the definition of "generosity" and whether the saying "the color of money is all the same no matter where it comes from" applies to charity.

Our discussion eventually centered on the question: how would you evaluate "charitableness"?

While there is common agreement that a person contributing to charity makes a positive impression, it is not clear how one would judge whether such a person is truly charitable or not.

I felt that a large part of the difficulty in answering the question lies in the fact that there is both a visible and invisible aspect to a person's generosity. In other words, there are two dimensions of charitableness:

– External: how charitableness is manifested to charities and the outside world

– Internal: the motivation behind an individual's charitable acts

External Manifestation

Often, when we say that a person is charitable, it is based on what we see, such as when a philanthropist donates a large sum of money to charity.

For example, most of us would regard Bill Gates as being very generous. He had given US$30 billion away to charity, and intends to give most of the rest (an estimated US$58 billion) [1] away as well. Gates and his wife, Melinda, have said that they plan to give away 95 percent of their wealth during their lifetimes. While they have not decided how much of what is left will go to their three children, they will follow Warren Buffet's philosophy to leave "enough to do anything, but not enough to do nothing." [2] Without in any way diminishing the Gates' largesse, five percent of several tens of billions of dollars is, of course, far from small change for most of us. Underlining this, my son, speculating on how much the Gates would leave their children, cheekily said to me, "Dad, I would fully support you following Bill Gates' example: give away all your money to charity, just be sure to also follow him and leave a hundred million dollars or so to me."

Bo Sanchez, a lay preacher and author, speaks of how, when he started out as a missionary, he struggled to give 10 percent of his earnings to charity.[3] Now that he is successfully earning more money through books and talks, he gives 40 percent to charity while still living a spartan life. His aim is to earn more so that he can afford to give 90 percent and more of his wealth to charity.

The relative versus absolute value of a gift from the giver's standpoint is illustrated in the Bible's parable of the widow's mite.[4] In the story, Jesus on witnessing the apparently large sums donated by rich men at the temple highlighted how a poor widow donated only two mites. A mite was the least valuable coin of that era, but this was everything she had, while the wealthy contributed only a small portion of their abundance.

In a recent charity collection at my church, one envelope out of the 7,000 donation envelopes stood out. It contained $10 and the donor had scribbled on it: "I am sorry, but this is all I have." He should not have apologized as he had, in fact, probably given proportionately a lot more than many.

So, the point here is that it is not the absolute sum that measures a person's generosity, but the relative amount—relative to his capacity.

When we talk about generosity in giving, it is not just in terms of money but also of time. In many ways, especially for the better-off in society, time is more precious and more difficult to give. Nevertheless, the decision reflects our priorities, and even some of the mega-rich are choosing to follow their hearts. Bill Gates transitioned out of a day-to-day role with Microsoft in mid-2008 to devote more time to working with his foundation.

To give totally means giving more than money and time—we can give blood, an organ or any part of our body. That would be literally giving of oneself.

One example of such an extreme giver is Zell Kravinsky, a mathematician and an American professor. He amassed a US$45 million real estate fortune expressly to give to charity. In 2003, he donated one of his kidneys to a complete stranger. He is said to be looking into other donations: his bone marrow, a lobe of a lung, "anything that someone might need."[5]

Thus, the external manifestation of charitableness is what we can see; a tangible determination of the proportion a man gives of his available capacity—his time, his money and himself.

Internal Motivation

However, true charity comes from the inside. It is, of course, hard to peer into a person's heart or mind when he gives, but motivation must count for an evaluation of how charitable a donor is.

People give to charity for a multitude of reasons. They may give because they want the publicity (visible giving), because of the tax deductions (tax-based giving), because they owe or want a favor from the person who asked (reciprocal giving), or because they were impressed with the sleekness of the event they attended which may have nothing to do with the cause (impulse giving). Many of these reasons are tied to the giver getting something back from his giving.

But to be truly charitable, some would argue that the basis for one's giving should not be based on any tangible return but be tied to pure feelings of altruism.

For some, especially the religious, pure giving sometimes go beyond any notion of feeling good. Rather, it is an obligation. A tenet of all great religions, including Christianity, Buddhism, Judaism and Islam, is that it is the duty of those who are well-off to aid the less fortunate of society. Christians, for example, are taught that they are mere stewards of God's creation, that they should take only enough for themselves and share the rest with those who need it.

Of course, there is the counter argument that even altruism confers benefits: feelings of fulfillment and goodness, rewards in the afterlife for the religious, and perhaps guilt reduction.

Whether it is out of duty or simple altruistic feelings, I would argue that motivations are pure when there is no intention by the giver of any material, social or political *quid pro quo*. In measuring this internal dimension, it is the intention of the giver that is important because often, charities may reward the giver with recognition, whether he or she seeks it or not.

The Charity Quotient

Can we effectively measure and combine these two dimensions of giving to produce a quotient for charitableness?

On the external aspect, if we are able to measure the level of giving, it would lie somewhere between giving zero to 100 percent of a person's capacity—his time, his money and his whole self to others.

On the internal dimension, the scale would range from a totally self-centered attitude to a pure altruistic heart.

Even if measurement is difficult, juxtaposing the two dimensions as shown in Figure 9.1 provides a useful conceptual framework to think about charitableness.

Figure 9.1 The Charity Quotient Chart

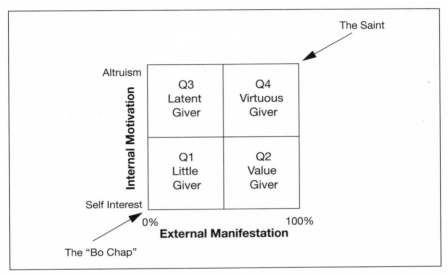

On this chart, we have two extremes. At the bottom left hand corner is the "bo chap" (a term taken from Hokkien, a Chinese dialect, meaning "don't care"), a person who neither cares nor gives. At the top right hand corner is the "saint," what mere mortals can only aspire to—giving all one has with no reservations or any expectation of returns.

Between these two extremes, the chart identifies four broad groups of givers:

Quadrant 1: Little Giver. This group generally believes in the edict that charity begins—and largely stays—at home. The Little Giver does give but it is usually spare change, and even then, there should be something given in return.

Quadrant 2: Value Giver. The people in this group give most of what they have away, but they believe in some give and take or, more aptly, give to take. They are also serving their enlightened self-interests.

Quadrant 3: Latent Giver. People in this group have a heart, but they have not yet given fully of their capacity.

Quadrant 4: Virtuous Giver. This group gives all it can for altruistic reasons. It is what ideally all givers should be. When you get into this quadrant, you are a true giver.

Those in Q1 (Little Giver) and Q2 (Value Giver) are motivated primarily by their self-interests. The difference between the two is how much proportionately they end up giving of their resources and themselves.

In modern society, where self and achievements are celebrated, many do give out of enlightened self-interest. We give to take something in exchange, even if the take may be less than the give. The take could manifest in tax breaks, special donor privileges, returning a favor or gaining one. In fact, the field of fundraising is replete with techniques to enhance "the power of the ask," from understanding the motivations (no matter how crass) of the donor to constructing an "ask" with benefits that the potential donor will hopefully agree to.

Even simple recognition—when craved—is part of this give-to-take approach. When Ted Turner started the ball of competitive philanthropy rolling with his US$1 billion pledge to the United Nations, he noted that in his conversations with his fellow mega-rich, they indicated they would give more if there "was a list of who did the giving rather than the having."[6] His remarks prompted *Slate* magazine to compile just such a list,[7] which led to greater media coverage and more lists of mega-philanthropic giving.

Being a Value Giver is politically more acceptable than being a Little Giver, as it would be evident that a person is giving away a lot even if you may question his or her motivation.

Few would therefore admit to being a Little Giver. That would mean celebrating selfishness and caring little for charity. That is, unless you are Ayn Rand, author of *The Virtue of Selfishness*.[8] She argued that each man should act in his own rational self-interest, which "does mean that he does not subordinate his life to the welfare of others, that he does not sacrifice himself to their needs, that the relief of their suffering is not his primary concern, [and] that any help he gives is an exception, not a rule." Her belief is that altruism would be an "evil" betrayal against one's own interests. To Rand, charity is neither a major virtue nor a moral duty. In the week of the 2004 Asian Tsunami, the Ayn Rand Institute, founded by Rand and modeled on her philosophy, sent out a press release that was headed "U.S. Should Not Help Tsunami Victims."[9]

Meanwhile, Q3 (Latent Giver) and Q4 (Virtuous Giver) people believe in altruism.

Some would argue that the Latent Giver is an oxymoron. How could you be altruistic but give away very little? Well, Q3 givers can exist if measured at a point in time of a person's life. When *Fortune* interviewed Warren Buffett[10] on the historic occasion of his pledge of more than US$30 billion to the Bill & Melinda Gates Foundation, he was asked why he did not do so earlier. He responded that he had much less to give before then and that "someone who was compounding money at a high rate… was the better party to be taking care of philanthropy that was be done 20 years out." (Buffet's investment company, Berkshire Hathaway had been earning an average annual return since 1990 that is twice that of the long-term average annual return of the Standard & Poor's 500 stock index.)[11] He also noted that he and his late wife had always intended for his wealth to go back to society, and he had previously communicated as much to Berkshire Hathaway's shareholders.

To be a Virtuous Giver suggests that the giver is close to sainthood, where motives are purer. Certainly, Mother Teresa who gave all of herself would be a paragon of sainted giving.

You could say that those who give much of what they have anonymously—foreclosing (or preempting) any possibility of recognition and benefits to themselves—could fall in this quadrant. *BusinessWeek*, in its annual philanthropy survey in 2003, ferreted out several major secret givers.[12]

Chief among them was Charles Feeney, who secretly donated his stake in Duty Free Shoppers to set up a charitable foundation while continuing to live a frugal life. At the time of the story, the foundation assets under his astute management were worth US$3.7 billion while his own personal net worth was only US$1.5 million. It was only with the sale of Duty Free Shoppers in 1997, some 13 years after he gave away his stake, that the existence and level of his giving became known.

A key difficulty with using this charity quotient framework lies in determining the internal dimension.

Who knows what lurks in the hearts of men? A secret giver whom one might place in Q4 (Virtuous Giver) could turn out to be doing so out of a guilt trip, or is simply avoiding the taxman or, worse, is supporting a charity that fronts a terrorist organization.

Corporate Charity Quotient

Applying the charity quotient model to a corporate context is easier. This is because the internal dimension of motivation, while difficult to determine for an individual human being, is obvious for an organization.

The constitution of an organization, the purpose for which it is set up, is known and open. For our purposes, there are two kinds of organizations: commercial organizations which exist primarily to make money for their owners, and social enterprises which are businesses with social missions. In that sense, commercial organizations, which are in the majority, are "selfish" as their ultimate interests lie with their shareholders. Social enterprises are altruistic as ultimately their profits benefit charities.

Applying the charity quotient framework in a corporate context enables us to identify these two types of organizations for the two halves of the y-axis.

For the x-axis, how much the corporation gives is similarly judged as people. It will be the amount of corporate philanthropy relative to its earnings and time spent by its employees with charitable causes.

The resultant chart is shown in Figure 9.2.

Figure 9.2 Charity Quotient for Corporations

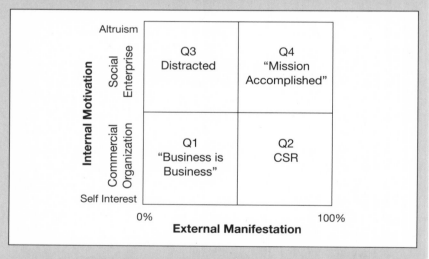

If a commercial company gives away very little or nothing to the community (Q1), it has simply taken the view that "the business of business is just business" and it has not found any business value in giving much back to the community.

If a commercial company falls into Q2, it gives a lot back to the community. You could argue whether it could give away *all* or even most of its money since that would be against its constitution. The company is probably giving away a lot because it has determined that it is good business to do so. That is why many companies that practice CSR (or Corporate Social Responsibility) extol its benefits in terms of branding, marketing synergy, employee motivation, etc. Thus, for a commercial company that is true to its constitution of maximizing profits for its shareholders, giving to the community is simply enlightened corporate self-interest.

Social enterprises, on the other hand, are set up specifically to benefit individual charities or charities in general. Some are set up by charities themselves, others by businessmen with a heart, and some are cooperatives serving a much larger community of stakeholders. Since their constitutions require them to give back all, doing so simply means that they are accomplishing their missions, and they naturally fall into Q4.

If a social enterprise fails to give all that it can (Q3), it means that it is distracted, has lost its way and failed to fulfill its mission.

Even if a person's intentions are pure, a paragon of virtue will eventually not go unnoticed in this connected world. Public attention and even adulation, such as in the case of Mother Teresa, may be inevitable. As Bill Gates Sr. noted with regards to the media attention accompanying the philanthropic giving of his son, Bill Gates III, an anonymous donation of that sheer size "was not an option my son had."[13]

Most of the time, we like to give the benefit of the doubt and assume the best of intentions. There are however situations, especially in business-related philanthropy, when businessmen run the risk of being accused of using their donations to further their business interests.[14]

I have developed this model of charity quotient in the context of individual (personal) giving, but it may also be applied to corporations (see box on "Corporate Charity Quotient").

Where Are We?

So, where would we be on this charity quotient chart?

Let us start with the x-axis. Where do we stand in terms of the external manifestation of giving? Table 8.3 provides data from various sources that can help us form a view on where the general population is in relation to the giving of time and money in, say, Singapore, the U.K. and the U.S.

As we discussed earlier, while the quantum of giving is important to the recipient, to determine charitableness, we need to compare the quantum given against the capacity of the individual to give.

Conceptually, a good measure of capacity for giving would be discretionary time and income. Economists define discretionary income as total income less taxes and the cost of necessities to maintain a suitable standard of living. Similarly, we can define discretionary time as the

Table 8.3 Giving of Time and Money

	Singapore	U.K.	U.S.
1. Giving of Time			
a. Volunteerism Rate[15]	15.2%	28.0%	44%
b. Economic value of volunteerism as % of GDP[16]	0.46%	2.97%	2.18%
d. Average annual volunteer hours per person[17]	12 hours	58 hours	127 hours
e. Average annual leisure hours per person[18]	657 hours	1,924 hours	1,825 hours
f. Ratio of leisure hours to volunteer hours (e) / (d)	55 : 1	33 : 1	14 : 1
2. Giving of Money			
a. Individual donations as % of per capita GNI[19]	0.28%	0.73%	1.63%
b. Annual donations by all individuals & households[20]	US$292m	US$19b	US$213b
c. Annual leisure expenditure by all households[21]	US$352m	US$190b	US$280b
d. Ratio of leisure expenditure to donations	1.2 : 1	10.0 : 1	1.3 : 1

waking hours available after time spent at work, and essential personal and household activities. However, data on discretionary time and income is not readily available. I have therefore sought to use leisure time and expenditure as a surrogate.

Thus, to measure charitableness in the giving of time, we can see how much time a person spends on volunteering versus leisure activities. For philanthropic giving, we can compare donations to leisure expenditure.

The U.S. is often viewed as being one of the most, if not the most, generous countries in the world,[22] and the data generally bears this out. For example, its volunteerism rate is at a high 44 percent compared to the U.K.'s 28 percent and Singapore's 15 percent. Its individual donations make up 1.63 percent of its Gross National Income, which is more than twice the U.K.'s rate and nearly six times Singapore's 0.28 percent.

Yet, in all countries and even in the U.S., more can be done in relation to our giving capacity.

In terms of time, Americans spend 14 times as much on leisure activities as they do volunteering. In the U.K., it is 33 times and in Singapore, it is 55 times.

In terms of money, the ratio of donations to leisure expenditure seems a lot healthier, with only slightly more spent by households on leisure compared to donations in the U.S. and Singapore. It should be noted that the amount of leisure expenditure is generally understated, as it does not include various luxury items that could have been classified by the respective household expenditure surveys under food, transportation and household goods.

Taking time and money together, the average person, no matter the country, would seem to fall on the left-hand side of the x-axis, putting us in the category of Little Givers (Q1) or Latent Givers (Q3).

It is more difficult to determine where people would lie on the y-axis—the internal motivation for giving—because this is subjective. Many surveys of volunteers and donors are usually not very useful in this area because they tend to be superficial and ask respondents to tick feel-good boxes such as "giving back to society," and others. Surveys of fundraisers and in-depth research by experts who study what motivates donors and volunteers provide a more accurate picture and are more useful, even if they may not always be very quantitative.

In its study of modern-day donors, nfpSynergy, a U.K.-based think tank and consultancy for the nonprofit sector, noted a trend towards "a more demanding, more reward driven and less dutiful generation of donors" and the need for "oven-ready, bite-size, fundraising niches" to succeed.[23] Similarly, nfpSynergy's analysis of volunteers noted that "while volunteers often cite altruistic motivations (belief in the cause and a desire to make a difference), some volunteer managers point to a worrying swing towards catering for the harder motivations and associated incentives for volunteering."[24] It identified two key trends as being "the rise of the selfish volunteer" and "the productization of volunteering."

A U.S. research of major donors and their motivations by Prince and File identified "seven faces of philanthropy."[25] Table 8.4 sorts the authors' segmentation of donors in sequence of how they might fit on the y-axis of our charity quotient chart.

Table 8.4 Seven Major Donor Types

Donor Type	Philosophy	Percentage
Altruists	It is right	9%
Devouts	It is God's will	21%
Dynasts	It is a family tradition	8%
Repayer	Repaying a benefit out of loyalty or obligation	10%
Socialites	It is fun	11%
Investors	It helps with personal tax and estate duty	15%
Communitarians	It makes good business sense and helps the community prosper	26%

Source: Russ Alan Prince and Karen Maru File, *The Seven Faces of Philanthropy*

The first two or three donor types would likely fall into the top half of the chart, while the rest would be in lower half. That makes, at most, 38 percent who are more motivated by selfless reasons and 62 percent who expect to take, or have taken, something in return.

Even if the research is not conclusive, sad as it may appear, we can tentatively conclude that the majority of us fall into the "Little Giver" quadrant. The good news is that the potential to move up and right is very high.

Meanwhile, where do you think you are on the charity quotient chart?

Endnotes:

Adapted from: "The Charity Quotient: How charitable are you, truly?" *SALT*, No. 24, January-April 2008.

1   The remaining wealth of Bill Gates is from *Forbes'* most recent annual billionaire listing: Luisa Kroll, "The world's billionaires," *Forbes*, March 5, 2008.

2   Patricia Sellers, "Melinda Gates goes public... about living with Bill, working with Warren Buffet and giving away their billions," *Fortune*, January 7, 2008.

3   Bo Sanchez spoke at a conference, "Christ@Work 2007" in Singapore on December 1, 2007. For more on Bo Sanchez, see www.preacherinbluejeans.com and www.bosanchez. ph.

4   Parable of the Widow's Mite is in the *Bible*: Gospel of Mark, Chapter 12, Verses 38-44. It is also found in Gospel of Luke, Chapter 20, Verses 45-47 and Chapter 21, Verses 1-4.

5   Peter Singer, "What should a billionaire give—and what should you?" *The New York Times Magazine*, December 17, 2006; Jerry Schwartz, "Zell Kravinsky doesn't get it," *The Oregonian*, November 28, 2003.

6   Maureen Dowd, "Ted Turner urges 'ol' skinflints' to open their purse strings wider," *The New York Times*, August 23, 1996.

7   David Plotz, "Competitive Philanthropy: The History of the Slate 60," *Slate*, February 20, 2006.

8   Ayn Rand, *The Virtue of Selfishness: A New Concept of Egoism*, (Signet, 1964). The book is a collection of essays and papers by Ayn Rand and Nathaniel Branden. Its themes include defining egoism as a rational code of ethics, the destructiveness of altruism and the nature of a proper government. Ayn Rand's philosophy is known as objectivism and the Ayn Rand Institute (www.aynrand.org), also known as the Center for the Advancement of Objectivism, promotes her philosophy.

9   "U.S. Should Not Help Tsunami Victims" was an op-ed piece written by David Holcberg, a research associate at the Ayn Rand Institute and released on December 30, 2004. It was printed in several publications. The piece attracted some criticism. A subsequent update by David Holcberg, "Clarification of ARI's Position on Government Help in Tsunami Victims," on January 7, 2005, which was published in the January 8, 2005 issue of *Capitalism Magazine*, stated that his earlier piece was "inappropriate and did not accurately convey the Institute's position." The clarification softened its stand on the donations but reiterated the stand that the government's only legitimate role is to protect individual citizen's rights and not to support altruism.

10   Carol J. Loomis, "A Conversation with Warren Buffett," *Fortune*, June 25, 2006.

11   Matt Krantz, "Berkshire Hathaway: Almost a screaming buy at more than $100,000 a share," *USA Today*, November 17, 2006.

12   Michelle Conlin and Jessi Hempel, with David Polek and Ron Grover, "Philanthropy 2003: The Secret Givers," *BusinessWeek*, December 1, 2003. See also Maureen Dowd, "One Life To Give," *The New York Times*, November 26, 1997, on a rare encounter with Charles Feeney.

13   Ibid.

14   For example, when Bill Gates gave $100 million to fight HIV/AIDS in India in 2002, there were questions as to whether this was a public relations exercise to "strengthen his company's brand and to keep people from dropping Microsoft Windows operating system and switching over to Linux." See "It was 70% generosity and the rest business," rediff. com, November 15, 2005 at www.rediff.com/money/2002/nov/15mess.htm; and Doc Searles, "SuitWatch: Views on Linux in Business," *Linux Journal*, November 14, 2002 at www.linuxjournal.com/xstatic/suitwatch/2002/sw31.html.

15   Volunteerism rate for the three countries is from *The State of Giving* (National Volunteer & Philanthropy Center, 2005).

16   Economic value of volunteerism for Singapore is from *The State of Giving* (National Volunteer & Philanthropy Center, 2005). For U.K. and U.S., the figures are from "Private philanthropy across the world," Johns Hopkins Comparative Nonprofit Sector Project, http://www.jhu.edu/cnp/pdf/comptable5_dec05.pdf.

17   Average annual volunteer hours person is computed as follows: Average annual hours per volunteer x Volunteerism rate. For Singapore, the data is from *The State of Giving* (National Volunteer & Philanthropy Center, 2005). For U.K., the data is from Elisha Evans and Joe Saxton, *The 21st Century Volunteer* (nfpSynergy, November 2005): page 4 shows that the 1997 national survey of volunteering is 4 hours per week for each volunteer, which works out to 4 x 52 x 28% = 58 annual volunteer hours per person. For U.S., the data is from *Giving & Volunteering in the United States* (Independent Sector, November 2001): the survey estimates 24 hours per month per volunteer, which works out to 24 x 12 x 44% = 127 annual volunteer hours per person.

18   Average annual leisure hours per person for Singapore is from *URA Survey of Lifestyles 2004* (Urban Renewal Authority of Singapore, 2004): leisure hours have been computed by taking the leisure time across five demographic segments and working out the national average. For U.K., the data is from Elisha Evans and Joe Saxton, *The 21st Century Volunteer* (nfpSynergy, Nov 2005): page 19 indicates that the average U.K. citizen spends 37 hours on leisure activities a week which works out to 37 x 52 = 1924 hours per year. For U.S., the data is from "American Time Use Survey—2006 Results," Bureau of Labor Statistics, U.S. Department of Labor, June 28, 2007: the data shows that more than 96 percent of men spend 5.6 hours and women spend 4.9 hours per day on leisure; I have averaged this to about 5 hours per person per day.

19   Individual donations as a percentage of per capita GNI for the three countries are from *The State of Giving* (National Volunteer & Philanthropy Center, 2005).

20   Annual donations for all individuals and households for Singapore is taken from *The State of Giving* (National Volunteer & Philanthropy Center, 2005). For U.K., the data is from *U.K. Giving 2007* (National Council for Voluntary Organizations and Charities Aid Foundation, 2007): note that data is based on year 2005/2006. For U.S., the data is from *Giving USA 2007, The Annual Report on Philanthropy for the Year 2006* (Giving USA Foundation, researched and written by the Center on Philanthropy at Indiana University, 2007): data used is 2005 donations by individuals and households.

21   Annual leisure expenditure by all households for Singapore is taken from *Report on The Household Expenditure Survey 2002/2003* (Singapore Department of Statistics, 2003); by adding up 2003 data for the following items under Recreation & Others—recreation & entertainment, alcoholic drinks & tobacco, personal care, personal effects, holidays, hobbies—the amount spent on leisure was S$523 per household. For U.K., the data

is from "Family Spending," Office of National Statistics, U.K., www.statistics.gov. uk; the average weekly expenditure by U.K. households in 2006 is £456 of which £58 is on recreation and culture. For U.S., the data is from "Consumer Expenditure in 2005," Bureau of Labor Statistics, U.S. Department of Labor, February 2007; only entertainment expenditure is used here, the other leisure expenditure such as travel, luxury goods are likely included in other categories and cannot be separated out.

22 Bhagyashree Garekar, "Why America is charity central," *The Straits Times,* November 18, 2007.

23 Joe Saxton, Michele Madden, Chris Greenwood & Brian Garvey, *The 21ˢᵗ Century Donor* (nfpSynergy, September 2007).

24 Elisha Evans and Joe Saxton, *The 21ˢᵗ Century Volunteer* (nfpSynergy, November 2005).

25 Russ Alan Prince and Karen Maru File, *The Seven Faces of Philanthropy* (John Wiley & Sons, 1994).

Chapter 10

Planned Giving

Raising Money from the Dead

The theory is that people should be most willing to part with their money for charitable causes when they are dead. The challenge is how to get them to commit to this course of action before it is too late for them to do so. Universities and healthcare institutions in the U.S. have led the way in getting bequests and legacies from donors—what has come to be known as "planned giving."

The level of planned giving in Asia is not as significant as it could be. This is probably due to the low level of estate duty, and an Asian culture that frowns on raising the subject of death. But the potential of cultivating this new source of giving is great. It should thus be proactively promoted, even to the extent of creating a mini-industry around it.

Several years ago, I had a great lunch with Winston Tan. A former investment banker, and well in his element, he regaled me with stories and philosophies of banking. In his view, bankers uniquely understand a very simple notion and, in fact, have very successfully built an entire industry around the exploitation of that notion—the time value of money.

The topic eventually turned to philanthropy and ideas for raising the level of philanthropic giving in Singapore.[1] Applying his banking insights, he advised, "Take the path of least resistance. Get people to give when the value of money matters least to them."

"Like, when?" I asked.

"Like, when they are dead," Winston replied simply, and added, "But of course, get them to commit before they are dead!"

Bequests and Planned Giving

The concept is, of course, not new.

Leaving estate assets to charities has long been promoted under the auspices of "planned giving," a term that generally refers to charitable bequests and other charitable gifts that are planned with forethought and that are usually effected upon the donor's death.

Some charitable bequests receive wide media attention. One of the most dramatic examples is the bequest made by Joan Kroc, the widow of Ray Kroc, founder of McDonalds Corp. She left US$1.9 billion to several charities when she died in October 2003 at the age of 75. The Salvation Army received the lion's share—more than US$1.5 billion, the single largest gift to a charity and more than what the Salvation Army received in 2002 from all sources. The money was for the development of community centers across the U.S., similar to the one that Kroc had opened in her and her husband's name in San Diego two years prior to her death. Recognizing the "unique fundraising challenge posed by this gift," the Salvation Army issued a statement. It highlighted that the gift might not be used for existing programs and services or for administrative costs, and it would therefore still need continuing support from its other donors.[2]

Another interesting charitable bequest was that of British millionaire, John George White.[3] He left £2 million (US$4 million) to charity in his will and only £40,000 (US$80,000) to his family. One of the major beneficiaries, the Royal Alexandra and Albert School did not even know of him and was totally surprised by his gift.

Certainly, not all bequests come as a surprise to the beneficiary organizations. In fact, most tend not to be, because they are promoted by the nonprofit organizations themselves. This is especially so in the U.S. where institutions of higher learning and healthcare-related charities are among the most proactive. Graduating students, patients and other potential donors are specifically asked to name these institutions in their wills or life insurance policies.

Over the years, more sophisticated planned giving instruments have also emerged to meet specific giver needs. These include Life Income Gifts where donors receive income for life after transferring their assets, and Pooled Income Funds where gifts are invested with similar gifts from other donors. An interesting innovative variation is a scheme by the Movement for the Intellectually Disabled of Singapore.[4] This is a charitable trust where parents can contribute and commit their money so that their children with disabilities will continue to be taken care of after they, the parents, have died.

Selling Planned Giving

When charities promote planned giving to potential donors, they would, of course, not do so on the basis of the convenience of the timing of the gift. They would not say that at the time of death, the gift is of least value to the donor. Or that what is available for giving would be known for certain at death.

Rather, they seek to persuade on the basis of the tangible benefits that can be derived from different planned giving instruments and the intangible benefits of leaving a legacy.

A wide range of planned giving instruments, as described above, has evolved to fit the income, security, tax and timing needs of donors. A significant aspect of these instruments relates to the tax benefits, of which there are several, that can be derived from such gifts.

In jurisdictions where there is estate duty (also known as estate tax or inheritance tax), charitable gifts made before and at death (those specified in the will) are excluded from estate duty. Since planned gifts remove property from probate, they reduce or even eliminate probate expenses. If appreciated assets (for example stocks that have gone up in value) are donated, there are savings from capital gains tax that could have applied to the increased asset value. In fact, depending upon the tax rules, financial planning experts may be able to structure planned gifts so that the total income, estate and capital gains tax can come close to the amount transferred while a donor receives income for life.

The intangible benefits of planned giving relate to leaving a legacy. Here, the donor usually receives recognition for his gift. If the gift is made through donor-advised funds or foundations, these can involve and teach the donor's children. The children can help decide who is to receive the gifts and continue the family's tradition of philanthropic giving.

The Potential of Planned Giving

Planned giving can be significant.

In the U.K., Legacy Foresight estimates legacy income received by charities at £1.6 billion (US$3.2 billion).[5] This represents about 12 percent of all voluntary income received by charities. For the largest charities (those with over £10 million or US$20 million income), legacy income contributed over 20 percent of all voluntary income. Interestingly, Fundratios, a narrower study of selected charities which have a strong focus on fundraising, shows that these selected charities derive as much as 36 percent of their voluntary income from legacies.[6]

In the U.S., charitable bequests amounted to nearly US$23 billion, or 7.8 percent of total giving in 2006.[7] Hopes are high that the future is even brighter. Experts have estimated that over the next 50 years, more than US$41 trillion will be transferred from one generation to the next, and a substantial percentage of this (conservatively estimated at US$6 trillion) will be donated to charitable causes.[8]

In Asia, not much official or industry data is available on planned giving. The sense is that legacy giving is low in Asia. In Singapore, for example, it is only promoted on a fairly low-key manner by a few large charitable organizations such as the Community Chest, the National Kidney Foundation and the National Heritage Board, while local universities follow the successful examples of their American counterparts and have specific legacy programs with their alumni.

But given the low base of planned giving, the high level of wealth and the high growth rate of wealth, the potential for planned giving in Asia should be high. High net worth individuals (those with US$1 million or more in financial assets) in the Asia Pacific region collectively own US$8.4 trillion in assets in 2006.[9] This represents over 22 percent of the global total. More importantly, Asian wealth is growing at a faster rate of 8.5 percent annually compared to the global rate of 6.8 percent.

Taking Singapore as an example, total wealth in the hands of high net worth individuals is US$320 billion. The National Volunteer & Philanthropy Center estimates that the intergenerational transfer of wealth each year easily exceeds S$2 billion (US$1.4 billion).[10] To put these figures into context, if just 10 percent go to charity, the total tax-deductible donations contributed by individuals each year would double.

Death and Taxes

Why, then, is planned giving not as significant as it could be in Asia?

I would hazard two guesses: estate duty and our attitude towards death.

As we have seen above, estate duty encourages charitable giving. The higher the level of estate duty, the greater the incentive. A 2004 U.S. government study concluded that a permanent repeal of the federal estate tax would reduce overall charitable giving by 6 to 12 percent.[11] The greater impact would be on charitable bequests which could decline by 16 to 28 percent.

The estate duty regime in most parts of Asia is typically generous, perhaps too generous. For a start, most countries in Asia have no estate duty: Singapore, China, Hong Kong, India, Indonesia, Australia, New Zealand, Malaysia and Thailand. For those that do, Philippines rests at a low 5 to 20 percent, while Japan, Korea and Taiwan have progressive rates that eventually go up to 50 percent. By contrast, in the U.K. and the U.S., the estate duty rate quickly reaches 40 percent and 45 percent respectively.[12] Hence, for the majority of Asian countries where there is a marginal or zero tax benefit for bequests, planned giving is not attractive from a tax standpoint.

Perhaps a stronger reason for the low level of bequests is that death is a taboo subject in our Asian upbringing. While this is true across most cultures, it is especially sensitive in many Asian cultures because of various superstitious beliefs. The Chinese, for instance, do not like to discuss death because it is associated with evil and bad luck. Talking about death, especially at the point near death, could be the harbinger of death and bring about its onset. If necessary, the traditional Chinese will talk about it in an indirect way, employing euphemisms such as "the end of the journey" or "time to go home."

The Asian attitude towards death makes it difficult for people to openly discuss matters of wills and life insurance. Insurers have argued that Asians are generally under-insured. The life insurance premium in Asia is US$155 per capita in 2006, while the premiums per capita in Europe and North America are seven times and 11 times more respectively.[13]

Partly as a result of this reticence to talk about and deal with death, charitable organizations that promote planned giving do not do much beyond putting up information about their planned giving programs on their websites.

Leaving the World a Better Place

What can we do about raising the level of planned giving in this part of the world?

More awareness and education would certainly help. Death may be a sensitive subject, but social entrepreneurs such as Dr. Mechai Viravaidya and Jack Sim have shown how they have overcome other taboo subjects (condoms and toilets, respectively).[14] The existence and growth of the life insurance industry in Asia is testimony that, perhaps, dealing with death is now becoming less of a taboo.

For the take-up to be greater, promotion of planned giving would need to be more proactive. Potential donors need to be actively engaged. One idea is to engage donors through the gatekeepers—the insurance agents, the financial planners, the private bankers and the estate lawyers. These people have the natural opportunity to discuss such matters and raise the giving question. The challenge, according to Charles Maclean of PhilanthropyNow, is that these gatekeepers need to be awakened first because they tend to raise the question only when it is initiated by their clients.[15] The reasons range from fear of losing their clients, to losing their fees because it is charity-related, to not participating in planned giving themselves.

Planned giving can also be institutionalized. Insurance and pension forms that require the naming of beneficiaries can have a simple checkbox or prompt for the naming of charities. This should, of course, come with the appropriate advisory on the implications, such as legacy and the avoidance of estate duty, of leaving the whole or part of an estate to a charitable cause.

It would be in the interest of the charity sector to develop planned giving as a concerted effort. The U.K. provides one good model where there is a whole ecosystem of planned giving. I counted at least four associations of charity organizations that are devoted to promoting the cause of planned giving. This number does not include the much larger number of generic fundraising related bodies which have departments or teams focused on planned giving. All major charities also have dedicated planned giving executives or teams. There are also consultancies, legal firms and software companies that focus on legacies and bequests.

The scale of the planned giving industry is a lot larger in the U.S. Both the U.S. and U.K. provide models which we can aspire to in Asia.

Endnotes:

Adapted from: "Living rites," *SALT*, November-December 2004.

1   At that time, I was chairman of the National Volunteer & Philanthropy Center and promoting philanthropic giving was part of our mission.

2   "Press release: Mrs. Joan Kroc gifts $1.5 billion to the Salvation Army to build community centers," The Salvation Army, January 20, 2004.

3   "Millionaire's 'surprise' legacy," *BBC News*, December 21, 2007, http://news.bbc.co.uk/2/hi/uk_news/wales/south_east/7155718.stm.

4   Arlina Arshad, "Trust scheme for special-needs children from 2007," *The Straits Times*, October 27, 2006. MINDS website is at www.minds.org.sg.

5   Figures from www.legacyforesight.co.uk. are as at March 31, 2008. Legacy Foresight is a research program on legacy income, funded by a charity consortium.

6   "Fundratios 2007—Summary Report," The Center for Interfirm Comparison with the Institute of Fundraising, at www.cifc.co.uk/Fundratios07.html.

7   *Giving USA 2007, The Annual Report on Philanthropy for the Year 2006*, (Giving USA Foundation, researched and written by the Center on Philanthropy at Indiana University, 2007).

8   This figure is found in various publications since 2003. See Betsy Brill, "Preparing for the intergenerational transfer of wealth: Opportunities and strategies for advisors," *Journal of Practical Estate Planning*, April-May 2003. See also endnote 15.

9   *Asia Pacific Wealth Report 2007* (Capgemini and Merrill Lynch, 2007).

10   This amount was estimated by the National Volunteer & Philanthropy Center based on estate duty data provided by the Inland Revenue Authority of Singapore in 2004. It was originally published in the article this chapter is adapted from: "Living Rites," *SALT*, November-December 2004.

11   Robert McClelland and Pamela Greene, *A CBO Paper: The estate tax and charitable giving* (Congressional Budget Office, Congress of the United States, July 2004).

12   U.S. estate tax rates are peculiar with recent tax laws changes. Since 2003, the top rate has been lowered from 49% by one percentage point per year; in 2007 through to 2009, the top rate will be 45%. If the U.S. Congress makes no changes to U.S. tax law, all estates will be taxed at 0% by 2010; and by 2011, the estate tax will return at a top rate of 55%. Most experts expect Congress to change the tax law before then. See Chapter 18, "Quitting quirky quagmires" for a further discussion on U.S. estate tax.

13 "World insurance in 2006: Premiums came back to 'life'," *Sigma*, No.4/2007, May 24, 2007.

14 See Chapter 15, "Innovating social change" for a description of Jack Sim's and Dr. Mechai Viravaidya's work.

15 Charles Maclean, "$41 trillion at stake," *Philanthropy World*, Volume 9, Issue 1, August 12, 2004; Charles Maclean, *Financial Advisors as Guiding Stars to Philanthropic Giving?* (PhilanthropyNow, May 2008).

Chapter 11

Elite Giving

Elite or e-Lite Giving?

You would think that society's elites have both the greater capacity and the greater reasons to give to charity than the less well-off. Yet, many studies show the opposite. They may donate more in absolute terms than those with lower income, but their donations are less in proportion to their income. Their reasons for not donating more are similar to those in the lower income bracket ("I cannot afford to"). Obviously, these reasons are not quite credible when they come from the elite rich.

Meanwhile, there are many other elites who personify exemplary giving. Their fellow elites should follow their lead, and preferably give from their strengths. They should not wait to be invited. Giving back to society is not a retirement affair. The time for the elites to contribute is now, not the proverbial later.

Mak Chee Wah is the chief executive officer of Melioris, a financial outsourcing company. He enjoys fencing in his spare time, and owns Z-Fencing, a fencing school. In 2004, during a casual lunch, Mak lamented the lack of facilities and support for children with brain disorders. He has a daughter who is afflicted with lissencephaly, a form of brain injury.

"Why not start a support group to network and help other families in similar situations?" I asked.

"Perhaps, when I retire," was his first response. But he saw the need.

Five months later, with some seed funding from the National Volunteer & Philanthropy Center, Mak launched a nonprofit charity called Amazing Kidz. The mission of the charity was to help families with children who are stricken with brain injuries.[1]

Mak's case is not untypical of many elites in Singapore. I suspect his initial response and subsequent action may be similar to other elites elsewhere. They usually respond positively when asked. This is good.

But often, it is the usual suspects who get invited to contribute, and usually, it is more about connections (that is, who asked) than the cause. Should not elites set the agenda for a civic society and be more proactive about their contributions?

Giving Back

There is a good reason for elites to contribute: they should be grateful for what they have.

The world we live in today is what it is because of the people before us and the people around us. Thus, we have a duty to do likewise for the people around us and after us. "Giving back" may sound trite, but this has been the basis on which the civilized world has been built through the generations.

Let there be no doubt about it. Most elites are where they are because they worked hard to get there. In one sense, such successful people do rightfully "earn" their wealth and positions in life. But who provided them the education to get on in life? The larger question, how did the education system come about?

It is a fine distinction between a privileged attitude versus an entitlement mentality. The former is grateful for the many blessings of life and seeks to bless others. The latter takes for granted all that has been provided by others and simply enjoys it without returning in kind.

Warren Buffet, the world's richest man in 2008, said that he became rich not because of "any special virtues of mine or even because of hard work, but simply because I was born with the right skills in the right place at the right time."[2] Thus, he felt that the only right thing to do when he did amass wealth "was to give it back to society."

Elites should have greater reasons to give back to society. After all, they have been endowed with so much more resources and talents, they should be more grateful. With their greater know-how and means, they have a lot more to give back to society.

e-Lite Giving

It is sad to say that although elites have the greater capacity and the greater reasons to do good, many studies show the opposite.

In an analysis of 2003 U.S. tax data, Claude Rosenberg and Tim Stone concluded that the middle class and below were two to three times more generous than the affluent (the upper middle class and the middle rich).[3] If the affluent had donated proportionately of their income as did those less well-off, the authors estimated that conservatively, there would be at least US$25 billion more in donations. That would increase total giving by 17 percent.

In the U.K., research consultancy nfpSynergy came to a similar conclusion.[4] While the absolute value of the donation from the highest income decile donors was twice that of the lowest income decile donors, it was less when one considers the relative capacity to give. As a percentage of income, it was only 0.8 percent of their income compared to 3.8 percent of the income of those earning the least.

Similar patterns were found in surveys in Singapore and Canada. In Singapore, a National Volunteer & Philanthropy Center survey showed that higher income earners gave much less proportionately to their income than lower income earners by a factor of more than five times.[5] Imagine Canada found that while donors from the lowest income range gave 1.7 percent of their income, this tapered off to 0.5 percent for those on the high end.[6]

Various studies have been undertaken to understand the psyche of the rich and what it takes to get them to donate more. The Institute for Policy Research, a U.K.-based independent think tank began research into this area on the premise that the better-off would have different attitudes towards and motivations for giving to charity than those with lower incomes.[7] It found that this may not be the case. The reasons for giving were similar across both groups: "I want to give something back;" "the cause is close to my heart;" and "that's the way I was brought up." The reasons for the rich not giving may be similar to those less well-off, but it was a lot less credible coming from them: "I have nothing to spare;" "it's not my responsibility;" "I don't have trust in charities;" "I don't want to feel guilty;" "I'm not wealthy, I'm just comfortable;" and "I do give <spare change>." .

The Luxury Institute surveyed the affluent of America on their giving and motivations.[8] The top two reasons for donating to nonprofits are the opportunity to make changes in the world in important areas, and seeing a compelling example of great need. The top two reasons for not donating are the fear of not having enough money for self and family, and the distrust of nonprofits.

I can relate to these findings. During my rounds of fundraising for charitable causes, I have sometimes been disappointed with the responses of some successful entrepreneurs. In my view, they have accumulated a fortune that would more than provide for themselves, their families and subsequent generations several times over. However, almost to a person, they were "not yet ready" to contribute a substantial but affordable portion of that wealth to charity or a foundation.

A recent book by Robert Frank, *Richistan*,[9] which is replete with stories of the nouveau riche, may help explain why many of them may never ever be ready. The more the rich have, they more they worry about it. These people "feel they need twice their current fortunes, no matter what their wealth." A large part of the drive seems to be an undercurrent of competition in hyper-luxury living that has taken "conspicuous consumption to new heights." Nevertheless, Frank remains hopeful that someday, the rich will see that their money "is not a gift but a responsibility." Then, they may use "their wealth to help target society's deepest problems."

Hopefully, this recognition will come sooner rather than later. Giving back to society should not be a retirement affair. Elites have "arrived" in society, even if they may not have reached their ultimate goals in life. The time to contribute should be now and not the proverbial later.

For most successful professionals and businessmen, one of the strongest motivators in contributing is the innate desire to make a difference and to leave a legacy. This is what Stephen Covey calls the Eighth Habit. He asserts that everyone has an inner longing to seize the day and live a life of contribution.

Giving With Strength

That's not to say that none of the rich are stepping up to the plate.

Certainly the likes of Bill Gates, Jeff Skoll and other mega philanthropists are leading the way.[10] But one does not need to be a multi-billionaire to make a big difference.

One of the most inspiring examples is Tracy Gary, who inherited a US$1.3 million trust fund at the age of 21.[11] She gave the bulk of the fortune to charity and started Inspired Legacies, a nonprofit dedicated to bringing donors, financial advisors and charities together. She donates 40 percent of the US$100,000 she earns from running Inspired Legacies. In addition, she has founded or co-founded 18 nonprofits. Her book, *Inspired Philanthropy*, provides a how-to for others to leave their own legacies in society.

Another uplifting example of elites is Responsible Wealth, a nonprofit that is open only to the wealthiest five percent of Americans (which includes those with assets of US$1 million and above).[12] The group is an offshoot of United for a Fair Economy which seeks to raise awareness of the risks of concentrated wealth and power. Responsible Wealth campaigns against unfair laws and policies in the areas of tax and corporate responsibility. They advocate against issues such as excessive compensation for chief executives, unfair corporate treatment of minorities and the repeal of the estate tax—some of the very policies that make their members rich. So, these wealthy activists are, in a sense, working against their own self-interests to reduce the deepening economic inequality and work for widespread prosperity.

Giving From Strength

As these exceptional elites show and as it is with any giving, when we give, we can make a much greater difference when we give from our strength by applying our unique talents and positions and not just from the strength of our dollars.

Mak was able to easily create a nonprofit, partly because he had previously helped start up two companies. In teaching people how to be philanthropic, Tracy Gary is sharing her own experience. Members of Responsible Wealth leverage their "economic privilege to contest economic privilege."[13]

From time to time, I have come across people who ask me about volunteer opportunities. Interestingly, about half of such senior volunteers I know ask to simply work directly with end-beneficiaries such as children, the aged or the handicapped. When I suggest that they could perhaps apply their professional expertise to work directly with the nonprofit's management to improve the organization's capacity, some say that they are looking for a change from what they do for a living.

I used to think that this is simply a case of different strokes for different folks. I would usually also ask them to think of how much greater the impact and contribution they would make by leveraging their strengths. The difference that a financial expert can make to a nonprofit's finances, or a public relations specialist to a nonprofit's media reach, should far outweigh the value of just an additional pair of hands, to say, clean the floor, helpful and necessary as that would be as well.

However, I have also come to realize that helping out in the bowels of a charity, be it building houses for disaster victims, cleaning up a nursing home and so forth, keeps one rooted in the humility and reality of charity work. So while it would be productive to make full use of our talents, I do think it is useful to maintain our perspectives by being involved at different levels of an organization, even if at first, some of the work may not be deemed befitting one's station in life.

Elite Giving

Thus, elites have more reasons as well as more resources to give. While many elites have not been, well elitist, about their giving, more need to come on board. When they do, they will make a much greater impact if they give with strength and from strength, leveraging their talents, resources and positions for the greater good.

Endnotes:

Adapted from: "Elite or e-lite giving?" *The Straits Times*, April 15, 2005.

1   Unfortunately, Amazing Kidz closed in August 2007. It was serving more than 100 families with disabilities but continually struggled with fundraising. When it was unable to receive IPC status (which allows for tax exemption for donations), partly due to the regulatory tightening on charities, it merged, as advised by the authorities, with a larger charity.

2   Carol J. Loomis, "A conversation with Warren Buffet," *Fortune*, June 25, 2006.

3   Claude Rosenberg and Tim Stone, "A new take on tithing," *Stanford Social Innovation Review*, Fall 2006. IRS data is for the year 2003.

4   Joe Saxton, Michele Madden, Chris Greenwood & Brian Garvey, *The 21ˢᵗ Century Donor* (nfpSynergy, September 2007).

5   *Individual Giving Survey 2006* (National Volunteer & Philanthropy Center, 2006). The data is not very conclusive for Singapore because the monthly income range was only up to S$10,000, and the sample size was limited at the upper range.

6   Michael Hall, David Lasby, Glenn Gumulka & Catherine Tyron, *Caring Canadians, Involved Canadians: Highlights from the 2004 Canada Survey of Giving, Volunteering and Participating* (Imagine Canada, 2006).

7   Laura Edwards, *A bit rich? What the wealthy think about giving* (Institute for Public Research, May 2002).

8   "Luxury Institute Philanthropy Survey: America's wealthy would be even more generous if they could have greater trust in nonprofits and greater engagement with financial advisors," *Market Wire*, October 9, 2006. News release is available from www.luxuryinstitute.com.

9   Robert Frank, *Richistan: A journey through the American wealth boom and the lives of the new rich* (Crown Publishers, 2007).

10 The giving by the mega-rich is covered in Chapter 14, "The second philanthropic revolution."

11 Jim Grote, "Extreme Philanthropy," *Financial Planning*, October 1, 2007; David Ian Miller, "Finding my religion: Born into great wealth, Tracy Gary finds happiness in giving her money away," *San Francisco Chronicle*, September 12, 2005; www.inspiredphilanthropy.org; www.inspiredlegacies.org.

12 Sandra Rothenberg & Maureen Scully, "Rolls-Royce Radicals," *Stanford Social Innovation Review*, Winter 2007; www.faireconomy.org/issues/responsible_wealth.

13 Ibid.

Chapter 12

International Giving & NGOs

Charity Without Borders

International giving is on the rise. A key reason for this is that modern technology and the media in an increasingly globalized world have helped to educate citizens in the developed world about the plights of those living in poorer countries, including those who are victims of globalization forces.

As a consequence, international non-governmental organizations (NGOs) have come into their own. They provide the vehicles through which donations, volunteers and ideas are harnessed to deal with the humanitarian, environmental and developmental issues in the developing world.

However, as NGOs go international, they face roadblocks from governments. Some governments perceive NGOs as undermining the role of the state and highlighting its inadequacies—more so when these NGOs are foreign.

But the use of charities for money laundering and terrorism financing is a valid concern of governments. In the wake of 9/11, authorities around the world have sought to clamp down hard on charities to ensure that they do not become conduits for the support of terrorism. Charities say the measures are too harsh and wonder if this is part of a broader recalibration of the relationship between them and governments.

In our increasingly globalized world, social causes and giving are also going global.

Both governments and the people are digging deep. The Hudson Institute, an international think tank, found that private donations from the U.S. to developing countries in 2003 exceeded US$62 billion or over three and a half times that of U.S. government aid, known as Official Development Assistance (ODA).[1] Interestingly, a University of Southampton's study of overseas giving in the U.K. showed that the general public assigns a greater importance to the work done by British charities for overseas causes than by the government.[2] In fact, two thirds of British adults believe that international charities make a major contribution towards reducing poverty in developing countries, while less than a fifth would view the governments of rich countries in the same light. Yet, in 2005, the British government's ODA actually exceeded private donations to charities that focus on overseas work by four times.

Meanwhile, in Singapore, the number of donors giving to overseas humanitarian effort increased four-folds between 2004 and 2006.[3]

The Asian tsunami of 2004 gave rise to its own tsunami of international giving. Within 14 months of the event, more than US$12 billion had been pledged as governments, corporations and individuals around the world "opened their hearts and their wallets."[4]

Indeed, the crises and disasters of recent years, such as Hurricane Katrina, the Kashmir earthquake and the September 11 attacks, have awakened an unprecedented level of global response and giving.

The increase in international giving has led to the emergence of organizations, such as Charities Aid Foundation,[5] that match donors with overseas causes. It has also led to the setting up of fundraising vehicles by non-resident charities or their supporters in major donor countries such as the U.S. and the U.K. Such vehicles may be foreign branches of charities or in some cases, "Friends Of" organizations. Thus, the Gawad Kalinga movement, which is based in the Philippines, has a network of international fundraising organizations under the Ancop name in 20 donor areas,[6] while Friends of Sunera Foundation is a British charity set up primarily to raise funds for and raise awareness of the Sunera Foundation, a Sri Lankan charitable trust dedicated to improving the lives of disabled persons.[7]

Beyond just money though, more people are giving their time internationally. Médecins Sans Frontières, or Doctors Without Borders,[8] is an independent medical humanitarian organization best known for emergency aid in war-torn regions and developing countries facing endemic diseases. Founded in 1971 by a group of French doctors, it seeks to observe neutrality and impartiality in the name of universal medical ethics. Every year, it mobilizes about 3,000 volunteer doctors worldwide. In addition, there is a larger group of volunteers for other administrative functions. In 1999, the organization received the Nobel Peace Prize for its work.

Since the advent of Médecins Sans Frontières, many other professional groups inspired by the *"sans frontières"* tag have emerged. There is "Engineers Without Borders," "Teachers Without Borders," "Bands Without Borders," and even "Magicians Without Borders." At last count, there were more than 30 "Without Borders" non-governmental organizations (NGOs).

It is not just professionals that are lending their much-needed expertise. The Peace Corps,[9] for example, was started in 1961 by President John F. Kennedy to challenge students to serve their country in the cause of peace by living and working in developing countries. Since then, it has mobilized more than 190,000 Americans of all ages, races and occupations to work in 139 host countries on issues ranging from AIDS education to information technology and environmental preservation.

Similarly, Voluntary Service Overseas[10] which was started to provide overseas experience for British school leavers, has evolved into an international development charity that has offices and partnerships in several countries, and provides diverse volunteer opportunities on international development projects. It has placed more than 30,000 experienced volunteers in developing countries.

Asia, which has been a significant recipient of donations and volunteers from the developed world, has also been paying it forward. During the Asian tsunami, Asian countries chipped in a fifth of the humanitarian aid that poured in. In Singapore, the tsunami may have been "the catalyst for the mindset change" of Singaporeans volunteering oversea.[11] The percentage of volunteers going on overseas humanitarian work jumped eight folds from 2004 to 2006.[12]

Why International Giving

There are a few reasons for the increase in international giving.

A large part of it stems from the world becoming smaller as a result of technology and other forces of globalization. The extensive reach of the media and the internet has helped to highlight, in real time, the plights of those affected by natural disasters, famines and disease, as well as those who are exploited by the forces of globalization.

In today's global village, the geographical distance of potential beneficiaries is a lot less of a consideration than the starkness of the contrasting living conditions between countries. Most volunteers and donors believe that they can make a much greater impact in the poor countries where the needs are more dire than in their home countries.

Much of charity is about the well-off giving to those less well-off. So, it has been with international giving that aid has been flowing mainly from the West to the East, from the North to the South, from the developed to the developing nations.

Giving back can also be given a push by emigrants from poorer nations. When they make good in their new communities, they want to make a difference in their countries of origin. According to the World Bank, diaspora communities remitted over US$206 billion in 2006 to developing countries. A part of this represents social investments for the public good, such as the building and financing of schools, community centers or health clinics, giving rise to an increased interest in and the study of "diaspora philanthropy."[13]

In some respects, international giving has a certain glamour to it. When high-profile entertainers such as Oprah Winfrey and Angelina Jolie, and public figures such as Bill Clinton and Nelson Mandela get involved in publicizing the needs of the developing world, they bring with them their reach and their sizzle. Through global charity concerts such as Band Aid, Live Aid and 8 Aid, helmed by the likes of Bob Geldof and Bono, the needs of the Third World have reached an audience of youths and other segments of the population that might not have been otherwise touched.

International NGO Growth

Globally, much of the private giving across borders is being funneled through groups, referred to variously as international NGOs or CSOs (civil society organizations),[14] to beneficiaries and causes in the host countries. These organizations tend to focus on humanitarian issues, sustainable development and developmental aid.

Their numbers have grown rapidly. The Union of International Associations,[15] an independent institution that documents NGO activity, listed over 51,000 international NGOs in 2005.

The scale of international NGO activity has also grown in tandem. In 2006, the Union of International Associations recorded over 8,800 international meetings held in 212 countries from the NGO community.[16] A prominent example is the World Social Forum,[17] which is a rival convention to the annual World Economic Forum held in Davos. It has become a movement against the ill effects of globalization. Members gather to coordinate world campaigns, share and refine strategies, and inform one another about movements and issues. The fifth World Social Forum in Porto Alegre, Brazil, held in January 2005, was the largest to date and saw 155,000 participants from 135 countries involved in 2,500 activities.

Border Checks

However, as many international NGOs have discovered, borders are not always easily crossed. Pursuing causes across borders is often fraught with complexities and governmental hurdles.

A basic factor lies in the nature of civil society. Civil society actors identify social issues and gaps, then either campaign for governments to resolve them or seek to provide their own solutions.

Enlightened governments, especially those from the developed world, view civil society, government and private enterprise as three integral and interdependent pillars of a modern nation. However, some governments see NGOs as undermining the role of the state, and highlighting its inadequacies—more so when these civil society actors are foreign.

The common argument against international NGOs is that they do not represent the constituents of the country they are operating in, whereas governments represent their people and have to take responsibility for the consequences of their actions. The NGOs counter that their legitimacy does not rest on representation but on their expertise, the popular support they have such as transparency on issues, or simply moral imperatives that transcend national borders, such as human rights.[18]

Critics argue that international NGOs walk a fine line between help and imperialism. The NGOs are accused of being "ideologically biased or religiously committed and, often, at the service of special interests." These special interests are often deemed to be the sponsoring states, where there is "a revolving door between the staff of NGOs and government bureaucracies."[19]

Russia, which had a limited culture of civil society, may have felt that sense of imperialism. It saw an explosion of NGOs with foreign funding following the introduction of glasnost and perestroika in the 1990s. In recent years, it has sought to rein in the NGOs. In 2006, it enacted an "NGO law" that is viewed as burdensome and even crippling, especially to foreign NGOs. For example, all NGOs have to submit bi-annual reports detailing their daily activities and expenses, even the cost of office supplies. Some NGOs have concluded that "if an NGO cannot be banned directly, the red tape, all-out control, endless check-ups, and a stepped-up financial burden could smother it."[20]

The paranoia can be extreme. When Cyclone Nargis devastated Myanmar's Irrawaddy Delta on May 2, 2008, the military rulers refused to allow in foreign aid workers although they reluctantly accepted some supplies.[21] Despite reports of two and a half million people severely affected by the disaster and limited local resources, the junta kept the world at bay even though "every day lost [meant] more avoidable casualties, more unconscionable human suffering." Finally, after appeals by the United Nations Secretary General and mediation by the Association of Southeast Asian Nations, Myanmar allowed in some international aid workers three weeks after the cyclone hit, by which time more than 100,000 were estimated to have died or gone missing.

Dirty Money

However, governments do have a valid concern that charities may be used as conduits for money laundering and terrorism financing.

To counter the use of the financial system by criminals, the G8 countries established the Financial Action Task Force on Money Laundering in 1989.[22] The Task Force has issued 40 recommendations and a blacklist of "non-cooperative countries or territories." The blacklist, in particular, has been very effective in applying pressure on countries to change their laws and practices to reduce or eliminate money laundering.

The unexpected "dirty" role of charities came under the spotlight after the September 11 terrorist attacks in New York in 2001. The Federal Bureau of Investigation found that there is a "systemic vulnerability" of charities that makes them a "tremendous funding mechanism" for terrorism.[23] *The Economist* reported that the experts "trying to track down Al Qaeda's money believe that charities are the terrorists' biggest source of money."[24]

Al Qaeda's affiliate in Southeast Asia is the Jemaah Islamiyah. With a small network of 500 to 1,000 terrorists, it has made a few suicide attacks on soft targets, such as tourist venues, with limited success. A study sponsored by the National Bureau of Asian Research noted that "much of Jemaah Islamiyah's funding is thought to come from charities, either unwittingly or intentionally siphoned off."[25] The organization had successfully inserted top operatives into leadership positions in several Islamic charities in the late 1990s. Indonesian intelligence officials estimated that 15 to 20 percent of Islamic charity funds were diverted to politically-motivated and terrorist groups.

The Financial Action Task Force identified numerous instances in which "the mechanism of charitable fundraising has been used to provide a cover for the financing of terror."[26] It also found that some nonprofits went further to provide cover and logistical support for the movement of terrorists and illicit arms. The Task Force issued an additional Eight Special Recommendations on Terrorist Financing in October 2001. In 2004, it added a ninth recommendation on cash couriers to the list. The special recommendation relating to nonprofits required improved practices in financial transparency, programmatic verification and directors' responsibilities. It also highlighted the role of the various regulatory bodies, private sector watchdog organizations and sanctions in the war against terrorism.

In the aftermath of 9/11, several governments came up with guidelines and regulations on how charities in their respective jurisdictions should manage their operations, especially internationally. The Charity Commission for England and Wales published *Operational Guidance: Charities and Terrorism.*[27] Canada enacted the *Charities Registration (Security Information) Act* and published *Charities in the International Context.*[28] The U.S. issued *Anti-Terrorism Financing Guidelines: Voluntary Best Practices for U.S.-Based Charities.*[29]

All the guidelines generally include rigorous financial oversight, high levels of disclosure and transparency, and significant new due diligence practices for charities with regards to the identity and certification of grantees.

The nonprofit sector responded strongly to the much tighter regime in the post 9/11 era. The National Council for Voluntary Organizations criticized the "draconian" approach taken by the British government, calling it "ineffective and counter-productive."[30] It pointed out that actual terrorist abuse of charities had been "extremely rare." It believed that the government should work within the present regulatory framework rather than propose additional regulations, and urged it to promote charity-led counter-terrorism initiatives.

The U.S. anti-terrorism guidelines also received protests from American nonprofits who complained that the government was effectively mandating the implementation of what was supposed to be "voluntary guidelines." Neither did they feel that the guidelines were truly representative of "best practices" as such.[31]

NGOs who received funding and grants from the U.S. government for overseas work had also been told that in this "new world," they had to function as "an arm of the U.S. government" to protect national security and foreign policy goals.[32] There are questions if this recalibration of the U.S. ODA is part of a broader reform of the nonprofit sector by the U.S. government.

A significant indication of just such a direction is the launch of NGO Watch in 2004 by two of the most influential and well-funded think tanks serving the U.S. Administration.[33] The stated mission of NGO Watch is "highlighting issues of transparency and accountability in the operations of NGOs and international organizations." In a sense, NGO Watch mocks the Watch-style NGOs[34] that scan and report on the behaviors of corporations and government agencies.

The launch of the NGO Watch was marked by a conference entitled "NGOs: The Growing Power of an Unelected Few."[35] A focus of the initiatives was "to expose funding, operations and agendas of international NGOs and particularly their alleged efforts to constrain U.S. freedom of action in international affairs and influence the behavior of corporations abroad."

Thus, 9/11 has also turned out to be a new day for charities. Governments are not stopping the rising tide of international compassion on which international NGOs have grown. What they are doing is putting in checks of a sort that some worry could be more of a brake to the functioning and growth of these international NGOs. Time will tell how all this will play out.

The Singapore Heartbeat

Singapore, as it enters the ranks of the First World, is an example of the balance and calibration that need to be made by civil society and progressive governments as each side seeks to progress its agenda.

Historically, the Singapore government has quite successfully created what some observers would say is "a supplementary role for civil society—a role of many helping hands to take over welfare functions that it chooses to withdraw from."[36] In such a climate, many local social activists have concluded that the way to change government policies is behind closed doors.[37]

Singapore's first major run-in with international NGOs occurred when it hosted Singapore 2006, the annual meetings of the International Monetary Fund (IMF) and the World Bank, and related events. This was the largest international meeting in Singapore's history with 23,000 participants.

A regular part of the annual meetings had been the participation of international NGOs, including staged protests by them. Singapore would only allow peaceful protests at designated indoor areas (outdoor demonstrations are outlawed in Singapore). It also denied entry to 27 activists and deported some of them. While the activists were accredited by the IMF-World Bank, some of them were said to have been previously involved in "violent activities at international meetings in Seattle, Cancun and Genoa." Singapore later allowed 22 of the 27 banned activists into the country.[38]

These actions resulted in adverse publicity. The President of the World Bank called the ban of the activists a "going-back on an explicit agreement" that was part of hosting the meeting. Some 160 organizations signed a petition to support a boycott of the meeting. When the meeting took place, many of the CSO Forum events were cancelled. Some of the protests did take place indoors, but they were quite muted.[39]

The handling of the protest issue marred what was otherwise deemed by most participants to be a well conducted conference.[40] While Singapore weathered the hiccup well, its image took a slight dent.

Image is important to Singapore as it is a global city that is now keen on being "a philanthropic hub."[41] Since 2004, the Economic Development Board, as part of its aim to add breadth to Singapore's business-hub status, has aimed to turn Singapore into "Asia's center for nonprofit organizations."[42] As other government agencies get involved, this has evolved into a vision of Singapore as a global philanthropic hub.

Unfortunately, this ambition has been somewhat stymied by charity regulations which are seen as discriminating against international charities and international giving.

Any registered charity that wishes to raise funds that will flow out of Singapore needs to get a permit from the Commissioner of Charities for each fundraising exercise. In addition, until recently, charities had to spend at least 80 percent of their funds raised in Singapore. That defeated the purpose of such overseas fundraising exercises. Waivers could be given for special cases, but tax deductions are not available for such overseas donations. Serving to highlight this, Médecins Sans Frontieres registered a branch in Singapore in 2000, only to decide two years later not to continue when it concluded that it was unable to overcome the restrictive fundraising conditions. Its Asian operations are currently supported out of Japan, Australia and Hong Kong.

Responding to such feedback, the Minister of Finance in the 2007 Budget announced changes that supported the charity sector.[43] One of the changes was the removal of the 80:20 fundraising rule for private donations for foreign charitable causes. However, it retained the rule for donations raised from the general public.

The Commissioner of Charities has also since worked with the other government agencies to enable a "lighter touch regime" for "qualifying grantmakers" and "qualifying international charitable organizations."[44] The criteria for qualifying international charitable organizations include non-political affiliation and commitment to meet at least one target which will benefit Singapore economically. The lighter regime primarily relates to flexibility on some of the charity registration rules.

While the relaxation of such rules is in the right direction, they appear to be primarily targeted at selected international organizations—the "iconic brand names, which are international or regional charters, and are not only economically self-sustaining but also help enhance our trust image and logistics positioning."[45] Consequently, the government's numerical target for international organizations is modest. In 2004, there were 33 international nonprofit organizations, including foundations, humanitarian organizations and industry associations in Singapore. By 2008, there were 60. The government aims to grow the number to 150 by 2015.[46]

This would likely not be enough. A global philanthropic hub would also require a hive of charitable activities and giving emanating from Singapore. The relaxation of the 80:20 rule only for private donations and not public fundraising, the continued lack of tax deductibility for overseas donations and the requirement for government permits for overseas fundraising mean that Singapore has actually not moved too far from "the principle that proceeds raised from Singaporeans should primarily be used to fund charitable activities that benefit the local community." Several international charities feel that these limitations and "bureaucratic hurdles" continue to make it difficult for charities to raise funds for international causes.[47]

Despite these policy hurdles, the ordinary Singaporean continues to be very willing to contribute to foreign neighbors who are in need. This was amply demonstrated in the 2004 tsunami crisis. The Singapore Red Cross had targeted to raise S$1 million (US$690,000) from the public but it very quickly ended up with S$88 million (US$61 million)—a fundraising record, especially considering that tax deductions were not given for the donations.[48] However, much of the resources from the government, as well as the nonprofit sector, were seen by some in the sector to be directed "in accordance with government's wishes" towards the tsunami cause.[49]

The Singapore government's approach of "humanitarian aid as an expression of foreign policy and as a tool of diplomacy" is not necessarily inconsistent with that of other countries. You could say that Singapore did well in the display of "soft power" in the exercise of "competitive compassion" by the major powers of the world in the immediate aftermath of the tsunami.[50]

Nevertheless, there is a yearning by some Singaporeans that international charity work should be divorced from the political and economic agenda of the country, that the focus should be on the recipients and their needs, and that people should be given leeway to "take the lead and work alongside the government rather than on behalf of the government."[51]

Hopefully, in time, Singapore and other nations would agree that First World countries and their citizens need not be calculating and measured in their generosity. That will be when the Singapore heartbeat will beat unfettered.

Endnotes:

Adapted from: "Charity without borders," *SALT*, November-December 2006; and "Charity without borders," *The Straits Times*, November 29, 2006.

1   *The Index of Global Philanthropy* (The Hudson Institute, 2006) at www.gpr.hudson.org/files/publications/GlobalPhilanthropy.pdf.

2   John Micklewright and Sylke V. Schnepf, "Giving to Development: Who gives to overseas causes?" (paper presented at the NCVO and VSSN's 13th Researching the Voluntary Sector Conference, July 2007).

3   *Individual Giving Survey 2004* and *Individual Giving Survey 2006* (National Volunteer & Philanthropy Center, 2004 and 2006). Data was in relation to a survey question on overseas humanitarian effort as a receiving sector: in 2004, it was 5% of donors and 1% of volunteers; in 2006, it was 21% and 8% respectively.

4   Chris Herlinger, "Where the world hit hardest: world's response best ever, but thousands yearn for housing," *National Catholic Reporter*, February 3, 2006.

5   CAF International is at www.cafonline.org; CAF USA is at www.cafamerica.org. Charities Aid Foundation's mission is to stimulate giving, social enterprise and the effective use

of funds by offering a range of financial services to donors and charities; its focus is on cross-border giving.

6　www.gawadkalinga.org/gk_ancop_directory.htm, www.ancopusa.org, and www.gawadkalinga.org. Further information on Gawad Kalinga is covered in Chapter 13, "Free labor wanted, but conditions apply."

7　www.friendsofsunera.org and www.sunerafoundation.org

8　www.msf.org. The U.S. website is at www.doctorswithoutborders.org.

9　www.peacecorps.gov

10　www.vso.org.uk

11　Daven Wu, "Beyond our shores," *SALT*, July-August 2005.

12　*National Volunteerism Survey 2006* (National Volunteer & Philanthropy Center, 2006). Percentage of respondents that indicated that they volunteer in overseas humanitarian effort rose from 1% to 8% between 2004 and 2006.

13　Paula Doherty Johnson, *Diaspora Philanthropy: Influences, initiatives and issues* (The Philanthropic Initiative Inc. and The Global Equity Initiative, Harvard University, May 2007)

14　"Civil Society Organization" or even "Citizen Sector Organization" are deemed to be more constructive and accurate terms because they avoid the "non" word and some NGOs, in fact, receive funding from governments.

15　NGO statistics are the figures of international organizations by year and type from Union of International Associations. See "Appendix 3: Table 1: Number of international organizations by type (2005/2006)" at www.uia.org/statistics/organizations/types-2004. pdf.

16　"Press release: International meeting statistics for the year 2006," Union of International Associations, August 2007.

17　www.forumsocialmundial.org.br

18　Lisa Jordan, "Civil society's role in global policy making," *Alliance*, March 2003, www.globalpolicy.org/ngos/intro/general/2003/0520role.htm.

19　Joseph Mudingu, "How genuine are NGOs," *New Times*, August 7, 2006; Sam Vaknin, "NGOs: the self appointed altruists," *Eco-Imperialism*, March 2005.

20　Elena Panfilova, "Freedom of civil society organizations in Russia," *Transparency Watch*, August 2006, www.transparency.org/publications/newsletter/2006/august_2006/spotlight; Yevgeny Volk, "Russia's NGO law: An attack on freedom and civil society," *WebMemo*, No. 1090, May 24, 2006, www.heritage.org/research/RussiaandEurasia/wm1090.cfm.

21　Aung Hla Tun, "Myanmar faces new cyclone worries," *International Herald Tribune*, May 14, 2008; "Forcing help on Myanmar," *The Economist*, May 22, 2008; "Singapore: Myanmar junta scared foreign aid workers will expose its 'incapability'," *International Herald Tribune*, May 30, 2008.

22　See www.fatf-gafi.org. The Group of Eight (G8) countries also known as Group of Seven and Russia, is an international forum of the governments of Canada, France, Germany, Italy, Japan, Russia, the U.K. and the U.S. Together they comprise 65% of the world economy.

23   Jeremy Scott-Joynt, "Charities in terror fund spotlight," *BBC News*, October 15, 2003, http://news.bbc.co.uk/2/hi/business/3186840.stm.

24   "The iceberg beneath the charity," *The Economist*, March 13, 2003.

25   Zachary Abuza, *NBR Analysis, Volume 14, Number 5. Funding terrorism in Southeast Asia: The financial network of Al Queda and Jemaah Islamiyah* (The National Bureau of Asia Research, December 2003).

26   *Combating the abuse of non-profit organizations: International best practices* (Financial Action Task Force Secretariat, OECD, October 11, 2002).

27   *OG 96: Operational Guidance—Charities and Terrorism* (Charity Commission for England and Wales, last update August 29, 2007).

28   *Charities in the international context* (Canada Revenue Agency, last update May 26, 2007).

29   *Anti-Terrorist Financing Guidelines: Voluntary best practices for U.S.-based charities* (U.S. Department of the Treasury, first issued November 2002, updated September 29, 2006).

30   Nolan Quigley & Belinda Pratten, *Security and civil society: The impact of counter-terrorism measures on civil society organizations* (NCVO, January 11, 2007); "Press release: Terrorism—charities part of the solution, not part of the problem, says new report," NCVO, January 19, 2007.

31   "Letter from Council on Foundations to Office of Terrorist Financing and Finance Crime," Council on Foundations, February 1, 2006. The letter responses to invitation for public comments on the revised *Anti-Terrorist Financing Guidelines, Voluntary best practices for U.S.-based charities* issued on December 5, 2005.

32   Traci Hukill, "U.S.: AID chief outlines change in strategy since 2001 terrorist attacks," *UN Wire*, June 30, 2003, http://comunica.org/pipermail/cr-afghan_comunica.org/2003-June/000043.html.

33   www.ngowatch.org. NGO Watch was launched by the American Enterprise Institute for Public Policy and the Federalist Society for Law and Public Policy Studies.

34   Examples are www.wombwatch.org, www.judicialwatch.org, www.governmentwatch.org, www.corpwatch.org, www.transnationale.org.

35   Jim Lobe, "Bringing the war home: right wing think tank turns wrath on NGOs," *Foreign Policy in Focus*, June 13, 2003. The conference was organized by American Enterprise Institute and the Australian think tank, the Institute of Public Affairs.

36   Constance Singam and Tan Chong Kee, "Available spaces, today and tomorrow" in Constance Singam, Tan Chong Kee, Tisa Ng and Leon Perera, *Building Social Space in Singapore* (Select Publishing, 2002).

37   Goh Chin Lian, "Singapore's quiet lobbyists: Civil groups tell Goh Chin Lian that making their views heard in Singapore requires working patiently behind closed doors," *The Straits Times*, October 28, 2006.

38   Chua Mui Hoong, "Tough S'pore can show softer side," *The Straits Times*, September 15, 2006; Pei Shing Huei, "Govt 'had decided to lift ban before the World Bank statement'," *The Straits Times*, September 21, 2006.

39 David Boey, Li Xueying, and Peh Shing Huei, "Singapore: We will honor obligations as host," *The Straits Times*, September 15, 2006; "Update: Civil society groups announce boycott of WB-IMF annual meetings in Singapore," *Bank Information Center Update*, September 15, 2006, www.bicusa.org/en/Article.2948.aspx; "CSO access in Singapore," *Civil Society Newsletter of the IMF*, November 2006, www.imf.org/External/NP/EXR/cs/eng/2006/111706.htm#access.

40 Andrew Duffy, "Eye on Singapore," *The Straits Times*, September 26, 2006; Goh Chin Lian, Li Xueying, "Spore, through foreign eyes," *The Straits Times*, September 16, 2006.

41 Pok Soy Yoong, "A master stroke of a blue ocean strategy," *The Business Times*, February 17, 2007.

42 Theresa Tan, "S'pore woos nonprofit organizations," *The Straits Times*, May 31, 2004.

43 "Turning S'pore into global charities center," *The Straits Times*, February 16, 2007.

44 *COC's Guidance on Regulation of Grantmakers and COC's Guidance on Regulation of International Charitable Organizations* are available at the Charity Portal, www.charities.gov.sg/charity/index.do. The rationale for a lighter touch regime for grantmakers is that no separate legislation exists for grantmakers who are therefore subjected to the regular and harder rules for normal charities.

45 Christie Loh, "A bit more give and take for charities?" *Today*, October 30, 2006.

46 Matthew Phan, "Tax incentives, training center to draw global bodies," *The Business Times*, February 14, 2008.

47 Chew Xiang, "Geography that gets in the way of charity," *The Business Times*, April 12, 2008.

48 The government waived the 80:20 rule for this public fundraising exercise.

49 Tan Chi Chiu, "Charity begins at home?" *Social Space* 2008.

50 Lee Kuan Yew, "Competition in compassion," *Forbes*, April 15, 2005.

51 Tan Chi Chiu, "Charity begins at home?" *Social Space* 2008.

Chapter 13

Volunteerism

Free Labor Wanted, but Conditions Apply!

It is a common perception, both within and outside the nonprofit sector, that volunteers are simply no more than free labor. Such a view underestimates the true value of volunteerism.

When you cut to the chase, it all boils down to engagement—engagement of the community with both the individual volunteer and the nonprofit organization. Many community projects and national programs would not have had the same meaning or level of impact without the participation of volunteers.

In fact, the value of recruiting and managing volunteers can far outweigh their economic value. Indeed, somewhat counter-intuitively, it is sometimes more worthwhile to spend more to get a volunteer than to use salaried staff.

O ccasionally, when working in the voluntary sector, a sign pops up in my mind. It reads in bold: **Free Labor Wanted*** and then in smaller print below, **Terms and Conditions Apply.*

Free but High-Maintenance

Three years ago, I attended a volunteer briefing for an overseas mission to Sri Lanka. To everyone's surprise, the volunteer manager started off by asking, "Who would you say are our customers?" His message was that he did not view the volunteers (those who were present) as his customers—the beneficiaries were. Hence, his main job was to worry about the faraway beneficiaries for whom the mission was set up, and as volunteers, we should just fall in line.

Apparently, he was peeved by earlier feedback given by some volunteers to his board of directors, saying that his organization needed CRM (customer relationship management). CRM is a business buzzword that refers to what a company need to do to better understand and value their customers, and to actively manage the relationship with these people who contribute to the company's revenues, and thus are critical to its existence.

While the volunteer manager was clearly trying to manage expectations ("Sorry, don't expect too much information or help from us in this strange land. After all, you had volunteered to go, knowing the risks and uncertainties"), the tone of the meeting was so bad that a volunteer meekly raised his hand and asked if he could be treated as a "secondary customer."

In all fairness, the volunteer manager may have felt overwhelmed by the barrage of questions posed to him from this batch of "spoilt-by-the-good-life" Singaporean volunteers who were anxious about the unknown terrain they were going to.

It is true that when volunteers become difficult, they can be a strain on the organization. Recently, I heard a term applied to volunteers that can be more than a handful: "volun-terrors," with the most extreme strain being called "volun-terrorists."

What then does an organization do when faced with volunteers who require a high level of maintenance?

When this question was posed at a conference I attended,[1] one of the panelists and good friend of mine, Robert Chew, replied spontaneously: "Why, just fire them, of course!" Robert's instinctive response reflects the typical human resource approach adopted to manage non-performers in corporations. After all, in the corporate world, when the cost of maintaining an employee outweighs the value he delivers, there is no business case for his continued employment.

Free but Valuable

These incidents illustrate a common perception, both within and outside the nonprofit sector, that volunteers are basically nothing more than free labor. Nonprofits simply use volunteers because they cannot afford to have paid labor do the same thing.

Such a view underestimates the true value of volunteerism.

For a group of us, the epiphany came during a National Volunteer & Philanthropy Center study to quantify the value of volunteerism in Singapore.[2] One of the drivers for the study was that we thought it important to demonstrate the economic value of volunteerism in a country driven largely by economic imperatives.

The results were a bit disappointing. Volunteers in Singapore contributed the equivalent of S$746 million (US$ 478 million) per annum of "unpaid labor" at fair market value, which was less than half a percent of our national GDP. In contrast, the U.S. volunteer contribution equivalent as a percentage of its GDP was over two percent, the U.K.'s was nearly three percent and Australia's was a high seven percent.

Interestingly, the study also compared the cost versus the economic value that volunteers contributed in 24 volunteer host organizations (VHOs).[3] Evaluations were based on the VIVA (Value Investment and Value Audit) ratio, which is the dollar value of the voluntary work compared to the cost of investing in the volunteers. If the ratio is 1:1, it means that the organization breaks even.

Even though a VHO does not pay a volunteer any wages, there is the cost of recruiting and managing them. In fact, enlightened VHOs have dedicated "volunteer coordinators" or "volunteer managers" and sound volunteer management practices to ensure the appropriate recruitment, integration and retention of volunteers for their organizations.

In the study, the majority of VHOs had VIVA ratios that showed returns ranging from a low six percent to over 480 percent more than their cost of recruiting and managing the volunteers, implying that the VHOs in Singapore were fairly effective. However, there were two VHOs that had negative returns; that is to say, the cost of recruiting and managing volunteers exceeded the equivalent labor costs (at fair market value) that they contributed.

This sparked strong internal debate. Had the VHOs known their true cost, would using paid labor not have been a better option? The answer is "yes" if you look at it from a purely economic standpoint.

However, it may not be the right answer if you consider the broader impact that volunteerism has on nonprofit organizations and the community they serve, and whose support they wish to have. Our debate led us to conclude that it was useful to devote a section in the report on the non-economic value of volunteerism.

Non-Economic Value

So what value is there to using volunteers beyond free labor? When you cut to the chase, it all boils down to engagement—engagement of the individual volunteer with the VHO and the community, and engagement of the VHO with the community. An engaged volunteer represents an extension of the VHO's personality into the very community it aspires to serve.

Without a doubt, volunteers are rewarded beyond any monetary return for their services, otherwise they would not have volunteered. Studies of volunteer motivation and their management provide a spectrum of rewards that volunteers get by helping out. These may range from simple relief of boredom to broadening their horizons and the immense personal satisfaction that comes from making a difference to other people's lives.[4]

For the VHOs, volunteers give them access to talent they could perhaps not afford or which is not otherwise available. However, beyond that replacement economic value, engagement of volunteers can benefit the community in ways that far outweigh the cost considerations.

The recent spate of natural disasters such as the Asian tsunami and Hurricane Katrina, and the subsequent relief and reconstruction efforts provide examples of how cost may not necessarily be a prime driver for the engagement of volunteers. Since those disasters, many charities have become involved in the building of replacement houses for the victims. Some do so by sending funds while a few such as Habitat for Humanity, Shelter and Mercy Relief[5] mobilize volunteers from other countries to go to the disaster sites to help build new homes.

Volunteers who go are usually required to pay for their own costs of travel and accommodation as well as to contribute to the costs of the construction materials. Depending upon the location, the expenses will vary. Costs ranging from US$500 to US$1,500 for each volunteer for a week's trip are not uncommon. However, critics commonly contend that the same money would go much further if it was spent on local labor.

Not only are the costs of local labor much lower than the imported well-heeled foreign volunteers, the latter, so the arguments go, are often inexperienced in construction and the local environment. Using local labor also helps to gainfully employ the displaced victims of the disaster. So much so that volunteers have risked being disparaged for being "volun-tourists" engaged in voyeurism.[6]

But ask any returned volunteer and it does not take long to be convinced of the value of such humanitarian trips. The impact on volunteer attitudes can never be adequately captured in slide shows and fanciful brochures. Many volunteers I know leave a lot more than their work or money at the site. It is not uncommon to hear volunteers share that they have gone through a life-changing experience and reach a different level of self-awareness. Some report emptying themselves of the material belongings they had brought with them and returning home renewed with a sense of mission and determination to be involved in future projects.[7]

What is more significant is that many realize they may have been less than forthcoming with their time and donations prior to the volunteering experience. But having gone and been engaged, they now give more of their time and money as they can better relate to the cause.

Studies bear out the observation that those who volunteer are more inclined to donate and to give more than the average donor. A National Volunteer & Philanthropy survey found that volunteers tend to donate 63 percent more than the average individual donor.[8] In a U.S. survey, the Independent Sector found that volunteering households donated more than twice the money compared to non-volunteering households.[9] A U.K. national survey also found that respondents who volunteered and donated were more likely to give money to an organization if they were involved in it through volunteering, the main reasons being that they knew and cared more about that charity.[10]

Community Raising

Beyond the costs, volunteerism encourages people from diverse backgrounds to bond with one another. The spirit of community that volunteerism generates benefits not just individual VHOs, but also the whole charity sector and the overall community. nfpSynergy's study of the *21st Century Volunteer* sees "volunteering as a factory for community social capital" because it builds "bonds of trust and reciprocity that seem to be crucial for a democratic polity and a market economy to function effectively."[11] Volunteering connects individuals and organizations, and teaches norms of collaboration that carry over into political and economic life.

Imagine Independence Day or National Day Parades[12] if the contingents and helpers were all paid. If national days are celebrated like commercial concerts, it may still be exciting but we would never capture that sense of national pride and community spirit that is an integral part of these events.

In 2000, I attended my first Olympics in Sydney. To my surprise, I was met at the airport and driven to my lodging by a volunteer. I learned that she was one of some 47,000 volunteers, mostly Australians, who had raised their hands for the simple joy and pride of being part of a historic moment in their country's hosting of the Games. She and the other volunteers we came into contact with during the trip were genuine and excellent ambassadors for Australia as well as the Olympics movement.

Five years ago, I ran my first marathon—the Standard Chartered Marathon.[13] I was pleasantly surprised and inspired by the number of spectators who cheered me all the way. They were nicknamed "runspirators" by the organizers. Some came to cheer their friends and loved ones, but there were many who came to support one and all, and they were having fun doing it. Many dressed up in funny and cheery outfits. They yelled, they played musical instruments and they banged on all sorts of tools and containers that helped add to the noise, excitement and experience of the "greatest race on earth." They were volunteers and as a runner, I truly appreciated those strangers who lightened my weary body as I struggled to complete 42 kilometers.

An impressive example of sustained "community raising" is that of SOLV (Stop Oregon Litter and Vandalism) (see box on "Case Study on Community Raising"). With only 26 staff members, SOLV has been able to mobilize nearly 100,000 volunteers a year to "build community through volunteer action to preserve this treasure called Oregon."

Beyond engaging and bonding the people, the community itself can be transformed through volunteer action. Gawad Kalinga,[15] a Filipino phrase meaning "to give care", is a great story of community transformation. It started in 1995 when Tony Meloto who was working with Couples for Christ, launched a work-with-the-poor ministry in Bagong Silang, a huge squatter relocation site in Manila. Meloto worked with volunteers and the beneficiaries to build houses in the neediest part of the squalid poverty-stricken area. In the process, they transformed a slum into a viable

Case Study on Community Raising:
"Be a SOLVer. Help Stop Oregon Litter and Vandalism"

SOLV (Stop Oregon Litter and Vandalism)[14] is a nonprofit organization that brings together government agencies, businesses and individual volunteers through programs and projects that enhance the livability of the American state of Oregon. It was founded in 1969 by Governor Tom McCall to address litter and vandalism problems.

Riding on the ethos of being a SOLVer, SOLV has successfully led the concept of individual and ownership in the country. It leverages its network to build the right kind of mindset amongst the citizens to love and care for their community and to focus on being part of the solution and not the problem.

Today, SOLV's vision and strategic intent have grown to encompass the wider effort to improve the community and the environment, so as to "preserve this treasure called Oregon." SOLV annually provides resources to more than 250 Oregon communities, focusing on clean-up, beautification and enhancement projects. It engages nearly 100,000 volunteers every year. It is impressive when you realize that this scale of volunteerism is being mobilized by a very small staff of 26 people led by its charismatic executive director, Jack McGowan.

SOLV's project model recognizes the episodic and gratification needs of today's volunteers. As McGowan puts it, "episodic volunteerism can be fast food for the soul." Specifically, it offers various programs to cater to different volunteer capacities. From the "Volunteer a Day" programs to the more extensive ongoing projects such as Oregon Adopt-A-River, Team Up For Watershed Health and SOLV's Earth Day Cleanup, SOLV is able to engage citizens in community bonding even as it gets the "good work for this good land" done. The good works include cleaning rivers and illegal dumpsites, restoring wetlands, painting out graffiti and so on, all of which make Oregon a "little bit better through their efforts."

SOLV has a cost budget of approximately US$2 million, but it delivers far more back. According to a University of Michigan study, for every public dollar invested in SOLV, the organization leverages the amount by US$64.08 in service back to the state.

But beyond the economic value it has delivered, it is SOLV's tireless engagement of the community in the task of environmental preservation that has made Oregon known as the "beach clean-up capital of the world," thanks to its beach clean-up program in 1984, the world's first. This concept has now spread to over 74 countries and sovereign territories.

For its efforts and its achievements, SOLV and McGowan have received several state and national awards over the years for volunteerism (The President's Volunteer Service Award), community building (Take Pride in America Award), leadership (Statesmen of the Year), governance (Effective Government Award) and environmental improvement (Best Environmental Program).

neighborhood which not only has safe, sturdy and attractive homes, but also shared values, a sense of community and a higher purpose.

As the Bagong Silang village blossomed, new sites for Gawad Kalinga villages were identified. Health, education and livelihood components were introduced to equip the villagers with skills and resources to rise in life. News of these villages and their success tapped into a reservoir of longing by many Filipinos to do something about the country's state of poverty. Nearly half of the Philippine's 84 million people are said to live below the poverty line and 40 percent of urban families live in slums. Donations poured in, and volunteers came flocking. Gawad Kalinga villages began to proliferate throughout the Philippines.

Gawad Kalinga became a national movement with a 777 goal: build 700,000 homes in 7,000 communities in seven years (2003-2010). By early 2008, Gawad Kalinga is in more than 900 communities. Whether it meets its ambitious timeline or not, the movement is steadily moving towards its vision of the Philippines as "a slum-free, squatter-free nation through a simple strategy of providing land for the landless, homes for the homeless, food for the hungry, and as a result, providing dignity and peace for every Filipino."

SOLV, Gawad Kalinga and other volunteer community projects show the power of volunteering in building and even transforming communities. Thus, the act of giving back is good for volunteers as well as the community.

When properly harnessed, you could say that volunteers are not merely free labor, but the soul of a free society.

Endnotes:

Adapted from: "Free labor wanted*," *SALT* May-June 2006, and "The true value of volunteers," *The Straits Times,* June 5, 2006.

1   *The V-Room Panel: Challenges of Raising and Getting a Return on Volunteer Capital,* at the National Volunteerism & Philanthropy Conference 2003.

2   *The Value of Volunteerism Study* conducted in 2003/2004 and related statistics cited in this chapter are contained in Section 5—Value of Volunteerism in *The State of Giving* (National Volunteer & Philanthropy Center, 2005).

3   Volunteer Host Organization or VHO is a term that NVPC and many in the volunteer sector use to describe the nonprofit organizations "hosting" or using volunteers.

4   Elisha Evans and Joe Saxton, *The 21st Century Volunteer* (nfpSynergy, November 2005). The report provides a list of volunteer motivations and describes the value of building social capital through volunteerism.

5   More information on these organizations can be found at www.habitat.org, www.england.shelter.org.uk and www.mercyrelief.org.

6   For articles debating voluntourism, see Tion Kwa, "Voluntourism: More tourist than volunteer," *The Straits Times*, July 28, 2007; Elizabeth Eaves, "Unusual Trips and Tours," *Forbes*, January 28, 2007; Vincent Crump, "Voluntourism: a guilt trip?" *The Sunday Times*, December 23, 2007; "Voluntourism scams do-gooders," *Daily Telegraph*, September 10, 2007.

7   For experiences of volunteers who have gone on housebuilding trips, view www.acct-sg.org/html/volunteer.html and habitat.org/faces_places/vol/list.aspx.

8   Computed from *Individual Philanthropy Survey 2004* (National Volunteer & Philanthropy Center, 2004) as the difference between the average donation per individual donor of $155 and average donation per volunteer of $253. The resultant difference in giving is $98 or 63.2%.

9   *Giving & Volunteering in the United States* (Independent Sector, 2001). For giving households, the average contributions were US$2,295 from volunteers and $1,009 from non-volunteers. The difference is 2295/1009 = 227% more.

10 Natalie Low, Sarah Butt, Angela Ellis Paine and Justin Davis Smith, *Helping out: A national survey on volunteering and charitable giving* (Office of the Third Sector, Cabinet Office, prepared by National Center for Social Research and the Institute for Volunteering Research, 2007).

11 Elisha Evans and Joe Saxton, *The 21st Century Volunteer* (nfpSynergy, November 2005).

12 National Day or Independence Day or its equivalent is celebrated in most countries. In Singapore, the National Day Parade is the biggest national event of the year. It includes not just the parade of various uniformed and community groups, but also performances climaxing in a fireworks display. About 30,000 to 60,000 Singaporeans watch it live depending on where it is held, while the rest catch it on TV and in the streets as the parade moves out. While the parade is run by the Singapore Armed Forces, it would not be a success without the widespread support of a multitude of private and public organizations and their volunteers.

13 www.singaporemarathon.com. The Singapore Standard Chartered Marathon is one of four in a series that has been branded "The Greatest Race on Earth: Race For a Living Planet" (www.thegreatestrace.com). The four marathons are Nairobi (The Highest Race), Singapore (The Island Race), Mumbai (The Historic Race) and Hong Kong (The Harbor Race).

14 www.solv.org

15 www.gawadkalinga.org, www.rmaf.org.ph/Awardees/Citation/CitationGawadKal.htm.

Social Innovation

Chapter 14

Philanthropy

The Second Philanthropic Revolution

Today's philanthropists are heeding Andrew Carnegie's advice: Give away your fortune while you are still alive, or die rich and die disgraced.

While the size of their mega giving has captured the public imagination, it is really the boldness and innovativeness of their approach that is driving the current philanthropic revolution. Compared to the previous generation, the neo-philanthropists are more ambitious (nothing short of solving the world's problems), more capitalistic (pushing the envelope of venture capital approaches), more personal (engaging directly with their time and talent on their areas of interest), and more collaborative (leveraging partnerships).

"The problem of our age," reflected the pioneer of modern philanthropy, Andrew Carnegie[1] in his enduring 1889 essay, *The Gospel of Wealth*,[2] "is the proper administration of wealth."

In Carnegie's view, "the true antidote for the temporary unequal distribution of wealth" was for the rich to distribute it for the common good during their lifetimes. In line with this philosophy, Carnegie applied himself diligently to giving away all his fortune.

The First Revolution

Up to the early 1900s, philanthropy had been mainly about localized giving to the needy. Carnegie and his contemporary, John D. Rockefeller[3] (see box on "Revolutionary Philanthropists") started a philanthropic revolution by creating foundations with hundreds of millions of dollars in assets.

They also changed the nature of philanthropy from alms-giving to organized philanthropy that is professionally managed in order to make a broader impact in their communities. They built and invested in institutions such as libraries, schools and research organizations.

Since then, this kind of philanthropic giving has grown steadily throughout the globe, but especially in the U.S. and developed world, where an increasing number of the nouveau riche are.

Foundations, the vehicles through which many of the wealthy channel their giving, had increased in the U.S. from 505 foundations in 1944 to more than 71,000 foundations in 2005. The size of their assets had likewise grown from about US$1.8 billion in assets to a whopping US$550 billion respectively. Still, the grants of more than US$36 billion which the foundations give out each year only represents about 12 percent of total philanthropic giving in the U.S. (about US$295 billion in 2006).[5]

Much of the growth in foundations has been in the last decade, with a doubling in the number of foundations and more than a doubling of foundation assets. So much so that many observers are calling these last few years the golden age of philanthropy.

Competitive Philanthropy

What is fueling this golden age? Perhaps it is the mega giving that has captured the headlines of recent years.

In a way, this phenomenon could be traced back to 1997 when Ted Turner,[6] founder of CNN, threw down the gauntlet with a dramatic billion dollar pledge to the United Nations.

Turner also openly challenged his fellow wealthy "skinflints" to "open their purse strings" wider. Turner suggested that instead of just fighting to be at the top of Forbes list of the world's richest men,[7] the wealthy

Revolutionary Philanthropists[4]

The Pioneers

Andrew Carnegie, an immigrant to the United States, founded the company Carnegie Steel, the largest and most profitable industrial enterprise in the world in the 1890s. In 1901, he sold the company to U.S. Steel and spent the rest of his life on large-scale philanthropy. He endowed and supported a long list of institutions and causes, especially local libraries, world peace and scientific research. By the time he died, he had given away more than US$350 million.

John D. Rockefeller founded Standard Oil Company, which became a monopoly and was later broken up into several oil companies which we see today. On the back of Standard Oil and the importance of gasoline, Rockefeller became the first U.S. dollar billionaire and is often regarded as the richest man in history.

Rockefeller was as generous as he was successful. He founded several institutions including the Rockefeller Foundation in 1913. By the 1920s, the Rockefeller Foundation was the largest grantmaking foundation in the world. Rockefeller hired Frederick T. Gates as his full-time philanthropic advisor.

During his lifetime, Rockefeller gave away $530 million to charity, a large part of which went to medicine and education. He transferred his remaining assets of about US$500 million to his son, John Jr. The latter and the generations that followed have continued the legacy of Rockefeller's philanthropy.

The New U.S. Heroes

Ted Turner is a media mogul. He founded CNN, the first dedicated and dominant 24-hour cable news channel. In addition, he founded WTBS which pioneered the superstation concept in cable television. He has a reputation for making controversial statements.

In 1990, he established the Turner Foundation which focuses its work on the environment and population growth. In 1997, Turner pledged to donate US$1 billion of his then US$3 billion fortune to the United Nations. The United Nations Foundation was set up to administer Turner's gift. It seeks to build and implement public-private partnerships to address the world's most pressing problems, and to broaden support for the U.N. through advocacy and public outreach programs.

Bill Gates is the co-founder and chairman of Microsoft Corporation, the world's largest software company. Between 1995 and 2007, *Forbes* ranked him the richest person in the world. He had a net worth valued at around US$58 billion in 2008.

In 2000, Gates and his wife established the charitable Bill & Melinda Gates Foundation. By 2007, it became the world's largest foundation with US$30 billion in assets, with much more to come from Gates and Buffet in future years. In 2006, it gave out US$1.56 billion in grants. With the Buffet donation, this amount is expected to double in future years.

The creed of the foundation is broad: "Guided by the belief that every life has equal value, the Bill & Melinda Gates Foundation works to reduce inequities and improve lives around the world." It spends 60 percent of its funds on tackling global health inequalities in six areas: infectious disease, HIV/AIDS, tuberculosis, reproductive health, global health strategies and global health technologies.

Warren Buffett made his fortune from astute investments through Berkshire Hathaway, a company in which he is the largest shareholder and CEO. He was ranked by *Forbes* as the richest man in the world in 2008, with an estimated net worth of US$62 billion.

In the mid-60s, Buffett started the Buffett Foundation (later renamed the Susan Thompson Buffett Foundation) which focuses on reproductive health, family planning, pro-choice causes and preventing the spread of nuclear weapons. In 2006, the value of its assets stood at over US$450 million.

In June 2006, Warren Buffett publicly committed to give away his entire fortune to charity, with 83 percent of it going to the Bill & Melinda Gates Foundation which he joined as a third trustee. The value of his gift of Berkshire shares in 2006 was US$37 billion but it is expected to gain in greater value over time.

Pierre Omidyar is the founder and chairman of eBay, the online auction site. After eBay went public in 1998, Omidyar and his wife Pam co-founded the Omidyar Foundation to fund nonprofits. In 2004, he shuttered the Foundation to set up the Omidyar Network to fund both nonprofit and for-profit enterprises that create social value. The nonprofit and the for-profit Fund were allocated US$200 million each. The Network's mission is to "enable individual self-empowerment on a global scale." It has invested in areas such as microfinance, technology and community-based initiatives expecting risk-appropriate returns on all for-profit investments.

Jeff Skoll is the first president of eBay. At 34, he used US$34 million from the proceeds of eBay's public offering to set up the Skoll Foundation, making him one of the youngest philanthropists in American history. The Skoll Foundation reflects his core belief that it is in everyone's interest to shift the overwhelming balance between the "haves" and the "have-nots." The foundation seeks to bridge this gap by largely focusing on developing social entrepreneurship.

Larry Page and Sergey Brin are two Stanford University classmates who founded and are still running Google, the Internet search and online advertising behemoth. At its initial public offering in 2004, Google was worth US$23 billion. By the end of March 2008, its market value was well over US$100 billion. Since its inception, the Google founders have reminded their employees that their work should "Do No Evil." That belief has now been revised to an active slogan, "Be Good." It was rated as the best company to work for by *Fortune* in 2007 and 2008.

In 2004, Google formed its for-profit philanthropic wing Google.org, with a starting fund of US$1 billion. Google.org hired Dr. Larry Brilliant, an iconoclastic multitalented entrepreneur to manage the foundation. The mission of the organization is to help with the issues of global poverty, global public health and global warming.

George Soros is a Hungarian-born billionaire investor and author. His Quantum Fund is one of the most successful managed investment funds in the world. He was once known as the "The man who broke the Bank of England" when he made US$1.1 billion speculating on the pound sterling. In 2008, his net worth was estimated to be US$9 billion.

Soros has been an active philanthropist since 1979, funding causes he believes in. To date, he has given away US$4 billion, much of it through the Soros Foundation and the Open Society Institute which promotes open societies throughout the world by shaping democratic governance, human rights, and economic, legal and social reform in more than 50 countries worldwide.

The Non-U.S. Philanthropists

Richard Branson is the flamboyant chairman of the Virgin group. He transformed Virgin from a fledgling record label, which he created in the 1970s, to a worldwide brand and conglomerate that dabbles in a host of business ventures, from airline business to cell phones and record stores. One of his most recent ventures is a space tourism company, Virgin Galactic, which will take paying passengers into suborbital space.

His net worth in 2008 was estimated at US$4.4 billion. In 2006, at the Clinton Global Initiative, Branson pledged to plow 100 percent of the proceeds from Virgin's airline and locomotive divisions, estimated at US$3 billion over 10 years, into investments in clean technologies. The initial focus is on producing "cellulosic" ethanol, a biofuel derived from agricultural waste and fast-growing crops, which produces no greenhouse-gas emissions, but which has yet to be proven in the marketplace.

Branson makes no bones that the move is as much about building the Virgin brand as it is about doing good by tackling climate change.

Sheikh Mohammed bin Rashid al-Maktoum is the ruler of Dubai. He is credited with transforming the tiny Persian Gulf emirate into an aviation, business and tourist hub. His efforts had helped to grow Dubai's GDP from US$8 billion in 1994 to over US$40 billion in 2006. In 2007, his fortune was estimated by *Forbes* to be around US$16 billion.

In May 2007, he established the Mohammed bin Rashid al-Maktoum Foundation with an endowment of US$10 billion. The foundation focuses on human development to create "a knowledge-based society" in the Middle East.

Li Ka-Shing is one of Asia's richest residents. His estimated wealth of US$26.5 billion (in 2008) centers on two conglomerates, Cheung Kong and Hutchinson Whampoa. Through them, he is the world's largest operator of container terminals, a major supplier of electricity to Hong Kong, a global cell phone provider and a major real estate developer.

The Li Ka-Shing Foundation was set up in 1980 and has since committed over US$1 billion to various medical and educational projects. In August 2006, Li announced that he would donate at least one-third of his personal wealth (then estimated at US$18.8 billion) over time to his foundation, calling it "his third son."

should just give a billion dollars each and move down the rankings accordingly. His remarks prompted *Slate,* the influential online magazine to start an annual listing of top donors.[8] This, in turn, sparked off more media coverage and other lists on philanthropy.

Three years later, Bill Gates[9] pumped a staggering US$16.5 billion into the Bill & Melinda Gates Foundation. In 2006, Warren Buffet[10] made a stunning announcement that he was going to inject over US$30 billion into the Bill & Melinda Gates Foundation which, by then, was already the world's largest, by far, with US$30 billion in assets.

Over the last decade, several of the other mega rich, led by the Americans, have set up foundations. A significant number seem to come from those who prospered with the surge in the information technology industry—people like Pierre Omidyar[11] and Jeff Skoll[12] of eBay, and most recently, Google founders Larry Page and Sergey Brin.[13] Others like George Soros,[14] who made their money through the financial and other traditional industries, have also contributed.

While the gifts that recent philanthropists have made may not have been in the same league as Gates and Buffet, they are still in the millions, hundreds of millions. Much more than just small change for us mere mortals.

Just as in the first philanthropic revolution, much of the big giving in the current era came out of the U.S. However in recent years, the wealthy outside America have begun following the example of the Americans.

Sir Richard Branson,[15] the British entrepreneur, jumped on board in September 2006 with a pledge of some US$3 billion, from the profits of his airline and train operations, to combat global warming over the next decade.

In May 2006, Sheikh Mohammed bin Rashid al-Maktoum,[16] ruler of Dubai, pumped in US$10 billion to set up his own educational foundation with the objective of increasing education, research, innovation and entrepreneurship in the Middle East.

Over in Asia, Li Ka-Shing,[17] Hong Kong entrepreneur extraordinaire, pledged in August 2006 to give away at least one-third of his fortune, then estimated at US$18.8 billion, to his charitable Li Ka-Shing Foundation.

Second Revolution

There are those who argue that these endowments, large as they are, do not really dwarf those of the early philanthropists.

To put things into context, the US$350 million and US$530 million that Carnegie and Rockefeller gave respectively in their lifetimes is worth more than US$3 billion and US$6 billion in today's dollars (adjusted for inflation).[18]

More significantly, the global economy has grown. Measured as a proportion of the annual GDP of their respective eras, Carnegie's gift is 0.44 percent and Rockefeller's gift is 0.59 percent. In comparison, Warren Buffet's large contribution of US$37 billion is only 0.3 percent, or about half that of Rockefeller's.

According to Lester Salamon, Director of Center for Civil Society Studies at the Johns Hopkins University, "philanthropy is not holding up its part of the bargain" in keeping up with the growth of the economy and the accompanying societal challenges.[19] He notes that while there is absolute growth of philanthropic giving, it is outpaced by the growth of nonprofit needs. Increasingly, these are being funded by other sources such as government grants and service fees.

However, more than the absolute size of their gifts, my take is that the new givers are changing the nature of philanthropic giving. Today's philanthropists, while building on the traditional vehicles of giving are not content with check-book writing and ribbon-cutting exercises. They are engaged with their philanthropy in innovative ways that have captured the imagination of many.

Although there is diversity in their approaches, we can distill some common characteristics of their giving:

- It's more ambitious
- It's more capitalistic
- It's more personal
- It's more collaborative

High-Impact Philanthropy

The agenda of these neo-philanthropists is both bold and global, nothing short of finding and implementing solutions to the world's problems. They are taking head-on issues, such as poverty and global warming that private enterprise and governments have been reluctant or unable to adequately tackle.

Turner's US$1 billion commitment to the U.N. was to address the world's pressing problems and broaden support for the body.

Bill Gates' push for getting into philanthropy is to redress "the awful inequities in the world—the appalling disparities of health, and wealth, and opportunity that condemn millions of people to lives of despair."[20] His big idea is to overcome the market failure afflicting poor consumers of health care by deploying his money on behalf of the poor to generate the supply of drugs and treatments they need. For instance, his money provides market incentives for drug companies to put some of their resources to work for the needy.

The money that Gates spends is bound to make an impact. The Bill & Melinda Gates Foundation supports global health initiatives with about US$800 million annually. This amount approaches the annual budget of the U.N. World Health Organization.

Meanwhile, social experts believe that microfinance, pioneered by Muhammad Yunus of the Grameen Bank, is a powerful tool for economic self-empowerment of the poor in developing countries. Recognizing that the sector is nascent and needs access to capital, Omidyar, together with Tufts University, launched a microfinance fund in 2005. His donation of US$100 million to the fund is the largest private allocation of capital to microfinance by an individual or company. Omidyar's goal is "to unleash at least US$1 billion in microloans to the poor throughout the world over the next decade as we make loans that are paid back and recycled."[21]

Global warming has found increasing support among the new social entrepreneurs. Richard Branson's initial focus on clean technologies aims to produce "cellulosic" ethanol, a bio-fuel derived from agricultural waste and fast-growing crops, which produces no greenhouse-gas emissions.

One of the goals of Google.org foundation's maiden project is to develop an extremely fuel-efficient, plug-in hybrid car engine that runs on ethanol, electricity and gasoline.

Philanthro-Capitalism

As many of the new philanthropists are corporate highflyers and successful entrepreneurs, it is no surprise that they seek to apply capitalistic ideas and approaches to the social arena. Not just straightforward corporate ideas of applying management discipline in planning and implementation, but sometimes going the whole hog, such as pushing the envelope of venture capital approaches which have come to be known as "venture philanthropy."

The venture model was initially posited in a landmark 1997 *Harvard Business Review* article.[22] The authors contend that traditional philanthropy, with its lackluster performance, would benefit from the infusion of venture capital techniques. These include adopting performance measures, placing fewer but larger bets on chosen organizations, engaging them closely to produce results, and exiting at the appropriate time.

Several hundreds of venture philanthropy groups are now active in the U.S., with a handful in Europe. The largest group is Seattle-based Social Venture Partners, which has affiliates in 23 American cities.[23] Comprising more than 1,700 individual partners, the network has benefited more than 250 nonprofit organizations with grants and countless hours of strategic volunteering support.

In taking a capitalistic approach, the line between profit and nonprofit organizations is blurring for some of these new philanthropists.

The Omidyar Network, for example, has two funds: one to make for-profit investments and another for philanthropic donations. The "investment team" is free to put its money in either for-profit or nonprofit projects. The team's main criterion is whether the investment will further the social mission of the organization.

Google.org had an initial fund of US$1 billion and has always shunned nonprofit status. It will pay taxes for any profits, but this then enables the foundation to fund startup companies, form partnerships with venture capitalists and even lobby Congress. Its founders Page and Brin have promised shareholders that they will make a social impact that will eventually "eclipse Google itself" by tackling the world's problems.

Branson's Virgin Fuels, set up to tackle climate change, is a regular enterprise that seeks "to do good through good investments," but it will be funded through donations from Branson's share of his profits from his other ventures.

In this sense, both Branson and Google have taken the view that the best way to accelerate the development of green technology is to let normal market competition dynamics work. They see their roles as helping with the initial capital injection to kick-start the process and further reinvestments from any profits made.

High-Engagement Philanthropy

The new rich want to make sure that their money is properly used, so they want to be personally involved in it. Bill Gates' view is that you have to work as hard at giving away your money as you do making it.[24]

Many of the newcomers, especially the dotcommers, are much younger, in their 30s and 40s, compared to the pioneer industrialists who started in their 60s. Being young, they want to give their time and youthful energy to mentor, guide and direct.

This certainly applies to venture philanthropists. Central to the venture model is the notion of treating funding as an investment with expectations of (social) return on investment, operating efficiencies and management oversight. This is in contrast to the traditional concept of a charitable grant which is viewed more as a gift, and the donor is noticeably hands-off. Social venture capitalists take a more direct hands-on role as an owner with shared responsibilities in socially positive ventures.

The focus areas of the new philanthropists usually reflect their personal interests and their methods often leverage their talents.

George Soros was heavily influenced by his early experiences of Nazi and Communist rule and the writings of the philosopher Karl Popper (author of *The Open Society and Its Enemies*). He campaigns for socio-political change in more than 60 countries, especially in Central and Eastern Europe and the former Soviet Union. He has authored or co-authored several books, some on the subject of open societies. The organizations and funds which he has created seek to free political prisoners from life-long confinement in state institutions, win releases for prisoners held without legal grounds, halt the spread of tuberculosis and AIDS, create open debate, and promote freedom of the press.

Jeff Skoll, among his many talents, is also a movie producer. He set up the media company, Participant Productions, to fund feature films and documentaries that promote social values while being commercially viable. An outstanding example is the Oscar winner, *An Inconvenient Truth*, which has been credited with raising the awareness of global warming.

Network Philanthropy

The aggregation of philanthropic resources occurred with the creation of community foundations. This, in turn, allowed mid-tier donors to essentially create their own "foundations" or donor-advised funds within a larger foundation on a very cost-effective basis.

The first community foundation was set up in Cleveland in 1914.[25] Today, there are more than 700 community foundations in the U.S. and about 1,000 around the world.

However, most foundations have traditionally worked their own programs and processed their grants individually. While multiple foundations may co-fund the same cause, this has traditionally resulted from fund-seeking on the part of the grantees.

As foundations become more proactive and ambitious in their quests for social change, they are also looking at new ways to collaborate. They are forming partnerships, not just with one another, but also with commercial partners, governments and the nonprofits themselves.

Even the world's largest foundations are collaborating to deal with the enormity of their global causes.

The Bill & Melinda Gates Foundation, which has enough money to go on its own in any project, emphasizes effective multi-sector collaborations. To that end, it has crafted a series of incentive-based investment partnerships. For instance, it teamed up with the Rockefeller Foundation in the Alliance for a Green Revolution to alleviate hunger and improve agriculture in Africa. In fact, about 80 percent of the foundation's grantmaking in the area of global health is undertaken with strategic partners.

Networks are also being formed to leverage money and experience. Peggy Rockefeller Dulany's Global Philanthropists Circle[26] brings together about 50 super-rich families from 20 countries to exchange ideas and experiences, mainly with a view to finding solutions to international poverty and inequality. Often, this involves the use of connections, influence as well as money.

Former U.S. President Bill Clinton established a non-partisan project, the Clinton Global Initiative in 2005, to bring together a community of global leaders. They meet annually to devise and implement innovative solutions to some of the world's problems such as global public health, poverty, and religious and ethnic conflict.[27] The organization does not give out grants, but only matches people with ideas and those with the means to help implement them. Its second annual meeting resulted in 262 commitments valued at over US$7.3 billion.

The Second Wind

Where is this second philanthropic revolution taking the world to?

First, the hopes are high. The potential of the size of giving is giving rise to many starry eyes.

So far, only a few billionaires have stepped up. But if the present rate of mega-giving snowballs, the amount of money and impact could be awesome. As at March 2008, there are more than a thousand billionaires on *Forbes* list with a total estimated net worth of US$4.4 trillion. That is more than six times the total asset base of foundations in the U.S.[28]

According to Jeff Sachs, special advisor to the U.N. Secretary General, "an annual five percent 'foundation' payout from these billionaires" which would amount to US$220 billion, would lift Africa out of poverty, obviating the need for aid from the G8 leading nations—aid which has not been forthcoming.[29]

But poverty in Africa is only one fraction of the world's problems and that does not leave much else on the table for other needs. The fact is that government funding is going to continue to be needed and philanthropic giving will not be able to fully replace it. For example, social welfare spending in the U.S. is 18 percent of GDP, in contrast to just over two percent for total philanthropic giving.

Secondly, the new innovative approaches take their cue very much from the business world. In fact, the lines between the two are blurring. In the long run, would or should business and charity converge into one seamless world? I do not have the answer, but hopefully, any transition to a converged world would be more smooth than chaotic.

Thirdly, the increasing amounts and visibility of mega-giving create concerns of accountability for these institutions. In the same way that foundations are demanding accountability of their grantees, lawmakers and the public are asking about measurable results and unjustifiably high administration costs of the foundations. America's Congress is showing increased interest in foundations and how they operate, and new tough laws that will "dramatically transform the relationship between the federal government and foundations" have been proposed.[30]

Finally, when you get past the targets, the methods and the amount of their giving, the broad intent of giving—as many of the philanthropists have articulated—has remained largely the same: benefiting society and humankind.

Or perhaps, they were simply heeding the message of Andrew Carnegie: "The man who dies leaving behind many millions of available wealth will pass away unwept, unhonored, and unsung.... The man who dies thus rich dies disgraced."[31]

Endnotes:

Adapted from: "The second philanthropic revolution," *SALT*, September-December 2007.

1   Andrew Carnegie references:
     – The Carnegie Corporation of New York at www.carnegie.org
     – *Autobiography of Andrew Carnegie,* ebook at www.zilliontech.com/knowledge/andrewcarnegie.html.

2   Andrew Carnegie, "Wealth," *North American Review*, No. CCCXCI, June 1889. Later republished in England as "The Gospel of Wealth," a title Carnegie subsequently adopted as his own.

3   John D. Rockefeller reference: The Rockefeller Foundation at www.rockfound.org.

4   The bibliography and references for each philanthropist are provided in the prior and subsequent endnotes. In addition, information on these philanthropists are also drawn from the following common sources:
    – Families of Philanthropy at www.familiesofphilanthropy.com
    – Faces of Philanthropy at www.facesofphilanthropy.com
    – *Slate*, the online magazine at www.slate.com has a philanthropy series
    – *Forbes* listing of the wealthy at www.forbes.com.

5   Giving statistics are extracted from:
    – *Foundation Yearbook 2007* (The Foundation Center)
    – *Philanthropy in the 21st Century: The Foundation Center's 50th Anniversary Interviews* (The Foundation Center, 2007)
    – *Giving USA 2007: The Annual Report on Philanthropy for the Year 2006* (Giving USA Foundation, researched and written by the Center on Philanthropy at Indiana University, 2007).

6   Ted Turner reference:
    – Ted Turner's website at www.tedturner.com/enterprises/home.asp
    – Maureen Dowd, "Ted Turner urges "ol' skinflints" to open their purse strings wider," *The New York Times*, August 23, 1996.

7   *Forbes* publishes an annual list of the world's richest people. Go to www.forbes.com for the latest list.

8   David Plotz, "Competitive Philanthropy: The History of the Slate 60," *Slate*, February 20, 2006; "The Fine Art of Giving", *Time*, December 16, 1996.

9   Bill Gates references:
    – Bill & Melinda Gates Foundation at www.gatesfoundation.org
    – Carol Loomis, "The global force called the Gates Foundation," *Fortune*, June 25, 2006
    – "Crafting partnerships for vaccinations and healthcare—The Bill & Melinda Gates Foundation," *Global Giving Matters*, December 2003-January 2004 feature, www.synergos.org/globalgiving matters/features/0401gates.htm
    – "Press release: Microsoft Announces Plans for July 2008 Transition for Bill Gates," Microsoft Corporation, June 15, 2006 at www.microsoft.com.

10 Warren Buffet references:
    – "Warren Buffet gives away his fortune," *Fortune*, June 25, 2006; Carol Loomis, "A Conversation with Warren Buffet," *Fortune*, June 25, 2006
    – "Special report Philanthropy: The new powers in giving," *The Economist*, July 1, 2006
    – See also online biography of Buffet at www.wwpidoo.com/biography/buffett/index.htm.

11 Pierre Omidyar references:
    – Omidyar Network at www.omidyar.net
    – Bill Breen, "Q&A: Pierre Omidyar—Empower Seller," *Fast Company*, Issue 113, March 2007

– "eBay and Omidyar Network Founder Launches $100 Million Microfinance Fund in Partnership with Tufts University," Tufts University, November 4, 2005 at www.tufts.edu/microfinancefund/.

12   Jeff Skoll references:
– Skoll Foundation at www.skollfoundation.org
– Participant Productions at www.participantproductions.com
– Tom Watson, "Skoll at Oxford: A Changing Time for Philanthropy," *onPhilanthroy*, April 2, 2007 at www.onphilanthropy.com.

13   Larry Page & Sergey Brin, and Google.org references:
– Google.org at www.google.org
– Jessi Hempel, "Google's Brilliant Philanthropist," *BusinessWeek*, February 22, 2006
– Katie Hafner, "Philanthropy the Google way: Doing good while making money," *International Herald Tribune*, September 14, 2006.

14   George Soros references:
– George Soros website at www.georgesoros.com
– Open Society Institute & Soros Foundations Network at www.soros.org.

15   Richard Branson references:
– Virgin Group at www.virgin.com
– "Branson pledges $3B to fight global warming," *CNNMoney.com*, September 21, 2006
– Amanda Griscom Little, "Branson With The Stars," *Grist*, September 28, 2006 at www.grist.org.

16   Sheikh Mohammed bin Rashid references:
– Official website at www.sheikhmohammed.co.ae/english/index.asp
– Mohammed Bin Rashid Al Maktoum Foundation at www.mbrfoundation.ae
– "Press release: Sheikh Mohammed bin Rashid Al Maktoum Launches Foundation to Promote Human Development with US$ 10 Billion Endowment," World Economic Forum, May 19, 2007 at www.weforum.org.

17   Li Ka-Shing reference:
– Li Ka-Shing Foundation at www.lksf.org
– Parmy Olson, "Li Ka-Shing can't take it with him," *Forbes*, August 25, 2006.

18   Gavyn Davies, "Who has the biggest heart in human history?" *The Guardian*, July 6, 2006. There are varying estimates of what Carnegie's and Rockefeller's gifts would be worth in today's dollars. Davies computes it at US$3b and US$6b respectively. Families of Philanthropy (www.familiesofphilanthropy.com) estimates are US$7.2 billion and US$14 billion respectively (the US$14 billion should include the gifts of both Rockefeller and Rockefeller Jr.). *Fortune* in 2006 puts the contributions at US$7.2b and US$12.6b respectively. The difference in the values would be due to estimates of the rate of inflation and in some cases, estimates of what might constitute a reasonable rate of return if the money had been invested.

19   Mark Hrywna, "Giving Hits Record $295 billion," *The Nonprofit Times*, July 1, 2007. This is an article on the *Giving USA 2007* yearbook published by Giving USA Foundation.

20   "Remarks of Bill Gates, Harvard Commencement," *Harvard University Gazette Online*, June 7, 2007, www.news.harvard.edu/gazette/2007/06.14/99-gates.html.

21   David Kirkpatrick, "Ebay's founder starts giving," *Fortune*, November 28, 2005.

22   Chris Letts, William Ryan, and Allen Grossman, "Virtuous Capital: What Foundations Can Learn from Venture Capitalists," *Harvard Business Review*, March 1997.

23   See Social Ventures Partners at www.svpseattle.org and www.svpi.org.

24   "Doing well and doing good," *The Economist*, July 29, 2004.

25   Established in 1914, the Cleveland Foundation is the world's first community foundation and the third largest in America. www.clevelandfoundation.org.

26   See Global Philanthropists Circle at www.synergos.org/philanthropistscircle.

27   www.clintonglobalinitiative.org

28   The asset base of U.S. foundations for 2005 (most recent available year) is $550 billion. Extrapolating by a historical growth trend of an annual average of 8%, by 2007, the figure should be about $641 billion. The total billionaires' worth of $4.4 trillion is from *Forbes* listing as of March 2008, which measures 2007 wealth. Thus, billionaires' wealth exceeds foundation assets by (4.4 trillion / 641 billion =) 6.9 times.

29   Leyla Boulton and James Lamont, "Philanthropy 'can eclipse G8' on poverty," *Financial Times*, April 8, 2007. Jeffrey Sachs had computed a figure of five percent "foundation payout" as being US$175 million using 2007 data of billionaires' worth. I have updated it using the most recent billionaires' worth from *Forbes* listing as of March 2008 (see previous endnote), hence it is (5% of 4.4 trillion =) US$220b.

30   "The birth of philanthrocapitalism," *The Economist*, February 25, 2006. The article highlights the tough new laws proposed by Senator Charles Grassley to deal with abuses in the nonprofit world. See Chapter 4, "Black box or glass house?" for a further discussion on the charity reforms in the U.S. and other countries.

31   Andrew Carnegie, "Wealth," *North American Review*, No. CCCXCI, June 1889. Later republished in England as "The Gospel of Wealth."

Chapter 15

Social Entrepreneurship

Innovating Social Change

Social entrepreneurs effect systemic, large scale social change through innovative approaches.

Studies of social entrepreneurs find and emphasize similarities with business entrepreneurs. However, it is the one crucial difference between the two that determines their methods and impact—money. When a business entrepreneur succeeds, the money flows freely to expand his business and his bank account. For a social entrepreneur, scaling up often requires more money which continues to be dependent upon the largesse of donors.

When you compare successful social entrepreneurs with successful business entrepreneurs who are philanthropic such as William Hewlett and David Packard, there is no question that the latter group has had a greater positive impact. However, there is a need in this world for both kinds of entrepreneurs and they can be symbiotic.

For a long time now, entrepreneurs like Steve Jobs, founder and chief executive officer (CEO) of Apple,[1] have been changing the world, and their personal bank accounts in the process. In recent times, however, a different genre of entrepreneurs called social entrepreneurs has been receiving some long overdue global recognition.

Social entrepreneurs effect systemic, large-scale social change through innovative approaches, but without reaping the corresponding financial benefits. For them, it is the fulfillment that comes from shifting paradigms rather than shifting blame and responsibility in the social arena. As David Bornstein, best-selling author of *How to Change the World: Social Entrepreneurs and the Power of New Ideas*, puts it: "Social entrepreneurs identify resources where people only see problems. They view the villagers as the solution, not the passive beneficiary. They begin with the assumption of competence and unleash resources in the communities they're serving."[2]

Celebrating Social Entrepreneurs

In his book, Bornstein profiles nine leading modern-day social entrepreneurs (see box on "People Who Are Changing The World"). Most of these extraordinary individuals are Fellows of Ashoka,[3] a global network of over 1,800 leading social entrepreneurs.

Ashoka: Innovators for the Public was founded by Bill Drayton who expects the rise of social entrepreneurs to bring about "a productivity miracle" in the citizen sector (government and nonprofits).[4] He sees social entrepreneurs, in helping those in need, as being not just content to give a fish or teach them how to fish. "They will not rest until they have revolutionized the fishing industry." Thus, Drayton aims to speed up and multiply the revolutions for social change by identifying and investing in these social entrepreneurs.

Another institution that was more recently created to honor social entrepreneurs is the Schwab Foundation for Social Entrepreneurship.[5] It was founded in 1998 by Klaus Schwab, president and founder of the World Economic Forum, together with his wife, to highlight and encourage individuals and organizations in "community-driven social entrepreneurship on a broad scale." By 2008, it had 140 social entrepreneurs in its network.

The Foundation organizes annual national "Social Entrepreneur of the Year" awards across the world. The inaugural event for Singapore was held in conjunction with *The Straits Times* in 2006. Jack Sim, founder of the World Toilet Organization (WTO),[6] was the first recipient of this prestigious award.

People Who Are Changing The World

Javed Abidi, India. Abidi, a paraplegic, is a champion of India's disability movement. Through his strategic leadership and tireless efforts, disability rights are now enshrined in India's legislation. He is working on making those rights a reality in economic and non-economic areas.

Jeroo Billimoria, India. Billimoria, an instructor in social sciences, set up Childline, a 24-hour toll-free telephone hotline that connects millions of vulnerable children living in India to an extensive network of child-service organizations. She then went on to replicate Childline internationally. More recently, she founded a global network, Aflatoun, that seeks to empower poor children through social and financial education.

Vera Cordeiro, Brazil. Cordeiro, a hospital worker, founded the Saude Crianca Renascer Association to provide emergency assistance to ill children from low-income families, during and immediately after hospitalization. Renascer has been duplicated in 14 other Brazilian public hospitals, assisting over 20,000 children.

Bill Drayton, U.S. Drayton is a former McKinsey consultant and assistant administrator of the Environmental Protection Agency where he launched emissions trading among other reforms. A social activist since young, he founded Ashoka: Innovators for the Public in 1980.

James Grant, U.S. Grant was the head of Unicef where he conceived and orchestrated a global campaign to stop the needless deaths of children from easily preventable illnesses. By 2000, this revolution was estimated to have saved 25 million young lives. He has also championed the legal rights of children globally.

Veronica Khosa, South Africa. Khosa was a nurse who, after visiting hundreds of AIDS patients suffering alone in their homes, founded Tateni and instituted a community-based model capable of addressing the AIDS pandemic. The government has adopted her model for the largest state in South Africa.

Fabio Rosa, Brazil. An agronomist and engineer, Rosa pioneered the use of low-cost transmissions systems to provide electricity to hundreds of thousands of impoverished rural Brazilians. Today, Rosa is spreading innovative "agro-electric" solutions and improved farming and grazing systems to simultaneously combat poverty, land degradation and global warming.

J.B. Schramm, U.S. Schramm who started work as a youth worker, designed and implemented a program to help low-income students across the US enroll and succeed in college. College Summit students enroll in college at a rate of 80 percent, against a national average of low-income enrollment of 46 percent.

Erzebet Szekeres, Hungary. The mother of a disabled child, Szekeres developed a program to address three of the most difficult programs disabled adults lack in her country—job training, employment and housing. Her organization, Alliance Industrial Union, now has centers across Hungary which provide for the needs of previously institutionalized disabled citizens.

Source: David Bornstein, *How To Change The World: Social Entrepreneurs and the Power of New Ideas*.

LOOse Change

Perhaps Jack Sim led the field in a country where major social gaps are proactively filled by the government because his cause and his impact are global. The fact that WTO is the first international non-governmental organization founded in Singapore is indication of his pioneering spirit.

In the space of five years, Sim (or Jack as he is fondly known in corporate and social circles) has taken a taboo subject and in his own inimitable way, put it on the international radar screen. The WTO has created a common global platform which now comprises over 120 organizational members in 49 countries. Its annual World Toilet Summit sees about 400 to 500 participants from across the world converge in one place to discuss the state of the world's toilets.

Through dogged persistence, a sometimes irreverent style mixed with a good sense of humor, Jack is able to engage governments and corporations alike; not only to support his cause, but even to compete for the privilege of having the cleanest public toilets.

Jack's tenacity has been key to the furtherance of his cause. As an example, he recounts how he gained access to the toilets of 300 institutions under a government ministry in Singapore. "The official told me that my request would be granted if I were to conclude that their toilets were good but could perhaps be better. However, if my view after visiting the various institutions was that the toilets needed to be significantly improved, I would not have access. I forwarded the official's note to his Minister, copied to him. The official called me up and scolded me for having sent that note. So, I sent another note to the Minister, copying the official, summarizing what the official said to me. After that, the doors were open."

Jack's ability to laugh at himself and the subject of toilets is obvious when you talk to him. He holds court with anyone willing to listen. WTO's promotional pictures feature Jack in comic poses with toilet-related paraphernalia.

Jack says that he takes his inspiration from the charismatic Dr. Mechai Viravaidya.[7] Dr. Mechai is the well-known Thai politician and social entrepreneur who popularized another taboo subject, this time in Thailand: condoms. Also known as "the condom king," Dr. Mechai has been employing attention-seeking and innovative means, such as a "cops and rubbers" program, mobile vasectomy bus, and restaurants themed around cabbages and condoms, to successfully tackle population growth, poverty, environmental conservation, and sexual health issues in Thailand.

While loos may be fodder for jokes, "toilet business is serious business" when you consider the stakes. There are more than 2.6 billion people in the world without toilets. A child dies of diarrhea every six seconds mostly from contaminated well water caused by poor sanitation. The United Nations has set a Millennium Development Goal[8] to halve the number of people without access to sanitation by 2015. According to Sim and other sanitation experts, this may be an impossible task given where we are today.

Besides governments, there are many other nonprofit organizations seeking to alleviate some of the world's problems caused by poor sanitation. Through the WTO, I met another impressive social entrepreneur, Dr. Bindeshwar Pathak, founder of the Sulabh International Social Service Organization. Sulabh builds affordable, eco-friendly and hygienic toilets in rural and urban India. It is the largest non-governmental organization in India. More than 10 million people use a Sulabh toilet daily. Unfortunately, this is literally a drop in a cistern for a country with a population of 1.1 billion people and where 65 percent still defecate in the open.

Beyond providing much-needed sanitation, Dr. Pathak, though a Brahmin[9] himself, has been a champion to more than 60,000 "scavengers," or untouchables who undertake the demeaning task of physically cleaning and carrying human waste. Sulabh programs include rehabilitating the scavengers and their families, to move on to other more dignified professions.

Unreasonable People

So what makes a social entrepreneur?

Authors Pamela Hartigan and John Elkington who have analyzed the work of more than 50 social entrepreneurs, explain that social entrepreneurs are often viewed as "unreasonable people"[10] because they want to change the system. They identify 10 characteristics of successful social entrepreneurs:[11]

- They shrug off the constraints of ideology or discipline
- They identify and apply practical solutions, combining innovation, resourcefulness, and opportunity
- They innovate

- They focus, first and foremost, on social value creation and, in that spirit, are willing to share their innovations and insights with others so that the results can be replicated
- They jump in before ensuring they are fully resourced
- They have an unwavering belief in everyone's innate capacity, often regardless of education, to meaningfully contribute
- They show a dogged determination that pushes them to take risks that others wouldn't dare
- They balance their passion for change with a zeal to measure and monitor their impact
- They have a great deal to teach change makers in other sectors
- They display a healthy impatience

Their primary thesis is that it is the "against all odds" tenacity that enables the innovations of these entrepreneurs to solve society's problems.

Social Entrepreneurs versus Business Entrepreneurs

As with other studies of social entrepreneurship, Hartigan and Elkington found similarities in the traits of social and business entrepreneurs. Both kinds of entrepreneurs tend to be driven people, deeply passionate of what they do, never say die, embrace change, innovate, create value, and bring people together to make things happen. The list goes on.

But perhaps there is one crucial difference between social and business entrepreneurs that determines their methods and impact—money. Successful business entrepreneurs roll in it. Social entrepreneurs often have to make do without enough of it.

By nature of—you could even argue by definition of—a social cause, normal market economics are not often present.

Some might contend otherwise. Well-known professor and strategist, C.K. Prahalad, believes that there really is tremendous buying power and profits from the billions of poor people in the world.[12]

Among his examples is the Grameen Bank of Bangladesh which pioneered the concept of microcredit to help villagers out of the poverty trap.[13] Each group of five individuals is loaned a very small sum but the whole group is denied credit if one person defaults. As of February 2008, statistics show that the Bank had more than seven million borrowers (97 percent of them women) across more than 80,000 villages. It had lent out Tk366 billion (US$6.8 billion), of which 89 percent had been repaid.

Muhammad Yunus, the founder of Grameen Bank is widely recognized as one of the world's most outstanding social entrepreneurs. He was awarded the 2006 Nobel Peace Prize for his work in microfinance. Even as he received the award, he was looking at another idea, a social business enterprise to provide low-cost, high-nutrition food for the poor. True to his instincts as a social entrepreneur, he has gone on to replicate the success of Grameen Bank internationally through the Grameen Foundation.[14]

Social entrepreneurship is sometimes confused with social enterprises—businesses with a social mission. For example, a café operated by a charity is considered a social enterprise. Most of such enterprises would not, in and of themselves, qualify as social entrepreneurship. A social enterprise is social entrepreneurship in action only if it achieves the large-scale social impact that comes from shifting paradigms.

Notwithstanding exceptions of social enterprises like the Grameen Bank, the reality is that most social entrepreneurs deal with social issues where getting an adequate economic return is a real challenge. Instead, their programs have to be justified on the "social return on investment."

It is very common for social entrepreneurs to function despite the lack of money. As Jack Sim, who operates on a shoestring budget, puts it, "We look at the problem first, not the resources available, otherwise we will never get going."

In contrast, a business entrepreneur may deal with initial funding challenges, but as his (or her) product or service succeeds, profits will roll in. He can then aggressively expand the business, as well as his and the other shareholders' wallets.

Scaling up good work is harder for a social entrepreneur. Although he may have the benefit of credibility from early successes, doing more requires more money. The requisite money to expand does not usually flow directly from the work itself. Instead, he must often depend upon the largesse of donors.

Social Entrepreneurs or Business Entrepreneurs

All this begets the question: would not successful business entrepreneurs who operate ethically and become philanthropists make a much greater positive impact on society than social entrepreneurs?

Take William Hewlett and David Packard who founded the Hewlett-Packard Company (HP).[15] The technology business they started in a garage in 1939 is now a US$100 billion global corporation providing jobs to 172,000 people around the world. It creates products and innovations that continue to change the way the world work, live and play. More than that, the duo created an exemplary corporate culture called the HP Way, one aspect of which was giving back to society. Both men have died, but they left behind an everlasting legacy and two foundations: The David and Lucile Packard Foundation, and The William and Flora Hewlett Foundation. In aggregate, these two foundations have more than US$15 billion in assets, and make grants of about US$500m annually.[16]

It really is hard to find social entrepreneurs who have made the same impact as Hewlett and Packard did in their lifetimes. There are, however, philanthropists who have accumulated wealth through their business ventures and are potentially moving into social entrepreneurship.

Such examples can be found in the technology world which is renowned for its mavericks. Larry Page and Sergey Brin of Google, Gordon Moore of Intel, Pierre Omidyar and Jeff Skolls of eBay, and of course Paul Allen and Bill Gates of Microsoft have all set up foundations, but at a much younger age. Some of them have also become more actively engaged with their foundations, giving not just large sums of money, but also their time, vision and expertise to shape the outcomes of their giving. In a sense, a couple of them are on the verge of crossing the line to become social entrepreneurs themselves.

But there's no need for successful businessmen to cross the line to become social entrepreneurs. They can do good, perhaps more good, simply by being philanthropic.

A good example of a businessman who decided to stick to his knitting is Warren Buffet. As the largest shareholder and CEO of Berkshire Hathaway, he had, by 2006, amassed a fortune valued at about US$37 billion. That was when he publicly committed to giving his fortune away to charity. But instead of doing so through his own foundation, he chose to donate most of it through the Bill & Melinda Gates Foundation. Why?

It is because Buffet is following his successful investment philosophy to be disciplined to stay within his circle of competence: "I don't think I'm as well cut out to be a philanthropist as Bill and Melinda are."[17] So, he has decided to focus his valuable time on investing and compounding his wealth at a rate that most investors can only dream of. Berkshire Hathaway share value grew at a compounded annual rate of 21.4 percent from 1964 to 2006.[18] Meanwhile the social sector benefits from the staggering amounts coming to it—probably a lot more than if Buffet were to roll up his sleeves to work in the social sector.

Celebrating Social and Business Entrepreneurship

So what's the bottom line?

First, the world has enough problems and opportunities to need both kinds of entrepreneurs. They can be symbiotic. Social entrepreneurs are needed to solve many of the world's social issues, and provide the same kind of focus and innovations that the business world has benefited from.

Secondly, business entrepreneurs can also be noble whether their businesses are or not.

Thirdly, money talks. So, businessmen with the entrepreneurial flair should be encouraged to continue to succeed in business and channel their gains into social causes. Those with a passion for social change can leverage off these donations to increase the social dividends.

Endnotes:

Adapted from: "Shifting Paradigms," *SALT* July-August 2006; and "Going beyond the profit principle," *The Straits Times*, July 12, 2006.

1   www.apple.com/pr/bios/jobs.html

2   David Bornstein, *How to Change the World: Social Entrepreneurs and the Power of New Ideas* (Oxford University Press, 2004). Quote is from www.pbs.org/opb/thenewheroes/whatis.

3   www.ashoka.org

4   "The rise of the social entrepreneur: Whatever he may be," *The Economist*, February 23, 2006.

5   www.schwabfound.org

6   Write-up on Jack Sim is at www.schwabfound.org/schwabentrepreneurs.htm?schwab id=3996&extended=yes. World Toilet Organization is at www.worldtoilet.org.

7   www.schwabfound.org/schwabentrepreneurs.htm?schwabid=332&extended=yes. PDA at www.pda.or.th/eng.

8   The Millennium Development Goals are eight goals that 189 United Nations member states have agreed to try to achieve by the year 2015. The goals are aimed at the reduction of poverty, hunger, disease, illiteracy, environmental degradation, and discrimination against women. For further information on the U.N. Millennium project and goals, go to www.unmilleniumproject.org.

9   Under India's caste system, the Brahmins occupy the top rank. They make up less than 5% of the population. The Dalits, also known as "untouchables," have the lowest social status. They tend to work in unhealthy, unpleasant or polluting jobs.

10 One of George Bernard Shaw's most famous quotes is: "The reasonable man adapts himself to the world; the unreasonable one persists in trying to adapt the world to himself. Therefore, all progress depends on the unreasonable man."

11 John Elkington and Pamela Hartigan, *The power of unreasonable people: How social entrepreneurs create markets that change the world* (Harvard Business School Press, 2008); John Elkington & Pamela, "Unreasonable people—Ten characteristics of successful social entrepreneurs," *The Social Edge*, February 26, 2008, at www.socialedge.org/blogs/unreasonable-people.

12 C.K. Prahalad, *The Fortune at the Bottom of the Pyramid* (Wharton School Publishing, 2005).

13 www.grameen-info.org/bank/GBGlance.htm

14 "Yunus wins Nobel Peace Prize," Associated Press, October 13, 2006; www.grameenfoundation.org.

15 www.hp.com. Statistics provided are as of March 2008.

16 For the David & Lucile Packard Foundation, see www.packard.org; for the William and Flora Hewlett Foundation, see www.hewlett.org. Statistics are based on the 2005 and 2006 annual reports of the foundations respectively.

17 Carol Loomis, "A conversation with Warren Buffet," *Fortune*, June 25, 2006.

18 "Berkshire's Corporate Performance vs. the S&P 500," from *Berkshire Hathaway, Annual Report* 2006.

Chapter 16

Social Enterprises

Profits for Nonprofits

In their search for financial sustainability, nonprofits are increasingly turning towards profits. Social enterprises, or businesses with social missions offering a variety of products and services, are mushrooming.

Despite the apparent unfair business advantage of grants, donations and widespread community support, the success rate of social enterprises has been low compared to commercial organizations. Multiple bottom lines, lack of scale and capabilities gaps are often cited as challenges. However, the key reason may be the differing cultures of the charity world as compared to the commercial world.

To encourage more successful social enterprises, it may be easier to change the heart of the business entrepreneur than the head of the social worker.

In their quest for the holy grail of financial sustainability, many nonprofits are increasingly turning their minds towards making profits. To achieve this goal, they set up social enterprises, or businesses with social objectives.

Compared to the effort involved in soliciting donations, applying for grants, or charging beneficiaries subsidized fees for services, some nonprofits find that setting up their own business is a more attractive way of securing funds. As Dr. Mechai Viravaidya, founder of the Population and Community Development Association (PDA), Thailand's largest non-governmental organization (NGO), declares: "This is the best way of financing an NGO—making your own donations. I have tried begging. It gets harder and harder. I have tried praying. It does not work."[1] In line with this philosophy, Dr. Mechai has set up 16 different for-profit ventures, offering services ranging from health services to resorts and restaurants. These companies contribute up to 70 percent of the funding for PDA's operations.[2]

Encouraged by successes like Dr. Mechai's and the active support of donors and governments, social enterprises are mushrooming across the nonprofit sector.

Mixed Business

The activities that social enterprises engage in are as myriad as those available to any business entrepreneur. These can range from setting up a café to providing house-moving services.

Just like regular businesses, there are many ways of categorizing social enterprises. For the purpose of this chapter, let us look at two attributes: ownership and integration with the charity.

From an ownership standpoint, a social enterprise can be started by a business entrepreneur with a heart, or by a charity itself.

A do-gooder can start a business with the intention of giving a part or all of the profits to charity, even if the charities may not be specifically identified until the profits start flowing. For example, the actor Paul Newman, together with a friend, set up a food company called Newman's Own[3] that sells all-natural salad dressing, pasta sauce and other food items. Newman then donates 100 percent of the profits. By end 2007, Newman and his franchise had given over US$ 200 million to educational and charitable causes, including Hole in the Wall Gang Camp, a summer camp for seriously ill children that Newman co-founded.

Such business-owned social enterprises are, however, few and far in between. Instead, most social enterprises are charity-owned, that is, they are started by a charity or those involved with the charity, for the purpose of funding the charity. Typical examples of these are Dr. Mechai's Cabbages & Condoms Restaurant and his other for-profit enterprises which are set up to fund PDA's work.

Another way of classifying social enterprises is based on whether they function separately and distinctly from the charity, or whether they are integrated.

A standalone social enterprise functions much like any other commercial operation. The only difference is that the profits go towards the cause of charity instead of somebody's pockets. Newman's Own is a standalone social enterprise.

However, if a standalone social enterprise is set up by a charity, the charity virtually has two autonomous arms—one that makes money through a commercial venture, and another that does the charitable work of looking after the beneficiaries. This is very much Dr. Mechai's philosophy and so, his famous Cabbages and Condoms Restaurants and the Birds and Bees Resort[4] are run separately from the PDA, even if the names and decor of the ventures may help link them with the owner.

Integrated social enterprises are business ventures where the mission of charity is, in some ways, an integral part of the business model. For example, a U.K. charity, Training for Life set up The Hoxton Apprentice, a Michelin-rated restaurant, to provide skills, training and employment opportunities for the long-term unemployed and homeless.[5]

Providing viable employment for beneficiaries is probably the most common approach to synergizing the charity's work with a business. Rubicon Programs[6] is a nonprofit agency in Richmond, California where its beneficiaries—low income, disabled and formerly homeless people—are the primary employees of businesses it has created. These include a wholesale dessert bakery, a landscape maintenance business and a home care worker business. Through these social enterprises, Rubicon employs more than 200 people in the Richmond area.

In some cases, charity and social enterprise are rolled into one. Thus, the Big Issue[7] was set up in the U.K. to offer homeless people the opportunity to earn a legitimate income as street vendors. They sell the weekly current affairs and entertainment magazine, *The Big Issue* which is written by professional journalists. *The Big Issue*, now has editions in five other countries.

Business with Unfair Advantage?

For most intents and purposes, it is relatively easy to set up a social enterprise compared to a business enterprise. Many people and organizations sometimes fall over one another to help a social enterprise get going.

Foundations and individual donors are generally supportive of the idea of one-off seed funding that allows a charity to be more financially self-sufficient. Even government grants can be readily available for this purpose. The U.K. government has anted up £100 million (US$200 million) into a Social Enterprise Investment Fund to help fund social enterprises that deliver health and social care services.[8] In Singapore, a smaller government-sponsored Comcare Enterprise Fund[9] provides seed funding for new social enterprises. For social enterprises, a big benefit is that the majority of such seed funding is given without any requirement of payback. By contrast, in commercial ventures, investors expect to be repaid with financial returns commensurate with the equity risk.

In many respects, it should also be easier to operate a social enterprise. A charity can leverage on its volunteers who will work for free, or hire employees who may be prepared to work for less than regular market wages since this is a charitable venture. Goods and services sold by social enterprises also tend to find more sympathetic and supportive buyers. Most significantly, running a social enterprise is, theoretically, easier since demands for accountability and outcomes are much less or sometimes absent, as the seed capital often does not have repayment criteria and the culture of charitable work is more forgiving.

In spite of these "unfair advantages" relative to their commercial counterparts, social enterprises as a whole actually do not fare very well in the marketplace.

An analysis in the *Harvard Business Review* by the Bridgespan Group, a nonprofit strategy consulting firm, showed that beyond the celebrated cases, few of the social enterprises that have been launched actually make money.[10] After getting past the hype of misleading statistics, it found that earned income only accounts for a small part of the funding of most nonprofit domains. Bridgespan's study of ventures that received philanthropic funding showed that 71 percent of them were unprofitable, 24 percent reported profits and 5 percent stated they were breaking even. Even then, "of those that claimed they were profitable, half did not fully account for indirect costs such as allocations of general overhead or senior management time."

A recent study of social enterprises in Singapore by the Lien Center for Social Innovation (the Lien Center)[11] seems to provide more positive results. Forty five percent of the social enterprises surveyed reported profits, 24 percent said they were breaking even and 21 percent were losing money. In reality, the actual statistics would be worse since such survey samples have survival bias (those social enterprises that have closed are not able to respond). Interestingly, only 33 percent of the respondents state that their operations are being funded by earned income; the majority continue to depend on private donations and government grants.

Why They Don't Succeed

The studies point to three major challenges that hinder a social enterprise's commercial success: multiple bottom lines, lack of scale and capability gaps.

A social enterprise has to juggle at least two bottom lines—one is economic and the other, social. A commercial enterprise, regardless of the nature of its business, has only one clear overriding mission—make as much money as possible for its shareholders.

Meeting multiple bottom lines can increase costs and add other operational constraints. An integrated social enterprise that employs beneficiaries will need to ensure an appropriate wage structure and working conditions, all of which may increase its costs beyond competitive market rates. Being a social enterprise, it is also expected to engage in socially responsible practices regardless of whether these fit in with its core social mission, adding further to costs. For example, a social enterprise factory that employs beneficiaries to manufacture the goods while being environmentally friendly effectively has three bottom lines.

Aspire (see box on "Two Case Studies in Contrast") is an example of a high-profile enterprise that struggled with this conflict of multiple bottom lines. Not only did Aspire want to employ the homeless to sell its products, it wanted to rehabilitate them. Its managers could not punish or fire employees in the same way that a commercial operation would. There was a "blurring of the roles of employee and client," leading to difficult managerial decisions, low morale, and the consequent collapse of the franchise business. However, the hurdle was not deemed insurmountable as Aspire could have employed fewer homeless people or be more selective in its recruitment of homeless employees.

The lack of scale is sometimes cited as a reason for the poor functioning of social enterprises. In the U.S., Juma Ventures focuses on developing and operating social enterprises to provide job opportunities for economically disadvantaged teens. Jim Schorr, its executive director, thinks that the first generation of social enterprises failed because they were "inherently small," being primarily small retail businesses such as ice cream shops, thrift stores and cafes.[14] He believes that a social enterprise's revenue

Two Case Studies in Contrast

Aspire Group[12]—A social enterprise failure

Aspire was founded by two Oxford graduates, Paul Harrod and Mark Richardson. It started off as a door-to-door catalog business, employing homeless people to sell fair-trade products. At its height in 2001, the company was doing US$1.6 million in business and received awards and praises from the likes of Prince Charles and then British Prime Minister, Tony Blair.

The group sought to grow by franchising. Their ambition was to create 30 outlets across the U.K. by the end of 2003. However, through a series of missteps, the group collapsed into bankruptcy by 2004.

One of its franchisees and a university lecturer analyzed the case and concluded that Aspire made two major mistakes. The first was that it became a franchise too soon—before it had become a strong and proven brand.

Its second mistake was that it paired a weak business model with ambitious social objectives. Franchise managers faced the challenge of "overseeing and supporting homeless and ex-homeless employees—many of whom still struggled with addiction, mental illness and a lack of basic skills like punctuality." In an effort to increase profitability, Aspire reduced its business cycle from 12 months to two four-month seasons. Franchisees saw this as pulling back from one of its primary social objectives of employing homeless people full time and year-round. This and other changes in the business model led to tensions between franchisees and the Aspire group, and the consequent collapse of the business.

BRAC[13]—A social phenomenon

BRAC (which started as Bangladesh Rural Advancement Committee, then Building Resources Across Communities, before becoming formally known just as BRAC) was established in 1972 by Dr. Fazle Hasan Abed to help Bangladesh recover from the Liberation War through small-scale relief and rehabilitation.

Today, it is the world's largest NGO in terms of the scale and diversity of its interventions. It employs nearly 100,000 people with the twin objectives of poverty alleviation and empowerment of the poor. It reaches more than 110 million people in Bangladesh and beyond. It has an annual budget of US$245 million, 77 percent of which is self-financed.

BRAC has set up over 150 enterprises in 23 different sectors, including a chain of retail handicraft shops, a vegetable export firm, chilling plant, fish hatcheries, a printing press, tea estates, a bank (BRAC Bank) and a university. The profits of these ventures are ploughed back into BRAC's core development fund.

BRAC's enterprises not only make money. Many of them help the beneficiaries directly. For example, by 2008, BRAC Bank had disbursed over US$3.9 billion as microcredit to 5 million people, with a recovery rate of 98.7 percent.

Using the experiences of its success in Bangladesh, BRAC went international in 2002 to assist other countries in Africa, the Middle East and Afghanistan to set up similar programs, further impacting the lives of millions more.

need to approach US$1 million annually to be sustainable for a double bottom line.

The ultimate social enterprises are those run by BRAC (see box on "Two Case Studies in Contrast"). There, the 150 enterprises which contribute to more than one percent of Bangladesh's GDP operate almost in a self-sustaining ecosystem that is a mini-economy or even "a parallel state."[15] BRAC's beneficiaries are effectively the employees, suppliers and customers of the various BRAC's enterprises which do cross-business with one another in the entire value chain of many businesses. Yet, even as it operates at scale, the advice of its chairman, Dr. Abed, is to start any program through small pilot projects, proving its effectiveness before scaling up.[16]

The Lien Center study found that the lack of capabilities is the single greatest challenge faced by social enterprises. Respondents speak of staff lacking business management skills and the organizations having difficulty tapping into the pool of volunteers for professional assistance.

This is echoed in the Bridgespan study which identifies the lack of business perspective to be a major reason for the gap between "rhetoric and reality" in social enterprise success. It finds that nonprofits tend to overlook the distinction between revenue and profit, and often misjudge actual financial contribution.

Yet, these reasons of multiple bottom lines, lack of scale and capability gaps are not quite sufficient in themselves to explain why social enterprises seem to consistently fare worse than commercial enterprises.

For starters, the pressure of bottom lines is relative. Many commercial companies will argue that the pressure they face for maximum returns from their shareholders is probably much greater than any pressure ever faced by a social enterprise, no matter the number of bottom lines. In the former, there are swift consequences for non-performance, whereas the latter is dealing with a much more forgiving charity looking for a "handout." A standalone social enterprise does not face much pressure from a double bottom line. Even an integrated social enterprise that works towards profit optimization instead of profit maximization, as it takes into account its social objectives, can be reasonably profitable. After all, there are ample cases of successful and socially responsible commercial organizations that employ disabled people.

Scale and capability gaps, as we have seen, also confront commercial companies. These are merely issues that any business needs to resolve.

Culture Shock

Perhaps the critical difference lies in the very different mindsets required to operate an enterprise versus running a charity. The commercial and charity worlds can be poles apart when it comes to basic fundamentals regarding the mission, markets, finance and perspectives of the different players. These differences are captured in Table 16.1

Table 16.1 Commercial versus Charity Environment

	COMMERCIAL	**CHARITY**
Mission Focus	Economic	Social
Market Basis	Economic value, Survival of the fittest	Generosity, Doing good
Funding	Market rate capital	Donations and grants
Workers	Staff at market-based compensation	Volunteers & staff paid below market rate
Recipients of goods & services	Customers pay market rate	Beneficiaries pay nothing or subsidized rate
Suppliers	Charge market rate	Charge subsidized rate & give donations-in-kind

The charity sector is a relatively easy-going one that thrives on the milk of human kindness. The commercial world, on the other hand, is Darwinian where only the most competitive survive.

Charities that step into the commercial environment with their culture and charity mindset (read "handout"), whether consciously or otherwise, set themselves on a path of non-sustainability if they choose not to change. A manager of a social enterprise in the Lien Center study lamented that government seed funding is only one-off and "wished donations and grants would be available in a more planned manner."

Understandably, this dependency mindset of social enterprises is pervasive since it is donations and grants, rather than shareholder funds, that kick-started the business. Sadly, it does not stop with expectations of (continued) financing. Some social enterprise managers expect that people would buy their goods and services out of charity notwithstanding their competitiveness. The mood of generosity and more forgiving nature of nonprofit culture also carry through to the accountability for results, and business performance suffers as a result.

If we examine the successes of PDA and BRAC, one of their common characteristics is the business-like approach they take to, well, business. Dr. Mechai has a firm philosophy of keeping social enterprises separate from the beneficiaries and work of PDA. Overall, he favors the standalone approach so that PDA's social enterprises need not be distracted by other priorities and, so, are able to focus only on business.

Dr. Abed, on the other hand, adopts the integrated approach, but even he advises that "a soft-hearted patronage approach of welfare organizations must give way to a hard-headed professional approach" for businesses like microfinance to be sustainable and effective.[17] The question of not being business-like has probably never occurred to Dr. Abed because he works in a culture where "business is the norm, not the exception, for Bangladeshi not-for-profit organizations."[18]

It is likely that both Dr. Mechai and Dr. Abed would equally be successful as business entrepreneurs if they had not started their respective nonprofits. Getting people with the right business acumen instead of a social worker with the interest to do business is probably the key to making a social enterprise successful.

Social Enterprise Version 2

In the last few years, much has been written about the promise of social enterprise. Overall, it is safe to say that the first generation of social enterprises has not quite delivered on that promise.

This raises the question: Should the sector continue to promote the social enterprise model?

On a macro-level, successful social enterprises will strengthen the charity sector because they add diversity to the kind of activities and funding sources available. They also instill a greater sense of self-reliance and business discipline that is much needed by nonprofit organizations.

However, the approach should not be to blindly seek to increase the number of social enterprises in play. Rather, the focus should be on cultivating the appropriate environment that promotes sustainable social enterprises.

A key part of this must be to remove the charity mindset from those operating social enterprises. In this respect, getting any charity to create and operate a social enterprise without this mindset change would likely start it on the wrong footing.

A good businessman who can continue to operate a business as a business, but with the proceeds going to charity, would be a better bet than a charity worker who has to learn business skills and unlearn the charity culture. In targeting the right people to create and run social enterprises, it may be easier changing the heart of the successful businessman than the head of a successful charity worker.

Endnotes:

1   Dr. Mechai Viravaidya made these remarks in his keynote address, "Show Me The Money," at the National Volunteer & Philanthropy Conference, October 28-29, 2003.

2   See www.pda.or.th. Information on social enterprises and funding as of March 2008. NGO is a non-governmental organization.

3   www.newmansown.com

4   www.cabbagesandcondoms.co.th provides information on both the restaurant and the resorts.

5   See www.trainingforlife-city.org and www.hoxtonapprentice.com.

6   www.rubiconprograms.org

7   www.bigissue.com

8   "News Release: Ivan Lewis announces £27 million extra for Social Enterprise," Department of Health, February 27, 2008 at www.nds.coi.gov.uk/environment/fullDetail.asp?ReleaseID=355787&NewsAreaID=2. For further information, see www.dh.gov.uk/en/Managingyourorganisation/Commissioning/Socialenterprise/DH_073426.

9   The ComCare Enterprise Fund (initially the Social Enterprise Fund) was set up by the Ministry of Community, Youth and Sports in March 2003. Its annual budget is about S$3 million. Typically, enterprises are funded between S$50,000 to S$300,000. As of February 2008, it had funded more than 60 social enterprises. For further information, see www.mcys.gov.sg/web/serv_E_CEF.html.

10   William Foster and Jeffrey Bradach, "Should nonprofits seek profits?" *Harvard Business Review*, February 2005.

11   *State of Social Enterprise in Singapore* (Lien Center for Social Innovation, August 2007).

12   See www.aspire-support.co.uk; Paul Tracey and Owen Jarvis, "An enterprising failure," *Stanford Social Innovation Review*, Spring 2006; Paul Tracey & Owen Jarvis, "Towards a theory of social venture franchising," *Entrepreneurship: Theory and Practice*, September 2007, www.entrepreneur.com/tradejournals/article/168630541_3.html.

13   www.brac.net. See also endnotes 15–18.

14   Jim Schorr, "Social Enterprise 2.0: Moving towards a sustainable model," *Stanford Social Innovation Review*, Summer 2006.

15   Annie Kelly, "Growing discontent," *The Guardian*, February 20, 2008.

16   "BRAC builds on Microcredit," *Countdown 2005*, Vol. 1, Issue 3 February/March 1998; Dr. Abed made the same point when he gave a talk at the Lien Center for Social Innovation Inaugural Distinguished Speaker Event on August 22, 2007 in Singapore.

17   Ibid.

18   Harriet Skinner Matsaert, *The Bangladeshi innovation take-away: How the not for profit sector in Bangladesh is breaking new ground in social entrepreneurship* (nfpSynergy, July 2006).

Doing Good Well?

Chapter 17

The Rich/Poor Divide

For Richer or For Poorer?

In our capitalist world, the rich get richer, the poor get poorer. Charity is meant to redress this uneven balance between rich and poor. Unfortunately, the gravitational forces that favor the well-off continue to do so in the charity world.

The dice seems to be loaded on both the supply (donors) and the demand (charities and their beneficiaries) side of the charity equation.

A large part of this is because the definition of charity has been broadened from being about helping the poor and needy (what most people understand it to be) to being about the community good.

The rich get richer, the poor get poorer. It is a hard reality of our capitalist world. In an increasingly globalized world, the gulf is widening. In recent years, the Gini coefficient, a measure of income equality, has been slowly rising, indicating a widening gap, in countries like the U.S., U.K. and Singapore.[1]

Charity is meant to help rebalance this uneven status between rich and poor. Yet, it seems that even in the charity world, there are similar forces that favor the better-heeled over those who are less so. This theme applies to both the supply (donors) and demand (charities and their beneficiaries) side of the charity equation.

The Supply Side

Let us start with donors—those who fund charities.

It should be apparent that rich donors get better treatment from charities compared to those who are less well off. They are courted and showered with attention because they have more to give. They get more recognition when they do give because they tend to give more in absolute terms.

What's more, most income tax regimes favor the rich when it comes to charitable donations. In most countries, income tax is imposed on a progressive basis, that is, the richer you are, the higher the percentage tax rates on your income. To encourage charitable giving, donations are generally tax deductible, that is, there is a tax savings on the donation which would not have occurred if the tax authorities had not allowed the deduction. Due of the progressive income tax structure, the tax savings is computed at the highest marginal tax rate which the taxpayer is subjected to.

To illustrate, a wealthy American taxpayer who is paying income tax at the top marginal tax rate[2] of 35 percent would be receiving a tax savings of $35 on every $100 of donations. In other words, he only effectively pays $65 for every $100 he donates. In contrast, a taxpayer whose highest marginal rate is only 10 percent would pay $90 for every $100 he donates. For a wage earner who has no taxable income (after various deductions), a $100 donation actually sets him back by $100.

In the U.K., the savings are even greater for the rich because the top marginal tax rate is higher, at 40 percent. Therefore, for the wealthy Englishman, a £100 donation will only cost him £60. The situation is even better in Singapore for the wealthy because, while the top marginal tax rate is only 20 percent (less absolute taxes for the wealthy), there is a generous double tax deduction for charitable donations (more tax savings for donations). Thus, a $100 donation costs a taxpayer, who is at the top marginal tax rate of 20 percent, only $60 (rather than $80 if it had only been a single tax deduction). In Singapore, two-thirds of the workforce do not pay income tax so they would have to fork out the full $100 for every $100 of donation.

So, who makes up for the $40 benefit (in the above British and Singaporean examples) that the wealthy taxpayer gets? Assuming that the total tax revenues remain unchanged, the shortfall must come from other taxation sources. Where these include income tax, the income tax net must be stretched wider to catch and thus penalize those earning less.

Alternatively, it could come from raising consumption tax revenues, such as sales tax, value added tax, and goods and services tax. In fact, this is the trend. Free-market economists and governments favor indirect taxes such as consumption tax, over direct taxes such as income tax.[3] Direct taxes are seen as harmful to the economy as they lessen the incentive to work, whereas indirect taxes have little or no impact on the incentive to work.

Where consumption tax is increased to make up for the fall in income tax, the poor must shoulder a greater tax burden again since the same rate applies to everyone regardless of one's income level. The lower a person's income, the higher the consumption tax as a proportion of his income. That is why consumption tax is regarded as regressive.

Of course, the rich can make up for their greater benefit by simply donating more. Yes, they do give more, but in terms of absolute and not relative dollars. We had seen previously[4] that surveys in several countries show quite consistently that the higher-income earners give less as a proportion of their income compared to the lower-income earners.

Therefore, from the donors' standpoint, the better-off give proportionately less than those who are less well-off, and yet they are better treated by charities and the tax authorities.

The Demand Side

Let us now look at the charities and their beneficiaries.

Not unlike for-profit organizations, charities also have to compete for resources. It should, therefore, not be a surprise that the larger players within the charity sector are richer and better off than the smaller ones. They have more resources and reserves, are able to attract funding more easily and enjoy economies of scale in their activities.

In a recent survey by nfpSynergy, big charities in the U.K. were perceived by small charities to have an overall negative effect on the charity sector.[5] Their feeling of being overwhelmed might be understandable. According to the National Council for Voluntary Organizations, the income of the U.K. charity sector is concentrated in a relatively small number of organizations.[6] Over two-thirds of the total sector income in 2004 was generated by two percent of the charities. The study pointed out the emergence of 14 "super-charities": brand-name organizations with an annual income of over £100 million (US$200 million), generating 10 percent of the sector's income. At the other end of the spectrum, 87 percent of charities have incomes of less than £100,000 (US$200,000) and they generated less than eight percent of the sector's total income. While the total number of general charities increased by more than 40 percent over a 10 year period, the larger charities have more than doubled in number during that time.

Size aside, charities serve a broad spectrum of beneficiaries. Those that serve the poor and the needy tend to be classified under the social service, or social welfare, or human services umbrella. The other charity segments such as arts, education, environment, sports, religious may have their share of poor beneficiaries, but their focus is on promoting their respective segment needs rather than alleviating poverty.

In general, the social service segment does not get the lion share of donations. In the U.K., the number one cause supported by donors in 2006 was medical research. Overseas disaster relief came in second, with social welfare and disabled people ranked fifth and sixth respectively.[7] In Singapore, the social service segment only gets about 25% of tax exempt donations, while the education sector gets 39%. For non-tax exempt giving from individuals, the bulk goes to religious causes.[8] In Canada, only 10 percent of total donations from Canadians go to social services, while the religious charities get 45 percent.[9] Similarly, in the U.S., only 10 percent of 2006 charitable donations went to human services, while nearly 33 percent went to religious causes.[10]

A more focused study conducted by the Center on Philanthropy indicates that less than one-third of all charitable giving by individuals in the U.S. in 2005 was directed towards the needs of the economically disadvantaged.[11] Further analysis showed that a mere eight percent of donated dollars were reported as contributions specifically to help meet basic needs such as providing food, shelter and other necessities. The rest went to programs that provided direct benefits ranging from medical treatment to scholarships, or to initiatives that created opportunity and empowerment through literacy, job training programs and so on.

So, from a beneficiary's standpoint, the majority of charitable giving does not go towards benefiting the poor, but to other causes that improve the community.

The Definition of Charity

A key reason for this state of affairs lies in the definition of charity.

The Oxford dictionary defines charity as "the voluntary giving of money to those in need," harking back to the Christian tradition of alms-giving. Ask the man in the street and he will likely define charity in similar terms: helping the poor and the needy of society.

However, the industry and legal definition of what constitutes charity or charitable purpose is much broader than that. The legal definition of "charitable purpose" in common law jurisdictions derives from the Charitable Uses Act 1601 of Elizabethan England, as interpreted and expanded by case law.[12] As a result, the modern definition of charitable purposes covers four main areas: the relief of poverty, the advancement of education, the advancement of religion and "other purposes beneficial to the community." Over time, the last catch-all clause has been interpreted to include areas such as health, arts, heritage, environment, animal welfare and sports. These other "miscellaneous" areas, which are generally beneficial to the community and would usually lessen the government's burden, are often explicitly added into the definition of charity by tax and charity legislation.

When the meaning of charity is stretched from alms-giving to promoting the community good, quirky outcomes with respect to the precept of closing the gap between rich and poor can arise. For example, the biggest donor in Singapore is the Singapore Totalisator Board, commonly known as the Tote Board. Annually, it gives out more than S$300 million (US$207 million), representing a third of total philanthropic giving in Singapore.[13] It also provided most of the S$600 million (US$414 million) funding needed to build the Esplanade, Singapore's center for the performing arts.

Now, the Tote Board's income comes from the very legitimate gambling operations of Singapore Pools (lottery) and the Singapore Turf Club (horse racing). The large proportion of gamblers comprises working class people, many looking for the windfall that can lift them from a mundane life or poverty. The arts, on the other hand, is typically associated with the more refined of the populace. Surely unintended, but this looks like a case of the less well-off helping to fund the more well-off. Sensitive to such possible perception, the Esplanade has, to its credit, worked hard to make the arts more accessible by showcasing a multitude of programs that reach out to the masses. To be fair, the Tote Board also channels a significant proportion of its giving to social services.

Singapore is not alone in its use of gambling proceeds to fund programs of national interest. Following the U.K.'s winning bid to host the 2012 Olympic Games, the National Lottery (its largest lottery) committed to initially provide £1.5 billion (US$3 billion) towards part of the infrastructure costs. About £750 million (US$1.5 billion) of that commitment was diverted from money that would otherwise have gone towards existing good causes between 2006 and 2012.

In early 2007, the charity sector learned about the possibility of the government dipping further into the National Lottery to fund the escalating costs of the Games. The National Council for Voluntary Organizations, as the umbrella body for the voluntary sector in the U.K., led a campaign to tell the Chancellor of the Exchequer: "Don't raid the Lottery to fund the Olympics." However, the government later announced that a further £675 million (US$1.35 billion) would be diverted from the National Lottery good cause funds for the Games. After further lobbying by the National Council for Voluntary Organizations and three other charity umbrella groups representing the sports, arts and heritage sectors, the U.K. government finally announced in January 2008 that there would be "no more diversion of funds away from lottery good causes to fund the Olympics."[14]

The question of whether charity should be about narrowly helping the poor and needy, or be broadened to serve the common good, goes beyond the matter of mere definition. By putting them under the same umbrella of tax breaks and government support, charitable giving to the poor, rather than being preferentially enabled, has to compete with community programs instead. The net result is that charity for the poor and needy will lose out; first, by having to compete and, secondly, by the glamour attached to (and the greater appeal of) some of these other causes.

Moreover, the degree of accountability is also impacted. The fundamental basis of charitable giving is generosity. Despite a ground swell of support for greater accountability of charities, the allocation of resources in the charity "marketplace" will continue to be driven less by economic value than by relationships between donors and beneficiaries, and their fundraisers.[15]

The basis of government programs, on the other hand, is rigorous cost-benefit analysis and public accountability. Having broad-based community programs funded under the aegis of charity reduces that level of public accountability.

In sectors such as education and healthcare, some observers have asked whether some of the programs funded through public donations should not be funded by, and remain the responsibility of, the government. Education, in particular, gets an extra boost from donations. In addition to tax exemptions and the intrinsic appeal of education, there are opportunities for naming rights and the government's encouragement through matching grants for donations (sometimes by as much as 3:1 in Singapore). Consequently, many universities around the world have amassed staggering endowments and other donations from loyal alumni and philanthropists. Their reserves will provide for current and future needs to no end. For example, Harvard University, which has close to a breakeven net operating budget, has more than US$35 billion in its investment portfolio.[16]

A Preferential Option for the Poor

In summary, it seems that the well-off are not just generally favored in life but in the charity space as well. To be true to the spirit of charity in providing for the poor and needy, we need to be vigilant of the gravitational forces that favor the well-off. Reviewing what constitutes charity and who is more deserving of the charity support mechanisms could be one big step towards this objective.

Endnotes:

Adapted from: "For Richer or For Poorer?" *SALT*, July-August 2007; and "In aid of the poorer or richer?" *The Straits Times*, September 4, 2007.

1. The Gini coefficient is the most widely used summary measure of the inequality of distribution of income. It represents an overall measure of the cumulative income share against the share of households in the population. It is expressed as a value between 0 (perfect equality) and 1 (perfect inequality—one person has all the income and all others have zero). The Gini coefficients for developed countries are: Singapore 0.49 in 2000, and 0.52 in 2005; U.K. 0.51 in 2000 and 0.52 in 2005; U.S. 0.462 in 2000 and 0.469 in 2005.

2. All tax rates used here are as of year of assessment 2007 in the respective countries. Thus, top tax rates are as follows: U.S. 35 percent, U.K. 40 percent, and Singapore 20 percent.

3. Singapore, for example, had progressively reduced its individual and corporate income tax rates since 2000, from 26 to 20 percent, and increased its goods and service tax (GST) rate since 1994 from 3 percent to 7 percent. However, each time the government raised the GST rate, it introduced an offset package to reduce the impact of the hike on the poor. See Audrey Tan, "7% GST / 2-point hike," *The Straits Times*, February 10, 2007.

4　See Chapter 11, "Elite or e-Lite Giving."

5　Chris Greenwood, *The State of the Third Sector 2007* (nfpSynergy, 2008). The survey polls senior executives of charities. Unsurprisingly, the majority of the respondents who felt that the statement "I think very big charities have a negative effect on the sector as a whole" was true, were from small charities.

6　Karl Wilding, Jenny Clark, Megan Griffith, Veronique Jochum and Susan Wainwright, *The UK Voluntary Sector Almanac 2006: The State of the Sector* (National Council for Voluntary Organizations).

7　Natalie Low, Sarah Butt, Angela Ellis Paine and Justin Davis Smith, *Helping out: A national survey on volunteering and charitable giving* (Office of the Third Sector, Cabinet Office, Prepared by National Center for Social Research and the Institute for Volunteering Research, 2007.) Since each survey respondent identified multiple causes, the report could only provide a sense of the relative ranking of the sectors.

8　*The State of Giving* (National Volunteer & Philanthropy Center, 2005).

9　*Caring Canadians, Involved Canadians: Highlights from the 2004 Canada Survey of Giving, Volunteering and Participating* (Imagine Canada, 2006).

10　*Giving USA 2007, The Annual Report on Philanthropy for the Year 2006*, (Giving USA Foundation, researched and written by the Center on Philanthropy at Indiana University, 2007). The report provides target of contributions. Apart from the sectors, 10 percent went to foundations and 8.8 percent related to contributions that were not tracked, deductions carried over and unallocated giving.

11　*Patterns of Household Charitable Giving by Income Group, 2005* (Google, prepared by The Center on Philanthropy at Indiana University, Summer 2007).

12　Common law legal systems are in widespread use and include the U.K., most of the U.S. and Canada, and the Commonwealth countries. The landmark case from which the modern definition of charitable purposes comes from is *Commissioners for Special Purposes of Income Tax v. Pemsel* (1891). In this case, Lord McNaughten identified the four heads of charity.

13　The last official figure (of more than S$300 million) on the Tote Board annual giving was provided in a parliamentary debate. Industry sources suggest that, in recent years, the Tote Board's grants have increased significantly. The amounts relative to total philanthropic giving is from *The State of Giving* (National Volunteer & Philanthropy Center, 2005.) For Tote Board, view www.singtote.gov.sg. For Esplanade, view www.esplanade.com.

14　See "Olympic Lottery Campaign" and related links at NCVO website www.ncvo-vol.org.uk/policy/index.asp?id=3852. The other three U.K. charity umbrella groups in the campaign are Voluntary Arts Network, CCPR and Heritage Link. National Lottery is at www.national-lottery.co.uk.

15　Chapter 1, "The missing hand of Adam Smith" and Chapter 20, "Doing good better," cover, in greater detail, the issues of the charity marketplace and the demand for greater accountability.

16　*Harvard University: Financial Report, Fiscal Year 2007.*

Chapter 18

Nonprofit Qwerties

Quitting Quirky Quagmires

Taking its name from the alphabet layout on the keyboard, the "qwerty effect" has come to be used in the business world to describe the practice of continuing with outdated and sub-optimal, but perhaps "good enough," methods. The reason for continuing is usually attributed to either inertia or the cost of implementing a new solution.

The nonprofit sector has its fair share of qwerties.

The fundraising efficiency ratio and other financial ratios have been created to assess the effectiveness and accountability of nonprofits. However, their use is fraught with implementation issues. Worse, they are inadequate to capture the nature and diversity of nonprofit organizations, leading to unintended and undesirable consequences.

It is a shame too, that estate duty, which has been a boost for charitable giving, is being reduced or abolished around the world. The basis for estate duty—rebalancing wealth and opportunities with each new generation—is sound, and the practical issues of enforcement, collection and acceptability can be overcome with proactive collaboration by governments.

Many of us take for granted the modern flush toilet and sewerage system, giving thanks for this boon of modern civilization. Well, while helping to build rural toilets in Sri Lanka, I was surprised to learn from the sanitation experts that the design of our modern toilet may be flawed.

As Jack Sim, founder of World Toilet Organization puts it: "God went through the trouble of designing our bodies so that the liquids and solids are separated into two different channels. And what do we do? As soon as they leave our body, we put them back together into one single receptacle! To make matters worse, we combine them with kitchen and bath water. We then create an expensive sewerage system to transport the mix over vast distances. Finally, at the end of the line, we expend a lot of energy and resources to, lo and behold, re-separate the liquids and the solids."

In dealing with the pressures of costs, space, health and water availability issues, alternative toilet solutions have emerged across the world. They range from dry toilets, where the liquids and solids are collected separately as they are discharged from the body, to various eco-san rural toilets. Sulabh, the largest toilet non-governmental organization (NGO) in India, for example, has introduced an eco-friendly, low-cost and hygienic twin-pit composting toilet that use less than two liters of water to flush, against the conventional modern toilets that require 12 to 14 liters.[1]

Most of these toilet solutions seek to cost-effectively recover the waste as source energy and yet not contaminate the surrounding environments. Despite these innovations, it would appear that none of these solutions is likely to displace the mainstream solution of the modern toilet bowl and urban sewerage system that we are all comfortable with.

You could say that the modern flush toilet is a "qwerty." It served its purpose when it was first conceived and implemented, but through widespread adoption, it continues to be in use even though certain changes made to the original solution could very well improve it. The reasons often offered for sticking with the status quo are inertia and/or the cost of implementing a different solution.

The Qwerty Effect

"Qwerty" refers to the layout of the modern-day keyboard and takes its name from the first six letters of the keyboard's top row of letters.[2] The layout was originally designed for the manual typewriter; its order was meant to prevent the most commonly used keys from jamming. Keyboard myth has it that it was designed to slow down the typing, by putting some commonly used letters such as "a" on the weaker fingers, so that the keys would not jam. Of course, modern keyboards do not suffer from the problems of older mechanical keyboards and so the raison d'être for the Qwerty layout no longer exists.

Interestingly, since the modern typewriter's invention in 1873, several other keyboard layouts have been proposed. Notable among these is the Dvorak layout which enjoyed some degree of widespread support. Several studies had shown the Dvorak layout to be more efficient and more comfortable than the Qwerty layout. Some computer manufacturers, such as Apple, even offered a dual "Dvorak-Qwerty" keyboard for a while. However, at the end of the day, the ubiquity of the Qwerty keyboard won out. The cost of the inefficient layout is much less than that of retraining typists and just about everyone in the world who are now used to a regular computer keyboard layout.

This explains why the term "qwerty effect" has come to be used, in the business world, to describe outdated and sub-optimal, but perhaps "good enough," approaches.

Well, we have our fair share of qwerties in the nonprofit sector. There are practices that have continued despite the need to change in order for the sector to move forward. I shall focus below on three such practices: fundraising efficiency; financial ratios; and estate duty.

Fundraising Efficiency

Besides making sure they achieve their fundraising targets, charities are often required by donors and regulators to be cost-effective in their fundraising.

This is often measured by taking the cost of the fundraising and dividing it by the total funds raised to create what is called the fundraising ratio. A ratio of 20 percent means that it costs 20 cents to raise $1. In some cases, the inverse ratio is used to denote the efficiency. So instead of 20 percent, the fundraising efficiency ratio, as it is called, is said to be 80 percent (100–20). So if the fundraising cost was zero, the fundraising ratio would be zero or the fundraising efficiency would be 100 percent.

What is a good ratio? A zero fundraising ratio would be the best, but that is usually not attainable unless you are, say a foundation and the money comes directly from the founding philanthropist without any effort required to secure the funds. The *Forbes'* list of the 200 largest

American charities in 2007 showed an average fundraising ratio of 10 percent.[3] nfpsynergy, a research consultancy in the U.K., found that the public's perception of an acceptable fundraising ratio was 20 percent, but the public believed that British charities were typically spending 38 percent.[4] In its annual benchmarking project, Fundratios found that the actual fundraising ratio of a group of British charities which focused on fundraising was about 13 percent in 2007.[5]

Most charity reporting standards require that the fundraising ratio or the efficiency ratio be disclosed to stakeholders by individual fundraising projects and/or the year in aggregate. In addition, many countries impose a cap on the ratio.

In Singapore, the limit imposed by the Commissioner of Charities on Institutions of a Public Character (in general, these are charities that are able to issue tax exempt receipts to donors) is 30 percent, which is why it is often known as the 30/70 Fundraising Rule.[6] Why 30 percent? I am told that it is a carryover from the 1970s when there was entertainment duty. The Customs & Excise department would waive this duty for charity shows on the condition that expenditure on the show did not exceed 30 percent of the revenue raised. Since then, this benchmark has found its way into the fundraising rules.

In Korea, the cap is 15 percent.[7] About a third of the American states impose limits ranging from 15 to 25 percent. Various charity watch groups in the U.S. (American Institute of Philanthropy, Better Business Bureau Wise Giving Alliance and Charity Navigator) seem to have a consensus on a recommended limit of 35 percent.[8]

On the other hand, Guidestar calls the fundraising ratio "the least useful of the ratios" because of the diversity of nonprofit organizations and the reality that reported fundraising expenses are not always reliable.[9]

Measuring and evaluating the fundraising efficiency makes sense to me. However, imposing a cap does not. A blanket 30 or 35 percent (or any percentage) is not a meaningful figure because a whole host of factors affect fundraising costs: the popularity of the cause, the profile of the constituency, the age of the organization, the methods used and so on.

Fundraising causes that tug at the heartstrings, such as those dealing with human suffering and children, find it easier and less costly to draw funds than, say, heritage and environmental causes. Even within human services, sudden emergencies such as the Asian tsunami or Hurricane Katrina attract more funds more easily than protracted problems such as AIDS and malaria.[10]

Size matters. Large established charities such as the United Way and the Salvation Army would typically find it easier to raise funds than their smaller counterparts which battle to not only get donors' attention but also to persuade them of their trustworthiness.

Having a ready base of supporters also helps fundraising. It would be much easier and less costly to reach out to a constituency that is already aligned with the organization, such as the alumni of a university or the congregation of a church, than seeking to fundraise from the general public.

However, among the variables that affect the relative cost of fundraising, the method of fundraising probably has the greatest impact.

Consider a charity golf tournament. It is typical to ask a golfer to contribute, say, $500 to play in a charity game. The effective cost of organizing the game and prize giving dinner could come to, say, $250 per golfer. That is a fundraising efficiency ratio of 50 percent. Is that bad? Well, if there was no golf tournament, the charity would not have received the net value of $250. A typical golf tournament (maximum of 36 flights of golfers on one 18-hole course) would not likely raise more than $60,000 to $70,000 without sponsorship.

Contrast this with the funds raised for the Lee Kuan Yew School of Public Policy. Largely as a result of "the pedigree of the man whose name the school bears," the school made waves early.[11] Even before it was officially opened in August 2004, it exceeded its fundraising target in just over three months. The cost of fundraising, in terms of the phone calls, networking meetings and so on, is likely to have been a fraction of one percent of the initial S$67 million (US$46 million) raised for the institution.

In 2007, the Lee Kuan Yew School received what was one of the largest ever donations of S$100 million (US$69 million) to an educational institution in Singapore, from Hong Kong tycoon, Li Ka-Shing. According to Professor Kishore Mahbubani, the school dean who broached the idea with the billionaire, "there is no way we could have raised $100 million from Li Ka-Shing if this was not called the Lee Kuan Yew School of Public Policy."[12]

In other words, using a single ratio does not appropriately factor in economies of scale. Donors, for example, would flip if they were told that it cost $30 million (which of course it did not), that is 30 percent (the acceptable fundraising ratio in Singapore), for the dean of the Lee Kuan Yew School of Public Policy to fly to Hong Kong to make his pitch for the $100 million.

What makes the fundraising ratio even less meaningful is that charities can, and often do, stretch accounting conventions to game the rule.[13] If a donor pays for all, or part of, the cost of the golf tournament for example, magically the fundraising ratio goes towards zero (if sponsorship costs are not added to the numerator and denominator of the fundraising ratio). There are also fundraising expenses, such as collaterals and staff costs, incurred by a charity, which can be channeled into other administrative costs buckets rather than be counted towards the costs of fundraising. Also, many charities do not allocate the costs of management and staff time to the fundraising efforts.

The fact that there are many well-established charities who do fundraising but show no fundraising costs in their reports suggests a lack of industry-wide accounting discipline in reporting fundraising costs. The *Forbes'* list of the top 200 American charities in 2007 showed 16 nonprofits with zero percent fundraising ratio.[14] Yet the websites and annual reports of these nonprofits show fundraising campaigns that include tribute cards, memorial gifts and cause marketing, so the cost of fundraising cannot be zero. As the American Institute of Philanthropy noted, "enlightened donors realize that charities who report zero fundraising costs are more likely to be advertising the poor quality of their financial reporting than their fundraising efficiency."[15]

An unintended consequence of a cap on the fundraising ratio is that it makes the cap the acceptable level. So instead of encouraging efficiency, it may encourage laxness in watching the fundraising costs if costs are clearly and safely below the radar of the fundraising ratio cap.

Since the cap is deemed acceptable, some commercial third-party fundraisers tend to use the cap as the guideline to set the success fees for their services. An investment banker called "unconscionable" the 30 percent proposal by one such professional fundraiser as the latter's cut for corporate funds raised for a charity. She commented that her own experience for similar fundraising in the commercial world was to charge five to 15 percent of funds raised. It is significant that the U.S.-based Association of Fundraising Professionals prohibits its members from taking compensation on a percentage basis.[16]

So what makes sense if 30 or 35 percent is not a good blanket figure for fundraising ratio?

My answer is not to have a limit. Under a disclosure-based regime, we would simply have clear accounting conventions on how the components of the fundraising efficiency ratio should be computed and require disclosure of fundraising efficiency for each fundraising project. Then we let the donating public judge how efficient a charity has been in its approach to fundraising.

Just as in the stock market where investors understand that margins and returns vary by industries and a range of other business factors, donors will likewise learn that they should expect different ratios for different kinds of fundraising exercises from different charities. Similarly, independent analysts, such as Charity Watch and Charity Navigator, will emerge to help donors better understand these differences.

Financial Ratios

The fundraising ratio is only one benchmark of a charity's effectiveness. In their quest for formulaic ways to conduct their due diligence, charity watchers and regulators have constructed a gamut of financial tools which have been eagerly embraced by donors and grantmakers as a litmus test of donation worthiness.

The idea of financial ratios has been adopted from the accounting and management practices of the commercial world. Thus, the majority of the financial ratios, as shown in the box "Some Financial Ratios used by Charity Watchers," bear striking similarity to what one would see in the financial analysis of a listed company.

However, there are a few ratios that reflect specific charity sector issues. Chief among them are the fundraising ratio, the reserves ratio and the program ratio. Other charity-specific ratios include the donor dependency ratio (subtract annual surplus/deficit from total donations and divide by total donations),

The fundraising ratio, probably the most maligned of all the ratios by critics, has already been covered in the previous section of this chapter.

The reserves ratio is computed by dividing the total (free) reserves by the net operating expenditure. It shows how many years a charity can last without further fundraising. The computational difficulties and debate over what constitutes a good benchmark on reserves ratio has been covered in a previous chapter.[18] In summary, outsiders of a charity frown upon too high a reserves ratio and some charities have thus sought to game the ratio. They do so by creatively defining what goes into the numerator (they can reduce it by creating and then excluding "designated funds") and the denominator (they can increase it by including fundraising expenses or by not taking into account recurring donations).

The program ratio, also known as charitable expense ratio, is computed by dividing expenses spent on the charity's programs by the total expenses. What would not be included in expenses would be fundraising costs, administration and general overhead. It thus measures how much the charity is spending on its core mission, as opposed to keeping the organization going.

Some Financial Ratios used by Charity Watchers*

- Accounts Payable Aging Indicator [(Accounts Payable x 12) ÷ Total Expenses]
  Measures creditworthiness. The lower the ratio, the faster the organization pays its bills.

- Administrative Expense Ratio [Administrative Expenses ÷ Total Expenses]
  Measures percentage of expenses spent on management and general overheads. The lower the ratio the better. If this is more than 30 percent, Charity Navigator assigns a score of zero.

- Current Ratio [Current Assets ÷ Current Liability]
  Measures ability to meet short-term obligations. Should be one or more, otherwise it could be a concern.

- Debt Ratio [Total Liabilities ÷ Total Assets]
  Indicates financial solvency. Higher ratios indicate financial problems in the future.

- Investment Rate of Return [(Investment Income + Gains — Loss — Investment Costs) ÷ Investments]
  Measures performance of investment holdings.

- Liquid Funds Indicator [{(Fund Balances — Permanently Restricted Funds — Lands, Buildings & Equipment) x 12} ÷ Total Expense]
  Measures operating liquidity. A low ratio could indicate hand-to-mouth existence while a high ratio could point to excessive savings.

- Savings Ratio [(Total Revenue — Total Expenses) ÷ Total Expense]
  Measures rate of savings and organization's longevity. However, a high ratio could also point to excessive savings.

- Solvency Ratio [Total Equity or Funds ÷ Total Assets]
  Measures ability to meet long-term obligations. Should tend towards one. Lower ratios mean charities have committed long-term spending.

* Source: Guidestar & Charity Navigator[17]

How do charities generally perform on this score? The *Forbes'* list of the 200 largest American charities in 2007 showed a range of 32 to 100 percent, with an average of 85 percent for the program ratio. Charity Navigator, which has over 5,000 American charities in its database, states that more than nine out of ten charities spend at least 65 percent on charitable expenses, while seven out of ten charities spend at least 75 percent. The National Council for Voluntary Organization indicates that 83 percent of the U.K.'s charity sector's expenditure in 2004 was accounted for by the direct delivery of missions.[19]

Donors would obviously prefer a higher program ratio. The American Institute of Philanthropy's Charity Watch indicates that a program ratio of 60 percent or greater is reasonable. The Better Business Bureau Giving Alliance specifies a higher benchmark of 65 percent. Charity Navigator, which also provides a scoring for charity, assigns a score of zero, the lowest, to any organization whose program ratio is below 30 percent.

Does using these ratios make sense? The answer is yes and no.

It is "yes" when the context in which the ratios are being used is relevant and applicable. That, in my view, would occur primarily in two situations. The first would be to use such ratios, as well as the raw financial data, to track the progress of the same organization over time. The second would be to use these ratios to compare two or more similar nonprofits, and then seek to understand the differences. The difference may not always be due to performance. For example, we would expect larger and more established organizations to enjoy economies of scale and hence, enjoy better performance ratios.

The answer is "no" when the ratios and benchmarks are used in a sweeping black/white manner without taking into account the specific nature and performance of the particular charities and context in which these ratios are applied. Unfortunately, it seems that this is how these ratios are commonly used, in a blanket way, without considering the diversity of charities.

The next natural question then is: if financial ratios are valid and widely used in the commercial world, which arguably has similar diversity in its population, why would the same approach not work in the nonprofit world?

First, while the commercial world has many different type of companies, its "bottom line" is the same: profits, sales and, ultimately, shareholder value. It is all about money. This universal language makes companies very comparable and easy to set benchmarks for.

Nonprofits, on the other hand, all have very different outcomes. They are mission-driven. Each nonprofit's mission and the measurement of how it accomplishes that mission cannot be reduced to a simple financial equation. With the diversity of their missions, defining what constitutes performance would naturally vary. Capturing this diversity through a few common benchmarks is nigh impossible.

Secondly, the commercial world has a wealth of historical experience and expertise that has been built up over time. This allows the refinement and validation of the ratios and benchmarks, and understanding how and when to apply them. Thus, when an analyst looks at the price/earnings ratio of a listed company, for example, his analysis is not based on that single ratio. Rather, he analyzes it in the context of the sector, the risks and other aspects of the company to make his buy/sell recommendation. Investors of stocks also expect that level of analysis.

Unfortunately, the charity sector does not have the same level of sophistication. Certainly, unlike investors, most donors do not have the interest or the time to do a lot of due diligence. They simply expect straightforward good/bad recommendations. Charity watchers have tended to simplify a much more diverse environment into a few ratios with little variations in order to aid understanding. This over-simplification may, in many cases, not take into account the need to properly segment the diverse charity sector. In fact, Charity Navigator has stated that its ratings are not rankings, but "qualitative designations" to help donors make informed decisions.[20]

However, with more attention and debate in this area, the use of financial ratios should hopefully improve.

Meanwhile, much needs to be done in the charity sector about improving the interpretation and definition of the ratios. The rigor and enforcement of standards here has not yet quite caught up with that of the commercial world. This creates confusion and leaves room for creatively engineering the accounts as charities seek to look good.

In the process, a study by Urban Institute and Indiana University observes that "more than being poor measures, [the unthinking use of financial ratios] threatens to lead to unintended consequences."[21] It describes these ratios as unhealthy and unfair "competition in creative accounting" that favors larger, longer established organizations and those with popular causes, and distracts regulators and watchers from dishonest charities with low costs to focus on worthwhile charities with higher costs. It concludes that the use of these financial ratios is not only misleading but harmful to nonprofits and the nonprofit sector as a whole. The study suggests that the focus of regulators, watchers and donors should be on "the question of how well nonprofits deliver their services rather than dwell on how they choose to spend their money."

Clearly, financial ratios, as they are currently being implemented, are creating a great deal of angst with good cause (no pun intended). The long-term answer is not to reject, out of hand, an otherwise sound commercial practice, but to judiciously apply ratios in the unique context in which the charity sector operates.

Estate Duty

Estate duty (or its various nomenclatures: estate tax or inheritance tax) is the levy imposed by the government on the estate of a deceased. It has long been both a source of revenue and a way of leveling wealth and opportunity.

Depending upon the jurisdiction, estate duty may be levied either at a flat (slab) rate on the whole estate, or progressively.

There are certain exemptions before estate duty kicks in. Generally, there is a qualifying amount so that less well-off families are not caught in the net. Typically, one of the properties in the estate could be exempted, subject to a ceiling on the property value, so that the family of the deceased will not be unduly burdened with having to sell the property and move out in order to pay the duty.

As we saw in an earlier chapter,[22] estate duty is good for charitable giving. This is because most tax jurisdictions would exempt gifts to charity given before or at death (left in the will). This encourages testators to give their assets to charity rather than have these taxed. A 2004 study done by the U.S. government concluded that a permanent repeal of the federal estate tax would reduce overall charitable giving by 6 to 12 percent, and that of charitable bequests by 16 to 28 percent. This is besides the US$1 trillion that would be lost in government revenues and interest payments on the national debt over the first 10 years of the repeal.[23]

Unfortunately, estate duty seems to be going the way of the dinosaur. A 2005 survey of 50 countries by PwC revealed that nearly half or 24 countries did not impose estate duty.[24] Sweden had just eliminated its estate tax. Soon after, Hong Kong followed suit in 2006 and Singapore in 2008 after some lobbying and debate.

Similar debates are taking place in other countries, and further repeals or reductions of estate duty rates can be expected. In the U.S. debate on the federal estate tax, an odd compromise has been struck. Since the tax cut legislation enacted in 2001, the top estate tax rate has been progressively reduced to 49 percent, where it will stay until 2009. At the same time, the exemption amount between 2002 and 2009 will increase. However, in 2010, under current legislation, the estate tax will be fully repealed and then resurrected a year later in 2011 with a top rate of 55 percent and an exemption amount of US$1 million. So the joke doing the rounds is that if you are a rich American, your heirs would appreciate it if your earthly departure can be timed to occur specifically in 2010. Most tax experts, however, expect the legislation to change before then.

Why the trend towards the reduction or removal of estate duty? Advocates argue on two fronts: principles and practicality.

The first argument goes like this: estate duty is unfair because it is effectively double taxation, and it becomes a disincentive for hard work. After all, the argument goes, the assets of the estate had been acquired through earned income by the deceased, for which he presumably had already paid income tax. So estate duty becomes a "double whammy" on top of income tax. Furthermore, why should any hardworking businessman struggle to build up his assets if the government takes away a large part through estate duty upon his death, rather than allow him to leave them to his descendants. In effect, "the death tax rewards a selfish 'die-broke' ethic whereby the wealthy spend down their wealth and socially beneficial intergenerational savings."[25] (Notice how the critics of the estate duty use the moniker, "death tax" because of its emotional appeal and ability to "kindle voter resentment.")[26]

When you look at the above arguments on principles, much of these are largely arguments against the principles of taxation. It is understandable that most of us do not like to pay taxes, but at the same time, we also recognize that it is an integral part of the economic system. Once we accept the need for taxation, we should accept that there is some level of "disincentive" for hard work which is necessary for the greater good. It then begs the question: at which point and at what rate do taxes become onerous and excessively discourage the work ethic?

A related question is whether estate duty is "fair" relative to other taxes. If you think about it, from a tax equity standpoint, inheritance is one income source that is not "earned." Windfalls are received by virtue of blood or other relationship. Estate duty makes for the equitable, albeit, partial redistribution of wealth back to society. Thus, Warren Buffet has called any repeal of the estate tax by the American Congress a terrible mistake, the equivalent of "choosing the 2020 Olympic team by picking the eldest sons of the gold-medal winners in the 2000 Olympics."[27]

As for the argument of double taxation, estate duty is really taxing a different taxpayer from the person who earned the money. It is taxing the heirs of the estate, people who did not originally "earn" the money. Where there are multiple tax systems, it can be argued that the taxes overlap. For example, many economies have income and consumption tax. A taxpayer who buys an item is really paying a second tax—the consumption tax, which is variously called goods and services tax, value added tax, or sales tax, with his net income by way of personal income tax. It has also been argued that in some cases, large estates comprise mostly "unrealized" capital gains that have never been taxed, and in fact, the estate duty is the only means of taxing such income.

My view therefore is that, from the standpoint of strict principle, contrary to it being unfair, estate duty is indeed the most equitable of all taxes.

Meanwhile, the arguments about the practicalities of estate duty focus on the costs to the taxpayer and the tax administration. Anecdotes of families having to liquidate their inherited assets or even their personal assets to deal with onerous estate duty and a protracted probate process are often cited to illustrate the burdens on the small man. The rich, on the other hand, are likely to have tax-planned their way out of any significant estate duty, defeating the very reason for having such inheritance taxes in the first place. In the process, estate tax has "created a large and wasteful estate-planning and avoidance industry."[28]

On the government side, tax revenues suffer since many of the rich would likely implement tax structures that avoid much of the estate duty. Those with lower assets tend to be caught in the net. However collections from this group may not fully justify the cost of tax administration for the government. The rich also have choices where they can live, and if the laws subject them to excessive estate duty, they may simply move their tax residency. So, as countries compete for the mobile rich by reducing or removing estate duty, they put further pressure on the cost/revenue equation until removing estate duty may be the only avenue that makes the most economic sense for a country.

That was the case for Singapore. To compete in a world where "wealth is being managed today on a global basis," Singapore brought its estate duty rates down from a high of 60 percent in 1984 to a top rate of 10 percent in the 2000s. It also increased its exemptions. However, these were apparently not good enough to attract the nomadic rich. In 2008, two years after Hong Kong abolished estate duty, Singapore followed suit and completely removed estate duty. The rationale was that Singapore wanted "to encourage wealthy individuals from all over Asia to bring their assets into Singapore, thus supporting the growth of the wealth management industry." It was probably not a difficult economic decision. Prior to the abolition of the estate duty, Singapore collected only S$98 million (US$68 million) in estate duties, a mere 0.4 percent of its total tax collections for that year. This is a small cost as the government expects that the scrapping of estate duty will "benefit the whole economy and society."[29]

The practical problems that arise with the enforcement and collection of estate duty may be solved with proactive global cooperation. First, the major tax jurisdictions of the world could unite on the beneficial impact of estate duty and agree to some consistent moderate rate, thus making the moving of tax domicile, for this purpose, unattractive. Secondly, governments could even agree for a part or all of estate duty to be directly channeled to charity, say, to a community foundation that gives out the money to those in need. That makes the whole idea of estate duty that much more palatable and attractive.

It is a shame, in my view, that many tax jurisdictions have either done away with estate duty, or are looking at ways of doing so. Aside from its boon to charitable giving, the basis of estate tax is sound as it rebalances wealth and opportunities with each new generation. Practical issues with respect to the enforcement, collection and acceptability of estate duty can be overcome if there is proactive collaboration by governments. After all, many of the affluent including Warren Buffet, Bill Gates Sr. and more than 100 other wealthy Americans,[30] have publicly declared their willingness to pay their fair share of taxes.

Other Nonprofit Qwerties

I asked some of my nonprofit colleagues what they consider to be other qwerties in this sector? Here are some of their examples:

- Even though charity staffs are not volunteers, we persist in paying them hugely discounted wages that value part of their time as free labor.

- The basis of giving by donors often bears little relation to the actual work done for beneficiaries. People give because of who asks, how it is being asked and so forth versus what and how the money is really used for.

- Endowments and reserves for end-beneficiary charities are considered good because they provide a sustained source of income for the charity's work. However, they require large donations that could have gone to other deserving charities and take away the need for the benefiting charity to continue to be relevant.

– Nonprofits are now being asked to generate profits, for example, through social enterprises, to provide for their existence. Why mix business and charity especially when the experience shows that failure rates are high?

– The more beneficiaries that a charity has, the more successful it is. Yet, it could also mean that the charity is dealing with the symptoms and not the root cause. The true measure of a charity should be its extinction, not its growth.

– Charities have typically been too conservative with the way they invest their assets, putting them in fixed deposits, instead of seeking a better return within managed risk parameters.

Many of these have, in fact, been covered in the other chapters in this book. Some of these may come across more as paradoxes or ironies of the nonprofit sector. It is only when we start to think in terms of "why" and "what else can we do?", with respect to what we are currently doing, that we can collectively and efficiently improve the sector.

Endnotes:

Adapted from: "Nonprofit qwerties," *SALT*, March-April 2007; and "Quirky qualities of qwerty quorums," *The Straits Times*, April 12, 2007.

1   For more information on Sulabh, see Chapter 15, "Innovating Social Change."

2   There are a number of articles about the origin of the Qwerty and Dvorak keyboards, and the Qwerty effect. A few are listed here: "The Qwerty Keyboard," Ideafinder, www.ideafinder.com/history/inventions/qwerty.htm; Richard Polt, "Typology: a phenomenology of early typewriters," The Classic Typewriter Page, http://staff.xu.edu/~polt/typewriters/typology.html; Stan Liebowitz and Stephen Margolis, "Typing Errors," *Reason*, June 1996, www.reason.com/news/show/29944.html.

3   William P. Barrett, "America's 200 largest charities," *Forbes*, November 21, 2007.

4   Joe Saxton, Michele Madden, Chris Greenwood and Brian Garvey, *The 21st Century Donor* (nfpSynergy, September 2007).

5   "Fundratios 2007—Summary Report," The Center for Interfirm Comparison with the Institute of Fundraising, www.cifc.co.uk/Fundratios07.html.

6   "Press release: Changes to 30/70 fundraising rule to facilitate fundraising efforts," The Office of the Commissioner of Charities, March 25, 2008.

7 Jung Sung-ki, "Donation rule to be relaxed," *Korea Times*, September 19, 2006, www.korea.net/News/News/NewsView.asp?serial_no=20060918030.

8 The fundraising and other ratios and standards are available as follows: American Institute of Philanthropy's Charity Rating Criteria, see www.charitywatch.org/criteria. html; BBB Wise Giving Alliance's Standards for Charity Accountability, see www. give.org/standards//newcbbbstds.asp; Charity Navigator's Ratings Table, see www. charitynavigator.org/index.cfm/bay/content.view/cpid/48.htm.

9 Chuck McLean & Suzanne E. Coffman, "Why ratios aren't the last word," Guidestar, June 2004, http://www.guidestar.org/DisplayArticle.do?articleId=850.

10 Keith Epstein, "Crisis Mentality," *Stanford Social Innovation Review*, Spring 2006.

11 Rebecca Lee, "New LKY school already making waves," *The Straits Times*, August 17, 2004; "Speech by Mr. Tharman Shanmugaratnam, Minister for Education, at the launch of the LKY SPP on Monday, August 16, 2004 at 4:00 pm at the NUS Guild Hall,"Ministry of Education, www.moe.gov.sg/media/speeches/2004/sp20040816a. htm.

12 Ho Ai Li, "Li Ka-Shing donates $100m to LKY school," *The Straits Times*, March 9, 2007; Clarissa Oon, "Telling it like it is to the West," *The Straits Times*, January 18, 2008.

13 For an example of how NKF gamed the 30/70 rule, see Chapter 19, "NKF: The saga and its paradigms."

14 William Barrett, "America's 200 largest charities," *Forbes*, November 21, 2007; Direct Relief International at www.directrelief.org.

15 "Zero fundraising costs may signify zero accountability," *Summer 2000 Watchdog Report*, American Institute of Philanthropy, 2000 at www.charitywatch.org/articles/zero.html.

16 The rule is in item 21 of "Code of Ethical Principles and Standards," Association for Fundraising Professionals, adopted 1964, last amended September 2007, at www.afpnet. org/ka/ka-3.cfm?content_item_id=1068&folder_id=897.

17 For Charity Navigator, see www.charitynavigator.org/index.cfm/bay/content.view/ cpid/48.htm. For Guidestar, see Chuck McLean & Suzanne E. Coffman, "Why ratios aren't the last word," Guidestar, June 2004, http://www.guidestar.org/DisplayArticle. do?articleId=850.

18 See Chapter 6, "The problem of plenty."

19 *The UK Voluntary Sector Almanac 2006: The State of the Sector* (National Council for Voluntary Organization). Direct charitable expense is about 67 percent and grantmaking is 15 percent of total expenditure.

20 "How do we rate charities?" Charity Navigator, www.charitynavigator.org/index. cfm?bay=content.view&cpid=35.

21 *The Nonprofit Overhead Cost Project. Brief No. 5: The pros and cons of financial efficiency standards* (Center on Nonprofits and Philanthropy of the Urban Institute, and Center on Philanthropy of the Indiana University, August 2004).

22 See Chapter 10, "Raising money from the dead."

23 Robert McClelland and Pamela Greene, "A CBO Paper: The estate tax and charitable giving," Congressional Budget Office, Congress of the United States, July 2004; *The Estate Tax: Myths and Realities* (Center on Budget and Policy Priorities, Revised October 11, 2007), www.cbpp.org/estatetaxmyths.pdf.

24 Chris Edwards, "Repealing the Federal Estate Tax," *Tax & Budget Bulletin, Cato Institute*, No. 36, June 2006.

25 Edward McCaffery, *Policy Analysis No. 353. Grave robbers: the moral case against the death tax* (Cato Institute, October 4, 1999).

26 William H. Gates, Sr. and Chuck Collins, "'Death Tax': What's in a name?," excerpted from their book, *Wealth and our Commonwealth: Why America should tax accumulated fortunes* (Beacon Press, 2002). See www.60plus.org/deathtax.asp?docID=347.

27 David Cay Johnston, "Dozens of rich Americans join in fight to retain the estate tax," *The New York Times*, February 14, 2001.

28 Chris Edwards, "Repealing the Federal Estate Tax," *Tax & Budget Bulletin, Cato Institute*, No. 36, June 2006.

29 Conrad Tan, "Analysts hail scrapping of estate duty," *The Business Times*, February 16, 2008; "Budget 2008, Extracts from Finance Minister Tharman Shanmugaratnam's Budget Speech," *The Straits Times*, February 16, 2008, Money Supplement.

30 David Cay Johnston, "Dozens of rich Americans join in fight to retain the estate tax," *The New York Times*, February 14, 2001.

Chapter 19

Case Study

NKF: The Saga and its Paradigms

As the largest and most controversial charity in Singapore for several years, the National Kidney Foundation (NKF) is replete with examples of nonprofit paradigms, and why they work or do not.

The NKF saga refers to a July 2005 scandal that followed the collapse of a defamation trial, which the NKF had brought against Singapore Press Holdings over an article the latter had published. The backlash that followed court revelations and the fallout of donors to the charity resulted in the resignation of and subsequent law suits against its chief executive officer (CEO) and some of its board members. A new board of directors and CEO then went on to overhaul the charity. Meanwhile, regulatory reforms were implemented in the charity sector.

This chapter provides context to the NKF saga and describes how the various paradigms covered in the other chapters of this book apply to the NKF.

The story of the National Kidney Foundation of Singapore (NKF) is hard to avoid. After all, it is, in many ways, Singapore's largest charity—highly visible, controversial and a prime example of many nonprofit paradigms.

Rather than to constantly use the NKF as an example in the previous chapters, I have sought to minimize the references and gather them all in this chapter as a case study of the various (but not all) charity paradigms.

Readers unfamiliar with the events will need a more complete context. Therefore, I shall briefly summarize the relevant history before covering the many paradigms which this case illustrates.

The NKF Saga

Table 19.1 summarizes the key dates and events leading to, and after, the NKF saga.

The NKF was set up in 1969 to respond to the high cost of dealing with kidney diseases. Since then, it has helped thousands of kidney patients through its 24 state-of-the-art dialysis centers. In early 2008, it was treating about 2,300 dialysis patients.

The rise of the NKF from the early 90s was due largely to the drive of one man, Thambirajah Thamadurai, better known as T.T. Durai. He quit the legal practice to join the NKF as its chief executive officer (CEO) in 1992 and quickly turned the organization into a credible and high-profiled charity with very effective fundraising appeals, a sizeable well-paid staff and an award-winning 12-storey headquarters building. Under his charge, the NKF rolled out new dialysis centers, expanded research, and branched out internationally and into new areas.

The NKF's success was not without its detractors. There was disquiet in the charity sector about its controversial fundraising methods and its perceived extravagance for a charity. Durai was sensitive about protecting his reputation and the NKF's. He took legal action against three people separately for having claimed that he flew first class on official NKF business trips and other allegations.[1] All three settled in the NKF's favor, although they were later vindicated.[2] However, Durai's penchant for suing[3] would lead to his downfall.

In April 2004, *The Straits Times*, Singapore's national newspaper, ran articles on two controversial topics. The first was the NKF-Aviva commercial tie-up, where the NKF would promote Aviva insurance products in exchange for sponsorship money and a cut of the premiums.[4] A week later, it started covering the NKF's high reserves of S$189 million (US$ 130 million).[5] Both topics attracted readers' response, much of it negative.

With the growing public interest, *The Straits Times* senior writer Susan Long wrote a feature piece titled, "The NKF: Controversially Ahead Of Its Time?" which was published on April 19, 2004. While the article was positive about the NKF's achievements, it also highlighted its lack of transparency and public accountability. The NKF promptly sued Singapore Press Holdings (SPH),[6] the publisher of *The Straits Times* and Susan Long for being defamatory, especially in relation to the article's lead-in story about the contractor who "lost it" when he was asked to install a gold-plated tap in Durai's office en suite toilet.[7]

Despite overtures and multiple opportunities to settle as the case awaited trial for more than a year, Durai and the NKF chose to go to court.[8] The court case that took place in July 2005 was originally scheduled for 10 days of hearings, but it lasted only two. At the end of the second day, Durai decided to withdraw his case "in the best interests of NKF, its supporters, donors and patients."[9]

However, it was too late. The revelations in court of Durai's $600,000 (US$414,000) annual salary, the fact that he did, in fact, fly first class and other eye-openers provoked a swift backlash that was quite un-Singaporean. The NKF's headquarters was vandalized. 6,800 donors cancelled their contributions. 18,000 signed online petitions, calling for Durai's resignation.

Two days after the court hearings ended, T.T. Durai and the board of directors of the NKF did just that—they resigned en masse. Six days later, the Minister of Health announced a new board of distinguished members led by Gerard Ee,[10] a well-known and respected public accountant and charity leader. The new board brought in an interim CEO and nine months later, appointed a new CEO.[11]

Calling itself "The New NKF," the new board and management set out to put things right. In its first two years, it achieved the following:

– Restructured the NKF and cut costs. Its manpower decreased from 1,000 to 630, with the reductions coming from non-clinical staff. The resulting savings amounted to S$3.4 million (US$2.3 million) annually.

– Built two more dialysis centers for needy clients.

– Improved patient service with a holistic rehabilitation program, and reduced dialysis charge by 35 percent.

Table 19.1 NKF Saga Key Dates and Events

The NKF Saga—Key Dates & Events	
Early History	
Apr 7, 1969	The NKF established by Dr. Khoo Oon Teik, a nephrologist and his friends.
Sep 1982	The NKF opens its first dialysis center at Kwong Wai Shiu Hospital.
Feb 1992	T.T. Durai becomes CEO of the NKF.
Feb 1995	The NKF moves to its new headquarters in Kim Keat Road.
Jun 1998	The NKF establishes the first Kidney Resource Center with its 14th dialysis center in Aljunied.
Apr 2001	The televised NKF Charity Show achieves several firsts in Singapore's fundraising history, with more than S$11.6 million (US$8 million) raised through 1.8 million phone calls and 447,000 SMS (cellphone text message) donations.
2001–2002	The National Council of Social Service refuses to renew the NKF's status as an Institution of a Public Character (IPC).
	The Ministry of Health takes over and renews the NKF's IPC status.
Oct 2001	The NKF Children's Medical Fund is set up.
Nov 2004	The NKF Cancer Fund is set up.
The Lawsuits	
Aug 1997	NKF volunteer Archie Ong is sued for defamation, for claiming that T.T. Durai flew first class and that the NKF squandered monies.
Dec 1998	Piragasam Singaravelu is sued for defamation for claiming to see T.T. Durai in the first class cabin of a Singapore Airlines flight.

Apr 1999	Tan Kiat Noi is sued for her email that said the NKF did not help the poor and needy, and that NKF staff were paid high bonuses. 48 others who forwarded the email are threatened with legal action.
Apr 2004	*The Straits Times* of SPH Group carries stories on the NKF-Aviva tie-up and the NKF's reserves level. It also publishes an article by Susan Long, "The NKF: Controversially ahead of its time?"
	The NKF and Durai file a defamation suit against SPH and Susan Long over Long's article.
11–12 Jul 2005	Court hearing of the defamation suit by the NKF against SPH and Susan Long ends abruptly, with the NKF withdrawing the case.
Aftermath	
Jul 2005	Negative public reaction to the court revelations.
	T.T. Durai and the NKF Board resign en masse.
	The Minister of Health announces a new Board.
Dec 2005	KPMG issues investigation report on the NKF's past practices.
Oct 2005– Mar 2006	Inter-Ministry Committee formulates recommendations on charity reforms which are accepted and implemented by the Government.
Nov 2006	The Inland Revenue Authority of Singapore reports tax irregularities in the old NKF.
Mar 2007	Charities Act amendments enacted.
Apr 2006– Jun 2007	Durai and two former board members face criminal charges and are convicted.
Apr 2006– Feb 2007	Durai and three former board members face a civil suit taken by the New NKF. All four concede liability.
May 2007	All three former board members are declared bankrupt.
May–Sep 2007	Former NKF chairman, Richard Yong becomes a fugitive but is arrested. He is sentenced to 15 months jail.
Jun 2008	Durai starts three months jail term after losing appeal.

- Increased community outreach through volunteer programs and open house events.

- Sought to clarify the reserves position, and transferred S$27.2 million (US$19 million) of non-dialysis designated funds to other charities.

- Improved corporate governance and transparency through the adoption of leading accounting and reporting guidelines.[12]

When the new board took office, it also called in the Commercial Affairs Department of the Singapore Police Force and commissioned KPMG, one of the big four public accounting firms, to conduct a thorough investigation into the NKF's past practices. On December 16, 2005, KPMG published a 442-page report (the "KPMG Report") that revealed numerous malpractices, a lack of meaningful governance and wasted opportunities by regulators to commence investigations earlier.[13]

As a result of the KPMG Report and further investigations, Durai and several former board members then faced several criminal and civil suits:

- In April 2006, Durai was charged under the Prevention of Corruptions Act for submitting false invoices for consultancy services that were never rendered. In June 2007, he was found guilty and sentenced to three months jail. He started the jail term in June 2008 after losing his appeal against the conviction.[14]

- At the same time, the former chairman Richard Yong and former treasurer Loo Say San faced criminal charges for failing in their duties as directors, particularly in relation to a botched Forte Systems computer software deal worth S$4.3 million (US$3 million). In May 2007, they were found guilty. Both escaped jail sentences but were each fined S$5,000 (US$3,500).[15]

- In April 2006, the New NKF board also brought a civil suit against Durai and three former board members, Richard Yong, Loo Say Sun and Matilda Chua, to recover S$12 million (US$ 8 million) for alleged breach of fiduciary duties.[16]

- On January 10, 2007, after three days of court hearings on the civil suit, Durai conceded that he had breached his duties as CEO and de facto director through mismanagement of the charity. He struck a settlement to repay the NKF S$4 million (US$2.8 million) over four years.[17]

– A month later, Yong, Loo and Chua conceded that they had abdicated their duties as directors of the NKF by leaving its operations in the hands of Durai. Full damages were to be assessed later in the year. However, the three were unable to pay both legal costs and certain damages that did not need to be assessed later. Consequently, all three were declared bankrupt on May 16, 2007.[18]

– The day after the bankruptcy order, Richard Yong fled to Hong Kong. It transpired that he had been disposing of his personal properties worth S$7.5 million (US$5.2 million) since February 2007. He was arrested on July 4, 2007, extradited and booked for criminal charges under the Penal Code and Bankruptcy Act. On September 18, 2007, Yong pleaded guilty and was sentenced to 15 months in jail.[19]

Following the NKF court case, the government formed, in October 2005, an Inter-Ministry Committee on the Regulation of Charities and Institutions of a Public Character (IPCs) to overhaul the charity regulatory framework. The Committee made its recommendations in January 2006.[20] After three months of public consultation, the government accepted the final recommendations, and the implementation of regulatory and other changes were effected from July 2006.[21]

The NKF saga left an indelible mark on Singapore and Singaporeans. It catalyzed major changes in the regulation of charities and raised public awareness of charity accountability. Without doubt, it was the disruptive force that triggered the tidal wave of charity reform in Singapore.[22]

Paradigms in Play

In the remainder of this chapter, I will discuss the NKF case in relation to the various paradigms described in the earlier chapters. The numbering of the paradigms follows the chapter numbering. Note that not all paradigms are covered since not all of them apply to this case. I have also assumed that the reader is already familiar with the paradigms as described in the respective chapters.

1. The Nonprofit Marketplace

The paradigm of the nonprofit marketplace, if we can call it a "marketplace," refers to the structural disconnect that occurs between the revenue and expenses of charities. It happens because givers respond to fundraising based on factors other than the true value of services delivered to beneficiaries.

The disproportionate size and financial success of the NKF compared to the Kidney Dialysis Foundation (KDF), despite both having the same cause, proves the point.[23] The NKF's fundraising success was due to very polished and focused efforts at understanding and catering to donor motivations. Its methods may have been controversial[24] but they were very effective in pulling in the donations.

For the annual televised NKF Charity Show, the NKF relied on two key elements to reel in the money: tearful and heart-wrenching testimonies by select patients and their families, and a lucky draw with large prizes[25] where the winning chances increased with the size of donations. In 2003, it raised a high of S$15.7 million (US$10.8 million). The NKF also offers free health screening services to the public. However, this has been seen by some as a barely disguised recruitment for Lifedrops, the NKF's sustained giving program.[26] At its peak, Lifedrops had about 300,000 donors contributing more than S$25 million (US$17 million) a year through monthly bank deductions.[27] Those who are on the NKF's mailing list will attest to the wonderfully personalized letters sent with their names mentioned several times, in the appeal or in appreciation for a donation.

The disconnect between revenue (what donors gave) and expenses (what it actually was spent on) at the NKF became evident later. (This is covered under "18. Nonprofit Qwerties.") Yet, in a way, you could also argue that the "marketplace" did work to some extent. Competition appeared for the NKF. The KDF was set up in 1996 by Dr. Gordon Ku, a kidney specialist in private practice, to fill what it saw as a gap in the NKF's service—helping only poor and needy patients since the NKF took on the full spectrum of patients, including full-paying patients.[28]

The old-fashioned approach of having another provider in the arena probably helped to raise standards and coverage of kidney patients. For one, dialysis rates for patients have come down over the years. However, despite its much greater economies of scale, the NKF, just before the saga was charging S$210 (US$145) per dialysis session for each patient while the KDF was only charging S$136 (US$94). When the new board took over, the New NKF reduced costs and brought dialysis charges down to S$130 (US$90) per session,[29] marginally below the KDF's.

Thus, while the competition provided by the KDF is useful to an extent, it cannot fully overcome the structural disconnect between revenue and expense for charities. For the nonprofit marketplace to function better, the paradigms of informed giving and charity governance must come into play.

2. *Informed Giving*

Informed giving means asking donors to be more discerning, discriminating and demanding of the charities they support. It is more practically achieved if donations can be channeled through grantmakers rather than come directly from the individual givers.

Looking back at the history of the NKF, it is clear that most donors did not operate on an informed basis. While this is to be generally expected of individual donors, in the NKF's case, donors were blindsided. Most were taken in by the slickness of the NKF's fundraising appeals. Even for those who did wish to understand how the organization operated or how it used its funds, there was inadequate information provided and in some cases, misinformation was provided as revealed by the KPMG Report.

A positive outcome of the case has been an increased awareness of the need to exert the hand of the donor. Both the public and charities themselves are now much more sensitized to the importance of informed giving. Surveys show that, after the scandal, donors were asking more discerning questions about the charities they supported, and how the funds donated were being used.[30] Fortunately, public confidence has not been so shaken as to affect the overall donation level. In the year of the scandal, overall donations actually increased but, interestingly, the proportion of the giving had shifted from individual giving to more institutionalized giving (including the grantmakers).[31] This would be moving the sector in the right direction.

3. *Nonprofit Governance*

Nonprofit governance exists at three levels:

- corporate governance
- regulation
- public opinion

With respect to the governance of the NKF, there were lapses in all three levels.

The first level, corporate governance, was present in form but not in substance. At the NKF, there was a board of directors and a proliferation of committees, such as Finance and Audit, that should have provided the necessary checks and balances required. The NKF also voluntarily accepted the *Code of Governance & Management for Voluntary Welfare Organizations* put out by the National Council of Social Service (NCSS) and indicated that it went beyond the code of best practices. However, these structures were merely a façade, giving the picture of good governance.

In its report, KPMG concluded that "there was no truly effective governance mechanism capable of challenging executives in their management of the business, and re-directing the NKF to its true purpose as and when needed." The board was largely ineffective because it delegated all its power to the Executive Committee, which in turn delegated almost all that power to Durai. KPMG went on to identify a litany of corporate excesses, conflicts of interest and accounting manipulations.

The subsequent criminal and civil suits illustrate the importance of fiduciary duty and care owed by the governing directors of an organization. However, the suits were only taken against three of the former directors: chairman Richard Yong, treasurer Loo Say San and Matilda Chua. They were the more active directors. There is the outstanding question of the extent of liability of directors who are not active and may have been there essentially to lend their name to a charitable cause. The former directors who were charged initially sought to bring in the entire former board, by naming the remaining four former directors as third parties in the suit. However, claims against three were dismissed with costs, while the defendants settled with the fourth.[32]

Interestingly, the NKF had changed its organizational form in 2001 from that of a society to a company limited by guarantee. The reasons for this move are not known. In general, a company structure allows easier concentration of power in a few people and is less transparent than a society. However, the duties and liabilities of directors are viewed as greater than that of elected officials of a society, which the former directors may have belatedly realized when they were charged.

While the three ex-directors may have been charged, there are some in the sector who feel that the price was too high. To be sure, the three enjoyed the trappings of luxury during their tenure as directors, but all of them have been made bankrupt and they will likely be socially ostracized. Their "sin" was failing to properly understand the role of a director and consequently delegating all their powers to, and following the directions of, the CEO. As a result of what these directors have gone through, would-be directors are now more conscious of the demands of directorships. In fact, this has also discouraged some from taking on governing positions in charities.

Durai had not set himself up as a director. Instead, though he was the one who made decisions on issues such as his own compensation, he was careful to arrange for them to come officially from the board. In other words, though he was not legally calling the shots, he was behind the scenes and for this reason, the New NKF took the position that Durai though "not formally a director, was a 'shadow' and 'de facto' director, and thus is just as liable as if he were an appointed director."[33]

There is also an expectation in corporate governance circles that auditing is a crucial part of the governance process. PwC (and its predecessor firm Coopers & Lybrand) was the external auditor of the NKF from 1988 to 2004, and its internal auditor from 1995 to 1998. Arthur Andersen took over the internal audit until 2002, and subsequently the function reverted to in-house.

Following KPMG's report of the NKF's financial lapses, the Minister of Health said that PwC had been found wanting and he was disappointed with their job. PwC's response was that it had discharged its primary responsibility of giving its opinion on the NKF financial statements.[34] A common misunderstanding by the public is the extent to which an auditor is supposed to be able to uncover fraud and malpractices, especially when these are deliberately concealed.

Prior to the NKF case, it was not uncommon for audit firms to take on the audit of charities as a case of, well, charity. That is to say, they delivered pro bono services or else charged discounted rates. Since the NKF saga, there has been a clear steering away from auditing charities, especially by the larger, more renowned public accounting firms.[35]

The second level of governance of a charity is regulation.

Prior to the NKF saga, the Commissioner of Inland Revenue doubled as the Commissioner of Charities, and the regulation of certain charities was devolved to 11 Central Fund Administrators. Two of these are the NCSS (for volunteer welfare organizations) and the Ministry of Health (for health-related charities).

The NKF had IPC (Institution of a Public Character) status. This allows a charity to issue tax-exempt receipts to donors. From 1995, the NKF came under the regulatory ambit of the NCSS. As part of its regulatory review, the Council brought to the NKF's attention several concerns with its administration and subsequently withdrew its IPC status in December 2001. In January 2002, the NKF was re-granted IPC status by the Ministry of Health for what KPMG termed an "unusual" period of three years since the NCSS was only prepared to do so for three months at a time.

The KPMG Report concluded that with the number of regulatory bodies involved (the Commissioner of Charities, the NCSS and the Ministry of Health), "there is no straightforward answer to the question as to whether and which or any of these bodies was responsible for more extensive audits of the operations of the NKF to ferret out earlier the abuses that we have learned of in our investigation." However, KPMG felt that there were sufficient triggers that the abuses could perhaps have been "either prevented or addressed some four years earlier." The Minister of Health, in responding to the report, accepted KPMG's sharp comments and acknowledged that "regulators could have done better."[36]

The Inter-Ministry Committee's recommendations for a revised regulatory framework included an approach based on self-regulation, a full time Commissioner of Charities with enhanced authority and the rationalization of the eleven Central Fund Administrators into six Sector Administrators. These recommendations were effected from July 2006.

That the NKF saga has resulted in an improvement of the regulatory framework for the charity sector cannot be doubted. That said, the changes have not been drastic and have not gone as far as to rationalize some of the myriad regulations that charities still have to follow.

The final level of governance lies with the community, through public opinion.

You could say that this level of governance kicked in after the SPH court case when it became evident that misinformation had been previously provided. Durai had maintained immediately after the court case that he did nothing wrong and saw no reason to step down.[37] However, the public furor became too obvious and too much, and he and the Board resigned two days later.

While that might have been the ultimate level of governance playing out, the discomfort with the NKF had been on the ground for a long time through "coffee-shop talk" and "published and unpublished feedback."[38] In part, it was the threat of the NKF's defamation suits and the support— even public praises of the NKF—from respected public figures that kept the situation going.[39]

A survey conducted by the National Volunteer & Philanthropy Center a year after the case erupted showed that while public confidence in charities had dropped from 55 percent to 28 percent, it has also sensitized the public to be more aware of the role it has to play.[40] Perhaps a future NKF situation is less likely to simmer for as long before it surfaces and gets corrected.

4. Regulation

In this paradigm, the regulator may position charities as trusted institutions with the government's seal of approval (the black box model) or as organizations that need to be transparent in a *caveat emptor* (buyer/donor beware) marketplace (the glass house model).

Both models are valid. In Singapore's context, the black box model is akin to the banking supervision provided by the Monetary Authority of Singapore, and the glass house model is akin to the public markets under the supervision of the Singapore Exchange.

It could be argued that before the NKF scandal came to light, the Singapore charity scene was operating on the black box model. Hence, the public outcry and calls for government accountability after the case broke.[41] Relying on the government is also a typical Singaporean trait.

However, the response and messages from the authorities suggest that the charity environment had been operating, and should continue to operate, on the glass house model. Political leaders have said that charities should run themselves and there should be self-governance.[42] The Inter-Ministry Committee report emphasized that the sector should be driven by the community, and that the revised regulatory framework should encourage self-regulation.

At the same time, the new regulations endow the regulator with increased duties and powers.[43] These include the power to suspend fundraising during an investigation prior to knowing the outcome, and to bar trustees from standing for elections. Such powers are extreme and would go against the grain of a glass house model of self-regulation and *caveat emptor*. If exercised, they should at least be done with due process and public accountability.

Perhaps part of the need for the authorities to reserve such powers is that the charity scene is not yet fully ready for a full glass house approach. Certainly, there is a noticeable increase in the public awareness of charities and what informed giving involves, but this is not yet prevalent. The tools and support infrastructure of extensive information sharing, charity watchers and a rating system which the Inter-Ministry Committee has already recommended, have not yet been put in place. More time will be needed.

Meanwhile, Singapore has drawn a line in the sand to adopt a glass house-based approach of self-regulation. Hopefully, over time, charities and the public will wean themselves from being over-dependent on the authorities to keep matters in check and work towards a stronger, more independent charity sector.

5.   Nonprofit Mission

In the business world, the paradigm is growth—of profits and shareholder value. On the other hand, nonprofits should be mission-driven, and hence their paradigm should be extinction, then its mission would be accomplished. But all too often, nonprofits get distracted by opportunities for growth and veer from their stated mission.

In that sense, the NKF was a typical nonprofit that was focused on growth. In the wake of its fundraising success, it ventured into non-kidney causes—children and cancer. In October 2001, it started the NKF Children's Medical Fund to provide subsidies for treatments and care for chronically ill children. In November 2004, it started the NKF Cancer Fund[44] to support needy patients undergoing cancer treatment. It held two television fundraisers in 2004 and 2005, using its usual and successful format to raise money for both these funds.

When the New NKF board took over, it decided that it should focus on the "core function of providing assistance and support to patients suffering from kidney failure."[45] It therefore dissolved the two funds and transferred the money to other relevant organizations: about S$2.95 million (US$2 million) to the Singapore Cancer Society in November 2005, and S$24.2 million (US$17 million) to the Singapore Children's Society in November 2006.[46]

In setting up the two funds, the NKF had not just entered two new healthcare areas (cancer and children's health), it extended its function to grantmaking as well. Since its inception, the NKF had primarily been an operational charity. Having the term "foundation" in its name was only a namesake; the NKF was not a grantmaker. With the two funds, it became more of a foundation by giving to the Rainbow Center, Spastics Children's Association of Singapore and others.

The NKF also sought to venture overseas. It helped the Samoan government to set up the Samoan Kidney Foundation-NKF Dialysis Center in early 2005.

The point is, the NKF's core mission relates to kidney care. In order to achieve its mission and become "extinct," its programs should probably have the following order of priority:

1. Education on kidney problems and prevention
2. Early screening of potential patients for kidney issues
3. Promotion and support of kidney donation and transplants
4. Support of peritoneal dialysis treatments
5. Support of hemodialysis treatments

In all fairness, the NKF was involved, at various degrees, in all five areas. However, it was the level of emphasis of the respective areas that was questioned. There were views, for example, that it could have promoted and supported peritoneal dialysis more than it did—which is what its much smaller competitor, the KDF, did.

In hemodialysis treatment, the patient is hooked up to a machine at a dialysis center three times a week for about four hours each time. The machine removes the blood from the body, cleans it and then returns it via tubes inserted into the veins.

Peritoneal dialysis, on the other hand, is done by the patients themselves. Dialysis fluid is fed through a small tube surgically inserted into the abdomen to clean the blood. The fluid is then drained after it extracts toxins and waste water. This is done either manually for about 30 minutes four times a day, or by a machine hooked up to the bed each time for about 10 hours every night.

Peritoneal dialysis is deemed more convenient and is cheaper than hemodialysis, although not all patients can undergo this treatment. The New NKF is now placing greater emphasis on facilitating transplants and peritoneal dialysis. Between January 2006 and July 2007, the New NKF nearly tripled the number of peritoneal dialysis beneficiaries from 68 to 198. It also helped 63 transplanted patients during that period.

It remains to be seen whether the New NKF will prove to be fully successful in meeting its core mission and finally become "extinct." In the meantime, the NKF saga has helped the organization to refocus and to take the necessary steps in the right direction of extinction rather than growth for growth's sake.

6.   Reserves

The debate over the NKF reserves reflects the conundrum common to charities with the happy "problem of plenty":

– Should the charity proactively disclose its reserves, and if so, what, when and how should it disclose it?

– What is an acceptable reserves ratio?

– How does one measure the different components of the reserves ratio?

One of the initial triggers of public concern with the NKF in 2004 was the disclosure of its reserves of S$189 million (US$ 130 million). Now, technically, based on the broad-brush calculation used at that time, this amount of reserves translated to only about three and a half years of its stated S$53.4 million (US$36.8 million) annual operating expenditure. This fell well below the NCSS' guideline of a maximum of five years of reserves. Yet, there was a lot of noise over what should be an acceptable reserves ratio. Why?

First, there was, at the time, no widely communicated understanding of a reserves ratio, let alone an acceptable reserves level.

Secondly, and more importantly, the absolute size of the reserves and the amount of funds raised each year by the NKF were seen by many to be staggering. S$189 million was just a lot of money for the man in the street. The NKF's sin was, therefore, in not highlighting its reserves upfront. Instead, the disclosure was made by the press.

In the NKF's defense, it probably had concerns, like many charities with high reserves, that disclosure whether proactively done or not, would chase donors away anyway. That said, there were many in the charity sector who felt that the sum of over S$67 million (US$46 million) that the NKF raised each year was out of proportion to the number of its beneficiaries, which was about 1,800 dialysis patients (although different numbers of up to 3,000 had been quoted by the NKF officials at that time). In contrast, the Community Chest raises about S$45 to 50 million (US$31 to 35 million) annually, and yet it provides for more than 350,000 beneficiaries across more than 60 Voluntary Welfare Organizations.

Certainly, there were several fundraisers and charities who felt strongly that the NKF was channeling away much-needed funds from others in the charity sector. So they joined in the mêlée.

Till today, the question of the reserves ratio, exactly how long the NKF's reserves could last, remains a point of contention. The range of numbers from a low of three years to a high of 40 years, quoted by various experts and those involved, largely reflects the lack of industry agreement on what constitutes the components of the reserves ratio.

Attention began to focus on the reserves ratio when figures quoted were torn apart by the defense counsel in the SPH defamation suit. The defense argued that since the NKF only subsidized dialysis patients to the tune of S$7.2 million (US$5 million) a year after netting out patient fees and other income, its reserves (which had by then risen to S$262 million or US$181 million) would last it somewhere between 30 to 40 years (262 / 7.2 = 36) if it were to focus only on its core mission of kidney dialysis. Indeed, during the trial, Durai conceded that the previous figure of three years of reserves was incorrect.[47]

For its part, KPMG concluded that the reserves could last 2.35 or 4.6 or 11.9 years depending upon what was taken into account:

- 2.35 years if the S$180.8 million (US$125 million) of reserves available for dialysis, excluding other designated funds, were used to fund the total annual operating expenses of S$77.1 million (US$53 million).

- 4.6 years if the S$180.8 million (US$125 million) of reserves were used to fund adjusted annual operating expenses (by excluding fundraising and non-dialysis activities costs), but assuming no dialysis income, which would mean patients were 100 percent subsidized for dialysis care.

- 11.9 years if the S$180.8 million (US$125 million) of reserves were used to fund net annual operating expenses, after excluding further fundraising and non-dialysis activities, and netting out its regular dialysis income, of S$15.2 million (US$10 million).

Just prior to the release of KPMG's report, the New NKF board stated that its reserves should last 6.7 years based on the following analysis:[48]

- Of its total reserves of S$260.3 million (US$180 million) as of October 31, 2005, only S$206.2 million (US$142 million) would be available for the NKF's dialysis operations. The remaining was designated for other purposes.

- Its net annual operating expenses was S$30.8 million (US$21 million) after taking into account the continuation of LifeDrops, its sustained giving program, new government subsidy for dialysis treatment, no more fundraising expenditure, expected cost of inflation and increases in patient numbers.

The New NKF board had computed the reserves ratio using a hybrid liberal-conservative approach. It was liberal (results in a higher ratio—less presentable to donors) by netting out the fundraising expenses and taking in new government subsidy. However, it was conservative (results in a lower ratio—more presentable to donors) by estimating future costs and patient increases, and not taking into account the significant investment income that could be generated from its capital reserves. The conservative aspects of the approach and the New NKF board's statement that it would ideally like 10 years of reserves ("since 57 percent of its patients survive beyond 10 years")[49] did not sit well in some quarters.[50]

There are two conclusions from the NKF reserves debate. First, while the reserves ratio is more important, the absolute level of reserves, if significant, can generate donor reluctance towards a charity. Secondly, the current state of accounting for reserves leaves room for varying presentation of reserves and reserves ratio.

7. Executive Compensation

In the paradigm of executive staff compensation, I made two observations:

- Charity sector pay is typically lower than that of the private sector.

- The gap between private and charity sector pay is due to two factors: a heart factor reflecting the noble spirit of altruism and a head factor for the environmental aspect of slower pace and less demanding expectations.

Were the NKF staff salaries lower than the private sector's? While there were rumors of high wages and bonuses of staff[51] and the KPMG Report provided instances of fundraising staff who received significant and multiple increments in a short space of time,[52] the information available only allows us to make good guesses with regards to Durai's compensation.

In the SPH court case, it was revealed that Durai made S$600,000 (US$414,000) a year. That was based on his declaration in court that he received 12 months bonus on a monthly salary of S$25,000 (US$17,000) per month (25,000 x 24 = 600,000). KPMG's report showed that Durai's compensation was more involved than that. In addition to eight to 12 months bonus, there was overtime payment, leave encashment, personal benefits and back-dated pay increases. In his last two years with the NKF, he should therefore have been paid more than S$600,000 a year on average, but it is not clear from the KPMG report how much higher the final amount would be.

Nevertheless, using the S$600,000 as the annual compensation to benchmark, where is the pay in relation to the market? There were a few who felt that it was fair wages for the size of the NKF's operation and its performance.[53] Also, Durai did get a job two years after he stepped down to start a firm at S$25,000 per month,[54] proving that he could command that monthly salary, albeit with a different scope and the bonus package being unknown. However, benchmarking Durai's compensation to Singapore's charity sector, it would be a clear outlier. Even if we used a more generous yardstick of the salaries of nonprofit CEOs from the U.S. or the U.K. where nonprofit compensation is generally higher, it would also be significantly outside the salary survey benchmark range of US$54,000 to US$290,000,[55] and £68,500 (US$137,000)[56] respectively.

So, there is no question of explaining whether the pay gap is due to a heart or head factor as the pay is outside the range. In fact, because the compensation is perceived to be much greater than what it should or needed to be, there is a "negative" heart factor. Instead of taking a "discount" on his compensation for charity work, Durai was receiving a "premium." Hence, the eruption of donors' anger when his compensation was first disclosed.

9.   The Charity Quotient

In the charity quotient model, there are two dimensions of charitableness: the external manifestation and the internal motivation. Juxtaposing the two dimensions, we have four different kinds of givers: the Little Giver, the Value Giver, the Latent Giver and the Virtuous Giver.

Which quadrant would the NKF's donors fit into?

The NKF donor base is large. Two in three Singaporeans are said to have contributed to the NKF, including many low-income families who bought into the appeals.[57] Let us examine the two dimensions of giving for the NKF donors.

For the external dimension on the level of giving, the data available does not allow for comparison of the NKF donor base with that of the national average. However, it may be useful to compare the NKF's Lifedrops program with the Community Chest's SHARE program. Both are sustained giving programs targeted at broadly the same constituency of wage earners. SHARE has about 200,000 donors, averaging nearly S$5 per donor per month.[58] At its peak, Lifedrops had nearly 300,000 donors with monthly contributions at nearly S$7 per donor.[59] On average, it would seem that the Lifedrops donor gave at least a third more than the SHARE contributor.

For the internal dimension, donor motivations would be mixed as one would expect with a large donor population base. For the NKF's TV spectaculars, those who responded did so either because they were attracted by the large prizes offered lottery-like for the donor calls (selfish motivation), or they were persuaded by the heart-rending stories of the beneficiaries (selfless motivation). While many who responded to the Lifedrops program may have done so out of a sense of obligation after a free health screening, the fact is that most of them continue doing so for years. This has given Lifedrops a donor base much larger than SHARE, even though the latter is almost a national scheme supported by employers. The many others who responded to the NKF appeal letters did so because of the well-crafted messages on the plight of the beneficiaries.

On balance, it would seem that more donors responded out of the goodness of their hearts than expecting something in return. Thus, the sense of betrayal and outrage by donors when they learned that they had been deceived. The NKF may have understood and exploited donors' motivations to be as successful with fundraising as it was, but it should also have taken heed of an old Chinese saying on motivations: that a man would rather give $100 to charity than be cheated of $1.

I concluded in Chapter 9 that most givers are Little Givers (Q1). Based on the above analysis, I would hazard a guess that the NKF donors are generally closer to the right and up of the chart compared to the average Singaporean giver. This means they tend towards the Virtuous Givers quadrant (Q4), uninformed and misinformed as they may have been.

10. Planned Giving

Planned giving refers to bequests and other charitable gifts that are planned with forethought and usually effected upon the donor's death.

The NKF's first major bequest was a S$700,000 (US$483,000) flat left by Rosslyn Mak, a teacher at a child-care center who died of cancer.[60] That gift probably led the NKF to start a formal NKF Planned Giving program in late 1998.

In the early 2000s, it supported this program in its collaterals and included announcements by live donors of their planned gifts.[61] In 2001, the NKF announced that it had received S$1.4 million (US$1 million) from nine benefactors. In 2003, it received its single largest bequest from Madam Chia Fong Ying. She had left S$3.4 million (US$2.3 million) to be shared equally between the NKF and the Community Chest.[62]

While little other information has been provided, the NKF's planned giving program is, in my view, probably the most proactive and successful in Singapore. The NKF said that it was receiving about 20 enquiries a month, even prior to the formal launch of its NKF Planned Giving Program.[63] That the response has, to date, not been significant, is more the result of the limitations in our environment: low estate duty (which was abolished in 2007), and an Asian culture that frowns upon discussions of death.

13. *Volunteerism*

In the paradigm on volunteerism, volunteers should be viewed as more than just "free labor" to charities. Charities should recognize the non-economic value of volunteering, much of it being engagement with the community. Thus, charities may use volunteers even when it can afford to hire staff to do it and volunteers cost more than staff.

Under Durai, the NKF had little room for volunteers. Which was a bit surprising, seeing that he himself was an NKF volunteer for two decades before he came on board full-time as its CEO. On the other hand, the NKF did not need much by way of "free labor" as it was well endowed with funds, and staff were likely viewed as more accountable and compliant. Of course, there were volunteers such as the board members, but as was revealed in the civil suits, they were compensated with perks and other benefits-in-kind.[64]

The NKF was run very much as a professional profit-based organization with the exception that it solicited for donations. The Minister of Health remarked that while this was contrary to the workings of a traditional charity, "there is nothing wrong with a large charity outfit run by professionals instead of volunteers, provided that it is properly governed and managed."[65] He did indicate, however, that a diversity of models would be good for the charity landscape.

The New NKF, however, has returned to the traditional charity model. It recognizes the importance of engagement with the community, and one way is through volunteers. Thus, the New NKF has initiated volunteer programs, such as the NKF Circle of Hearts, to provide befrienders to the kidney patients and to enrich their lives. In its commitment to volunteerism, it has also introduced a Staff Volunteer Program so that its employees can walk the talk.

Beyond volunteers, the New NKF has also sought to reach out to the broader community through an "open-door" policy, collaborating with grassroots organizations to organize "open house" events and public education campaigns.

15. Social Entrepreneurship

A social entrepreneur is one who effects systemic, large scale social change through innovative approaches. Unlike business entrepreneurs who work to enrich themselves, social entrepreneurs labor for the betterment of others and the fulfillment of changing the world.

Was Durai a social entrepreneur? I get mixed reactions when I broached this topic.

Durai received praises from many, before and immediately after, the saga, for his numerous achievements in building up the NKF.[66] As one writer puts it, "I see Mr. Durai as, first and foremost, an entrepreneur. He is a man of vision.... He transformed the NKF into a cutting-edge charity organization."[67] Even Susan Long in her allegedly defamatory article called the NKF such "a trail-blazing model of social entrepreneurship that American universities like Harvard, Johns Hopkins and the Massachusetts Institute of Technology have done case studies on it."

However, critics say that running a large and professional organization does not equate to social entrepreneurship. There must be innovation, impact and heart.

Certainly, the NKF was innovative in its fundraising approaches. For example, it pioneered the use of SMS (cellphone text messages) appeals with tele-polling for its television charity appeals. This proved extremely successful and helped achieved new records of calls and donations. What is significant is that there was noticeably less innovation in the provision of healthcare services to its patients, although the facilities and equipment provided were modern and often state-of-the-art.

From an impact standpoint, the NKF certainly had scale on its side when it came to offering kidney dialysis. It treated more than half of the population with kidney disorders. However, the New NKF board was able to, in a short period of time, substantially increase even these already impressive statistics—more patients, more focus on alternative and better treatments beyond hemodialysis and greater outreach to community. All of this was achieved at significantly reduced expense, with cost savings being passed back to patients.

On balance, few people today would regard Durai as a social entrepreneur. It is not for want of making short shrift of his achievements. It is because in doing so, we would be holding Durai out as a role model of a social savior, and he has been far from exemplary as one. With the revelations in the court cases, it is increasingly difficult for many to maintain he acted with the right motivations of selflessly serving the community. He may have started out doing so, but unfortunately, he lost the plot along the way.

17. The Rich/Poor Divide

In this paradigm, the gravitational forces favoring the better-off over those who are not continue to exert their pull in the nonprofit world. This is notwithstanding that the role of charity is to bridge the gap between the poor and rich.

The NKF was first established at a time when thousands of Singaporeans were dying of kidney failure, many of them unable to pay for the "exorbitant" cost of dialysis.[68] Through the years, the NKF went about fulfilling its mission primarily through dialysis care. By 1997, it had 900 patients. But there were rumblings among private kidney specialists that the NKF was "diluting its mission of helping the poor by taking in those who could afford to pay as well." It was also accused of being discriminatory towards the older and more sickly patients. Hence, KDF emerged to fill the gap of providing for poor and needy patients.[69]

The New NKF board is moving the organization back to a focus on the poor and needy. Within two years, it brought dialysis rates down by 35 percent to below KDF's levels. It capped full-paying patients at 10 percent, and increased the subsidy for needy kidney patients.[70] It is also seeking to ensure a more holistic care with social and community support for their needs beyond dialysis.[71]

In this paradigm, a key reason for the continuing disparity between rich and poor lies in the definition of charity. Over the years, the legal definition of charity has morphed from being about the alleviation of poverty to a range of causes that are generally about the community good. Interestingly, when NCSS refused to renew the NKF's IPC status in 2001, it suggested that the NKF apply to the Ministry of Health because the NKF's services were "more health-related than welfare-related." NCSS being the outreach arm for the poor and disadvantaged of society would, in the eyes of many, be truly what charity is about. On the other hand, some would argue that healthcare, while important to the community, should be provided by the government, and therefore should not be subsidized by charity dollars. If healthcare had not been a charitable cause, the NKF might have continued to be policed by NCSS, and the outcome may well have been different.

18. *Nonprofit Qwerties*

Two of the nonprofit qwerties covered are fundraising efficiency and financial ratios.

In Singapore, fundraising efficiency is achieved through the 30/70 Fundraising Rule: the cost of fundraising should not exceed 30 percent of the funds raised. I highlighted two major disadvantages of the fundraising efficiency rule: (1) lack of accounting clarity allows charities to game the ratio and (2) the ratio is not very meaningful by itself. Both of these came to the fore with the NKF.

According to the KPMG Report, in order to comply with the 30/70 rule, the NKF did not just game the system, it repeatedly manipulated the accounts so that its fundraising events that would otherwise have exceeded the 30 percent limit, would come in just under the limit. This result was achieved by a number of ways, including recording unrelated sponsorship or rebates as donation income which increases the denominator, and reversing expenditure from fundraising projects into other projects, which reduces the numerator.

Even if the numbers provided by the NKF were correct, the fundraising costs, which may have complied with the 30/70 rule, would, in my view, still have been far too high. In fundraising, as in most other business activities, there must be economies of scale. If it takes $30,000 to raise $100,000, it may not necessarily need to take $3 million to raise $10 million.

The NKF raised S$68 million (US$47 million) in 2003, the highest in public fundraising in Singapore that year. At least a third of the money raised would have been contributed by Lifedrops,[72] a program of recurring donations which should have been gathered at minimal cost. However, NKF sought to manage its fundraising expense in such a way that they came in at just below the radar screen of 30 percent. In contrast, the Community Chest, which raises a large but smaller amount of S$45 to 50 million (US$31 to 35 million) a year, has a fundraising efficiency of two to four percent.[73]

Thus, the NKF had scale but not the economies of scale. That is the fundamental flaw of the 30/70 Fundraising Rule: it makes a 30-percent fundraising expenses acceptable, no matter the type of fundraising methods and the size of funds raised. Rather, the right approach is for there to be full and proper disclosure of funds raised and methods used. The informed donor can then decide what makes sense for him.

With regards to the qwerty on financial ratios, the point is that broad-based benchmarking is not useful in the charity sector. Rather, ratios should be judiciously applied. One of the key financial ratios that many observers look at is the program ratio. Also known as charitable expense ratio, this is computed by dividing expenses spent on the charity's programs by the total expenses.

KPMG's report highlighted that only 10 cents out of every charity dollar received by the NKF actually went towards the direct treatment costs of the patients. That sounds extremely low. However, on closer examination, 41 cents of every dollar went into reserves. Now, reserves are presumably for future use of patients and so forth. So in fairness to the NKF, really we should say that 17 percent (10 cents out of 59 cents) of its operating expenditure was for patients, the remaining were for non-charitable purposes such as fundraising, public relations and overheads.

Unfortunately, this is still a very poor use of funds. According to the American Institute of Philanthropy, at least 60 percent of total expenditure should be spent on charitable programs.[74] The BBB Wise Giving Alliance sets a higher benchmark of at least 65 percent.[75] The New NKF says it is targeting for more than 70 percent of total expenses to be spent on dialysis patients.[76]

The watchdog benchmarks set the lowest general limit. The right comparison would be against a comparable charity. KDF's program ratio for 2006 would be 47 percent if government subsidies were netted against its expense, or 74 percent if government subsidies were included in its income line.[77] In both instances, the KDF fared much better than the NKF despite the former not having the economies of scale of the latter.

Thus, the program ratio, in this instance, properly benchmarked, does provide some sense of how well the charity is doing. In NKF's case, its usage of funds for non-charitable purposes was way off. Based on the subsequent court revelations, it became clear that the NKF's excesses were not just limited to the luxurious bathroom fittings of the CEO, but also on a high-end executive lifestyle and high wages. If the program ratio for NKF was analyzed earlier, it might have avoided the situation deteriorating as much as it did.

Endnotes:

1   The defamation suits are summarized in Table 19.1 Stories from *The Straits Times* (unless otherwise indicated) regarding these three cases are as follows: (1) Archie Ong, Sharon Vasoo, "NKF chief, 5 members suing ex-volunteer for slander," August 13, 1997; Geraldine Yeo, "Sorry what I said about NKF is untrue," April 15, 1998; Esther Au Yong, "I forgive Durai, Sad that I lost a friend," *The New Paper*, December 23, 2005; (2) Piragasam Singaravelu: "NKF chief gets public apology," December 11, 1998; Arlina

Arshad, "Accused of libel in 1998, he's happy skeletons are out," July 14, 2005; (3) Tan Kiat Noi: Samantha Santa Maria, "NKF acts against e-defamation," May 5, 1999; "NKF action is to reinforce transparency," May 13, 1999; Samantha Santa Maria, "Smear on the Net: NKF to let matter rest," May 22, 1999.

2   The subsequent revelations of the NKF from the various court proceedings and the KPMG report showed that allegations such as flying first class and high bonuses were true.

3   Conrad Raj, "Mr. NKF, the court-happy combatant," *The New Paper*, July 13, 2005.

4   When *The Straits Times* first broke the story, the nature of the Aviva-NKF tie up which was worth S$5 million was unclear as the parties were in negotiations. A key controversy was over whether NKF's patient data should or would be made available to a commercial entity; when the deal was finalized, the data was not made available. The stories were mainly covered by Lorna Tan of *The Straits Times* and some of them were: "Aviva to tap NKF for referrals," April 2, 2004; "NKF S$5m tie-up with Aviva: Creative move or invasion of privacy?" April 3, 2004; "Business and charity don't mix, even for $5m," April 6, 2004; "It's a dangerous' precedent, says Case of NKF-Aviva deal," April 7, 2004.

5   Theresa Tan of *The Straits Times* picked up the NKF's reserves level from my article, "The missing hand of Adam Smith," *SALT*, March–April 2004 and featured it. Some of the stories on NKF's reserves in *The Straits Times*, many of them covered by Theresa Tan included: "NKF's reserve of $189m sparks debate," April 7, 2004; "Tell us how it's being spent, NKF," April 8, 2004; "Big NKF reserves OK, says Minister," April 10, 2004; "MPs seek answers on fund-raising issues," April 14, 2004; "Govt prefers a light touch for charities," April 20, 2004; "More transparency please: NMP," April 20, 2004.

6   When the saga occurred and to the time of publication of this book, I am a director of SPH. However, the views expressed in this chapter which are not specifically attributed to any party, are my own and do not represent the views of SPH or other organizations. The materials that are used and referred to in this chapter are based largely on publicly available information.

7   Susan Long, "The NKF: Controversially ahead of its time?" *The Straits Times*, April 19, 2004. NKF filed the lawsuit four days after the publication of the article. An overview of the lawsuit is provided in the article: Siva Arasu, "How NKF vs. SPH became The People vs. T.T. Durai," *The Sunday Times*, July 17, 2005.

8   "Why Durai killed offer to settle with SPH," *The Straits Times*, January 10, 2007.

9   Michelle Quah, "Durai withdraws suit against SPH," *The Business Times*, July 13, 2005.

10   Gerard Ee was then Chairman of National Council of Social Service, the umbrella body for social service organizations in Singapore, among his several other appointments in the charity sector. He had also just retired as a public accountant from Ernst & Young.

11   Professor Goh Chee Leok, former head of the National Skin Center was brought in as the interim CEO. In May 2006, the board appointed Eunice Tay, former chief operating officer of the National Neuroscience Institute, as the CEO of NKF.

12   These are Financial Reporting Standards and Recommended Accounting Practices for Charities—RAP6.

13 *A Report on the National Kidney Foundation, Commissioned by the Board of Directors, the National Kidney Foundation* (KPMG, December 16, 2005). The report was publicly released by The NKF on December 19, 2005.

14 Bertha Henson, "NKF saga: Durai, four others charged," *The Straits Times*, April 19, 2006; Chong Chee Kin, "Durai given 3-month jail term," *The Straits Times*, June 22, 2007; Selina Lum, "Ex-NKF chief Durai will go to jail," *The Straits Times*, May 30, 2008.

15 Chong Chee Kin, "Two ex-NKF directors fined $5,000 each for failing in their duties," *The Straits Times*, May 17, 2007.

16 Michelle Quah, "NKF seeks $12m from Durai and four others," *The Business Times*, April 26, 2006.

17 Michelle Quah, "Durai throws in towel, admits liability," *The Business Times*, January 11, 2007; Selina Lum, "Durai to repay NKF $4m over 4 years," *The Straits Times*, June 22, 2007.

18 Bertha Henson, "NKF suit: Ex-directors give in," *The Straits Times*, February 9, 2007; Michelle Quah, "Former NKF directors Chua, Loo and Yong declared bankrupt," *The Business Times*, May 17, 2007.

19 Michelle Quah, "Richard Yong's flight from law ends in Hong Kong," *The Business Times*, July 5, 2007; Elena Chong, "Ex-NKF chairman Yong jailed 15 months," *The Straits Times*, September 19, 2007.

20 *Interim Report by the Inter-Ministry Committee on Regulation of Charities and Institutions of a Public Character* (IMC on Regulation of Charities and IPCs, January 27, 2006).

21 "Move towards more transparency. New rules for charity," *The Straits Times*, June 26, 2006.

22 See Chapter 20, "Doing good better" for description of the S-curve of change and the inflexion point of the change curve.

23 The comparison of the NKF and the KDF is provided in Chapter 1, "The missing hand of Adam Smith."

24 Examples of some of these criticisms are in: Aaron Low, "Unethical to make patients appear in fundraiser," *The Straits Times*, July 22, 2005.

25 In 2005, the top prize in 2005 was a car and condominium worth S$750,000 (US$517,000).

26 "The NKF responds," *The Straits Times*, April 9, 2004; Lee Hui Chieh, "NKF plans to woo back 50,000 donors," *The Straits Times*, December 9, 2005; Susan Long, "The NKF: Controversially ahead of its time?" *The Straits Times*, April 19, 2004.

27 Yap Su Yin, "Supporters helping new NKF get back on its feet," *The Straits Times*, August 1, 2006. Before the saga, Lifedrops donations amounted to S$2.14 million a month, which works out to S$25.68 million (US$17.71 million) a year.

28 Allison Lum, "Kidney war of words—the nub of the issue," *The Straits Times*, May 11, 1997.

29 The charge of S$130 is effective from July 2007. According to the New NKF, more than 50 percent of its patients actually end up paying only S$0 to S$50 because of various other subsidies for the patients.

30 Yap Su-Yin & Theresa Tan, "Survey: Public trust in charities hit by NKF scandal," *The Straits Times*, July 14, 2006. The surveys were done by the National Volunteer & Philanthropy Center.

31 Ibid; Kevin Lee, "$340m came only from individuals," ST Forum Page, *The Straits Times*, July 26, 2006; Theresa Tan & Yap Su-Yin, "Surprise! Charities drew record $644m last year," *The Straits Times*, June 8, 2006.

32 Chong Chee Kin & Khushwant Singh, "NKF suit now involves entire former board," *The Straits Times*, June 20, 2006; Selina Lum & Chong Chee Kin, "NKF suit ends as Yong, Loo drop third party claims," *The Straits Times*, February 14, 2007.

33 Selina Lum, "Landmark $12m NKF suit set to begin," *The Straits Times*, January 8, 2007.

34 Lee Su Shyan, "PwC rapped for not spotting lapses," *The Straits Times*, December 22, 2005.

35 Theresa Tan & Yap Su-Yin, "Accounting firms seen as reluctant to audit charities," *The Straits Times*, June 26, 2006. Prior to the scandal, the regulator of public accountants (the Accounting & Corporate Regulatory Authority) had introduced a new regime whereby audit firms that audit "public interest entities" such as charities are subjected to closer scrutiny. That move caused some reluctance on the part of the audit firms to take on charities, and the NKF case sealed the reluctance.

36 "Statement by Health Minister Khaw Boon Wan on KPMG's report on the National Kidney Foundation", Ministry of Health, December 21, 2005.

37 "T.T. Durai: I have done nothing wrong," *The Straits Times*, July 13, 2005.

38 Theresa Tan, "NCSS warned NKF and raised alarm back in 2001," *The Straits Times*, December 22, 2005; Willie Cheng, "Beyond the headlines," *SALT* May/June 2004.

39 Alex Au, "Singapore's spleen over kidney scandal," *Asia Times Online*, January 5, 2006, www.atimes.com/atimes/Southeast_Asia/HA05Ae01.html; Li Xueying, "Minister says he's a donor and will still give," *The Straits Times*, April 11, 2004.

40 Yap Su-Yin & Theresa Tan, "Public trust in charities hit by NKF scandal," *The Straits Times*, July 14, 2006. The survey by NVPC took place shortly after the NKF saga.

41 Chua Mui Hoong, "Who watches the regulators?" *The Straits Times*, December 28, 2005.

42 Zuraidah Ibrahim, Li Xueying, "A very smooth transition and quite a good year. Interview with PM Lee," *The Straits Times*, September 18, 2005.

43 Bertha Henson, "More duties and powers proposed for regulator of charities," *The Straits Times*, January 28, 2006.

44 The official name of the fund had been the "NKF Cancer Fund," although it has sometimes been called the "NKF Children Cancer Fund."

45 "Press Release: NKF hands over the NKF Cancer Fund to the Singapore Cancer Society," The New NKF, November 16, 2005.

46 "Press Release: NKF hands over Children's Medical Fund to the Singapore Children's Society," The New NKF, November 29, 2006.

47 Wong Wei Kong, "Durai concedes NKF view of reserves misleading," *The Business Times*, July 13, 2005.

48 "Press Release: NKF Interim Board's position on reserves and the urgent need to resume fund-raising," The New NKF, December 8, 2005.

49 "Press Release: KPMG's report on investigation into the National Kidney Foundation (NKF)," The New NKF, December 9, 2005.

50 Cheong Wing Lee, "Be more realistic in assessing NKF reserves," ST Forum Page, *The Straits Times*, December 15, 2005.

51 Theresa Tan & Tracy Sua, "Slew of changes at NKF, 92 staff laid off," *The Straits Times*, September 17, 2006.

52 Arti Mulchand, "Fund-raising staff got more perks," *The Straits Times*, December 21, 2005.

53 Arti Mulchand, "Durai's $25K monthly salary 'not excessive', " *The Straits Times*, February 2, 2007; "Mrs. Goh: I've full trust in NKF and its CEO," *The Straits Times*, July 13, 2005; "Charity still saving lives and still needs support," *The Straits Times*, July 18, 2005.

54 Selina Lum, "Durai's got a new job—and it pays $25k a month," *The Straits Times*, September 8, 2007. The job was to start a firm in the United Arab Emirates offering health care and human resource services in the Middle East.

55 See Chapter 7, "Heart Work, Less Pay," and survey result in Mark Hrywna, "Special Report: NPT Salary Survey 2007," *The Nonprofit Times*, February 1, 2007.

56 Based on survey data published by NCVO and Remuneration Economics in: "The 19th Annual Voluntary Sector Salary Survey," *Inside Research*, December 2007.

57 "'Besieged' over NKF issue," *The Straits Times*, July 21, 2005.

58 Radha Basu, "Ordinary folks lead the way when it comes to charity," *The Straits Times*, May 11, 2007. According to the report, 200,000 donors contribute to a quarter of the S$47 million raised for SHARE. This works out to S$4.90 per month.

59 Michelle Quah, "NKF has reserves to last only 6.7 years," *The Straits Times*, December 9, 2005. Based on NKF's then reported S$1.7m per month from 248,532 donors, it comes to $6.84 cents a month.

60 Siti Andrianie, "Woman who died of cancer leaves $700,000 flat to NKF," *The Straits Times*, September 25, 1997.

61 Andre Yeo, "Her giant hongbao: She donates her flat to NKF, $1.4 million pledged," *The New Paper*, January 25, 2001; Cheong Suk-Wai, "Another donor pledges flat to NKF," *The Straits Times*, May 19, 2001.

62 Wendy Tan, "She leaves—$3.4m to charity, $32,100 to children," *The Straits Times*, January 23, 2003.

63 David Miller, "More bequeath money to charity," *The Straits Times*, August 29, 1997.

64 "Durai and friends travelled in luxury, 'on NKF money'," *The Straits Times*, January 10, 2007.

65   "Ministerial Statement in Parliament on the National Kidney Foundation, by Minister for Health, Mr. Khaw Boon Wan," Ministry of Health, July 20, 2005.

66   Natalie Soh, "When praise flowed for the charity," *The Straits Times*, December 22, 2005.

67   Chua Lee Hoong, "Don't tar all charities with NKF brush," *The Straits Times*, July 14, 2005.

68   "History of the NKF" on NKF website: www.nkfs.org/index.php?option=com_content&task=view&id=86&Itemid=83.

69   See Section on "1. The nonprofit marketplace," and Allison Lum, "Kidney war of words—the nub of the issue," *The Straits Times*, May 11, 1997.

70   *The New NKF, Annual Report, January 1. 2006 to June 30, 2007.*

71   Radha Basu, "The NKF's new mantra: Care beyond dialysis," *The Straits Times*, January 18, 2008.

72   Yap Su Yin, "Supporters helping new NKF get back on its feet," *The Straits Times*, August 1, 2006. Before the saga, Lifedrops donations amounted to S$2.14 million a month, which works out to S$25.68 million (US$17.71 million) a year. Lifedrops of US$25.68 million is 37.7 percent of total donations of S$68million (US$47million) (from the financial year 2003 figure as provided in the NKF SPH court case).

73   See NCSS financial disclosure for 2004–2007 at http://www.ncss.org.sg/documents/financial_disclosure.pdf.

74   www.charitywatch.org/criteria.html

75   www.give.org/standards//newcbbbstds.asp

76   "Press Release: KPMG's report on investigation into the National Kidney Foundation," The New NKF, December 19, 2005.

77   *Kidney Dialysis Foundation Annual Report 2006/07.*

Chapter 20

The Charity Ecosystem

Doing Good Better

Cultural and structural issues have led the charity world to be less effective than what we might be used to in the commercial world. But the winds of change are blowing.

The nonprofit sector is gradually and surely moving from an era of simply "Just Doing Good" to one of "Doing Good Well."

This new era requires the various components of an effective and self sustaining charity ecosystem—the regulator, capacity builders, charities, beneficiaries and the community (individuals, corporations, media and government)—to be in place and to function properly.

The previous chapters have covered paradigms on specific aspects of nonprofit reality. As I struggled with how to make sense of each of these specific areas, I also wondered if this complex process of understanding and influencing change in the charity world could be assisted with the development of a macro, all-encompassing framework.

Drawing upon my systems background, I thought about how we often look at the ecosystems of industry clusters in the corporate world. So, perhaps defining and working towards a full-functioning charity ecosystem may provide a possible answer.

The Charity Ecosystem

The term "ecosystem," which originates from biology, refers to a self-sustaining community of organisms. For our purposes, an ecosystem can be defined as a system through which members benefit from one another's participation via symbiotic relationships.

Just as systems can comprise sub-systems, an ecosystem can comprise sub-ecosystems which interact with, and benefit, one another. Thus, the ecosystem of a country comprises three sub-ecosystems: the enterprise ecosystem (the private sector), the state ecosystem (the public sector) and the charity/civil society ecosystem (the people sector).

The beauty of the ecosystem paradigm is the way it applies systems thinking to a complex environment. Biological ecosystems comprise interdependent organisms that interact, sometimes in deadly competition, with one another and the environment to create a self-sustaining community. Non-biological ecosystems, such as the charity ecosystem, may not necessarily function well or self-adjust unless the relationships and interactions of the component parts are designed for, and they work towards, that end.

By taking an ecosystem approach to the charity sector, we can obtain a holistic and integrated perspective of how the different players can and should interact with each other to create a more effective charity sector.

A framework of what the charity ecosystem and its players could look like is shown in Figure 20.1.

There are five main components of the charity ecosystem: Beneficiaries, Charities, Capacity Builders, the Regulator and the Community. Each has an important role to play in order to create and sustain the necessary balance within the system.

Beneficiaries

Beneficiaries are the most important component. They are the *raison d'être* for charities and other stakeholders, yet we often lose sight of this vital group because they have the least voice.

Figure 20.1 The Charity Ecosystem

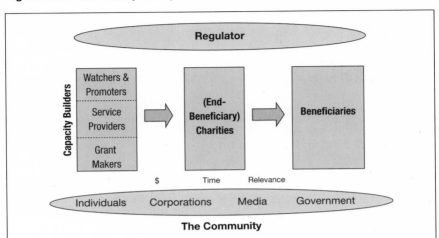

The key question is: who should be beneficiaries? Integral to the answer is the definition of a "charity."[1] There is a surprising disconnect between what different people see as constituting a charity and its beneficiaries.

If you ask the man in the street, the common response you will get is that charity is simply about helping the poor and the needy. Implicit in this answer is the notion that charity is about redressing the gap between the rich and poor.

However, as we have seen, the legal definition of charity is much broader than that. While different jurisdictions define "charity" slightly differently, by and large, there are common elements in the definition. The scope of what legally constitutes charity would extend beyond the poor and the disadvantaged to cover the general community good—sports, arts, the environment, heritage and even animals.

While there may be nothing wrong with this broadened definition in itself, there are two important implications.

First, with the same support mechanisms, such as tax breaks, community mobilization, being made available generally for the community good, we lose that preferential option for the poor.

Secondly, the level of accountability for charitable projects is different when it comes to non-charitable projects. Charity is very much about generosity and so, the process of cost-benefit analysis that should be performed for many community projects will likely not be as rigorous as that for government or commercially funded projects.

Charities

The charity ecosystem has two main types of charitable organizations—end-beneficiary charities and capacity builders. End-beneficiary charities, or often simply known as charities, are what most people commonly understand charities to be: they serve beneficiaries. Capacity builders, on the other hand, support the (end-beneficiary) charities.

A charity is set up for a social cause. However, its real role often gets lost as corporate thinking and empire building take hold of those running it.

In business, the mantra is growth and more growth in profits and revenues. The moment growth declines, shareholders get worried and share prices tumble. This triggers an exploration of mergers and acquisitions to either inorganically grow the company or else find a way for it to be part of some other corporation's growth plans.

But this mentality should not be taken into the charity world. Charities exist not to make a profit, but to further social causes. So, the success of a charity must be judged by whether or not that cause has been fulfilled. And when it is, the organization would no longer be needed. So the end-game for charities must be their eventual extinction, rather than growth.[2]

Yet, when the purpose for which a nonprofit organization is founded becomes less relevant, it may not naturally seek to scale down. Instead, the organization explores other ways to scale up—much like in the commercial world.

Related to the issue of fulfilling mission is the question of services versus advocacy. There are two ways to deal with a social issue: we can deal with the symptoms, or we can deal with the root causes.

To illustrate, there are two approaches to dealing with the abuse of low-income foreign workers such as maids and construction workers in Singapore. The first is to help those who are abused. To this end, several organizations such as Humanitarian Organization for Migrant Economics and the Archdiocesan Commission for the Pastoral Care of Migrants and Itinerant People[3] have set up shelters and counseling services for the abused foreign workers.

The second is to nip the problem in the bud and avoid having to deal with cases of abuse in the first place. This requires education of employers on the fair treatment of their employees and the creation of the legal structures and framework that deter and punish offenders. Transient

Workers Count Too (TWC2)[4] has taken the lead to champion this approach.

The measure of success for the charity sector in dealing with this issue must lie in the reduction of abuse cases and a decline in the need to build any more shelters for abused workers. Thus, I would consider the advocacy role played by TWC2 to be more critical in the long term.

But advocacy is less appealing to charities than providing a service. There are several reasons for this. First, the results are less tangible and visible. It is easier (even though it is still a challenge) to announce an increase in the number of abused worker cases treated, than it is to describe a campaign for worker rights and fair treatment.

Moreover, the process of advocacy can be difficult. It involves changing mindsets, policies and rules which are not only challenging, but which can often be controversial.

What's more, the road can be long and winding. William Wilberforce, the British politician, campaigned for 46 years against slavery before the Slavery Abolition Act was passed in England in 1833.[5]

Add all these factors together, getting support and funding to deal directly with the visible symptoms of a problem is usually easier than getting money to campaign for a change in policies and mindsets to remove the problem. Despite the lesser sums needed compared to the other more service-oriented charities, one of TWC2's challenges has continually been finding enough money to do its work.[6]

It is therefore not a surprise that, by and large, most charities are service providers that prefer dealing with symptoms rather than necessarily understanding and redressing the root causes.

Capacity Builders

Capacity builders, as the name suggests, are intermediaries that help build the capacity of the charity sector.

The role and need for intermediaries is generally not very well appreciated. The fact is that all ecosystems need intermediaries to facilitate the core activities and oil the wheels of the marketplace. A good parallel for intermediaries in the charity sector is the public commercial market.

In this analogy, charities are like public listed companies. They need funds from their investors—the donors. However, for donors to know who to invest their limited funds in, they require independent analysts to evaluate and rate the charities. Instead of donating directly, they could actually do so through grantmakers, the equivalent of fund managers in the public markets. Just as the commercial companies service one another, there are charities that service other charities.

There is a range of intermediary organizations in the charity sector and I have grouped them into three categories: grantmakers, service providers, and promoters and watchers.

Grantmakers comprise foundations (for example, The Rockefeller Foundation) and funds (for example, Community Chest, United Way). They take money from donors, big and small, and give them out as grants to the charities. They should do so through a rigorous process that ensures the money is given for the right use and is properly used to achieve the desired result.

Grantmakers play a crucial role in that they are the best positioned to bridge the disconnect between revenue and expenditure in the charity sector.[7] They can ensure the alignment of funds received and the value delivered to the beneficiaries.

Meanwhile, service providers assist charities in areas such as strategic advice (Bridgespan), training (Social Service Training Institute), professional development (Compass Point), human capital matching (Bridgestar, BoardnetUSA), brokering (Charity Choice Goodwill Gallery, Ammado) and technical services (Hackers for Charity).[8]

One issue with charity service providers is that there are very few of them, especially outside of the developed countries. This stems from the lack of maturity within our ecosystem to develop this type of service, and a general lack of recognition that they are an important part of the infrastructural needs of any ecosystem.

In fact, many people do not regard service providers as charities. This view has been further clouded by the many regular commercial service providers who provide their services to charities at discounted rates. For example, Computer Troubleshooters is the world's largest computer service franchise. It also has a Charity Service Program that provides discounted or donated computer services to charities.[9] The end result is that the charity service providers are not always differentiated.

The good news is that, increasingly, more foundations are willing to fund and even set up such charity service providers.

The third group within the capacity builders is the industry watchers and the promoters. They usually sprout up from within the sector to help govern and grow the sector.

Promoters seek to grow and develop the sector or a specific segment within the sector. For example, the National Council for Voluntary

Organizations[10] is a British independent body with 5,700 organizational members that represents more than half the voluntary sector workforce. Its mission is to provide the voice and support for a vibrant voluntary and community sector in the U.K. The Institute for Philanthropy,[11] on the other hand, focuses on the supply side to increase effective philanthropy in the U.K. and internationally.

Watchers facilitate informed giving.[12] Like Standards and Poor in the commercial world, they are the rating agencies and analysts that monitor, evaluate and rate charities so that grantmakers and donors have benchmarks by which they can make informed decisions. In the U.S., there are several organizations that fill this gap. They include GuideStar (which also has a presence in the U.K.), Charity Navigator, the Better Business Bureau Wise Giving Alliance and the American Institute of Philanthropy's Charity Watch.[13]

Regulator

At the very top of the charity ecosystem is the regulator such as the Charity Commission for England and Wales. Regulations and rules are necessary to ensure that charities operate for the public benefit and not private advantage. The regulator ensures compliance by charities within a legal framework so that public trust and confidence in charities are achieved.

Regulators often come under pressure from charities to lighten up and allow them to focus on their mission with minimal administrative and other constraints. But when things go wrong, the regulator will likely be criticized by the public for any perceived lack of preemptive action.

Fundamentally, the regulator should be clear as to which approach it wishes to adopt in fulfilling its role:

- A black box approach, where the regulator vets charities to the nth level; or
- A glass house approach, where the regulator supervises with a light touch and donors have to take a *caveat emptor* (buyer/donor beware) approach to dealing with charities.[14]

The main difference between the two approaches lies in the nature of the regulations, and the powers and resources that need to be given to the regulator. A black box approach would be somewhat akin to the banking system where a lot of detailed rules exist, frequent inspections are undertaken and the regulator needs a significant level of resources to conduct its work. A glass house approach is more akin to a stock exchange where the regulations are primarily focused on disclosures to the public who invest at their own risk.

The Community

The community provides the underlying support for charities by supplying three things: money (donations), time (volunteers), and legitimacy. The third is seldom thought of, but some charities have learned the hard way that relevance to the community is critical to their survival.

Within the community, there are several distinct groups: the public, corporations, media and government.

Historically, the role of the public has been to give money, give time to help out at the charities and provide general support. In recent years, donors and volunteers have been asked to do more. There has been a call for them to be more discerning, discriminating and even demanding of the charities, in other words, to be more informed in their giving.

The underlying notion is that the public represents the ultimate level of governance for charities. Except for extreme situations such as the National Kidney Foundation,[15] this call is not very practical for the average giver. The reaction would likely be: "You mean if I am generous enough to give $1,000 or a few hours a month to a charity, I now have to do all this additional due diligence work to figure out what, why, how the charity is doing before I give?" As previously noted, the long-term solution to better informed giving is to encourage donors to direct their donations to grantmakers who are organized professionally with the resources, rigor and clout to ensure accountability.[16]

That is what many neo-philanthropists are now doing in what is being seen as a philanthropic revolution. They are setting up grantmaking organizations with mega-bucks that are not just pushing accountability, but finding new and innovative ways to accomplish their ambitions to solve some of the world's social problems. Their approaches have moved from the check-signing and ribbon-cutting exercises of the past to a more personal engagement with the charities, using capitalistic approaches such as venture philanthropy.[17]

The second group within the community is the corporations. While their role is similar to that of individuals, their motivation is different.

Corporations face the perpetual question of whether or not they should be a corporate giver.

Because the constitution of a corporation drives it to generate profits and value for its shareholders, the basis of its response to the giving question is really a very selfish one—does corporate social responsibility make business sense? This is why many concerned government agencies and nonprofit watchdogs advocate mandatory corporate social responsibility, especially in the areas of environmental control, ethical conduct and corporate governance.[18]

The third group is the media. Its role is similar to the one it has in the commercial and public sector space—keeping the public informed and shaping public opinion for the benefit of the charity sector. That said, there is a question among many as to whether the media should or should not be a watchdog, or even a bloodhound with regards to wrongdoings by charities.[19]

Government

Government is a unique player in the ecosystem. It has multiple roles: regulator (as we have already seen), funder, promoter and even provider.

How each government actually discharges these roles depends heavily on its history and attitudes towards the nonprofit organizations. The dilemma for governments is that the nonprofit sector is really about filling up the social gaps left behind by governments and private enterprises. For private enterprises, it is understandable that, in their pursuit of profits, they may legitimately ignore the community interests and create unintended social inequalities.

Governments, however, are meant to look after the overall interests of their citizens, and thus, may be loath to admit that they have failed in some areas. The reality is that no government can cover every ground, so more enlightened legislatures seek out and support nonprofit organizations which, with their smaller scale and close connections to the community, are able to more nimbly mobilize resources and solve social issues.

When it comes to supporting the nonprofit sector, there is a spectrum of government responses. On one end are developed countries like the U.K. and the U.S. where, historically, there has been a focus on a smaller role of the state and a larger reliance on private charitable activities. On the other hand, there are the former communist states in Eastern and Central

Europe, which traditionally have relied on the state for the provision of social services and inherited a culture of low tolerance for dissent.

Notwithstanding the kind of support it gives the charity sector, it is not unusual for a government to want to steer it. Thus, even in liberal U.K. where government actively supports the sector, a 2007 survey of charity executives indicated that 54 percent felt that the government was exerting too much control over the sector.[20]

One way in which governments seek to steer the sector is through funding. The Johns Hopkins project estimates that about 35 percent of the nonprofit organizations' revenue in its surveyed countries comes from the government through grants, contracts or reimbursement payments of governmental agencies.[21] Government funding tends to be highest in the social service and health care segments.

Governments can also promote and support the growth of nonprofits through their policies and initiatives. A common policy mechanism by which governments support charity is through tax benefits, for example, double tax deductions for donors in Singapore or Gift Aid for charities in the U.K.[22] ChangeUp[23] is a good example of a wide-ranging initiative by an enlightened British government that seeks to proactively improve the sustainability, quality and reach of the infrastructure of the voluntary and community sector.

The last role, government as provider, is often debated in charity circles. The question is which services should be provided by the government and which by the charities? The boundaries are not always clear, especially in the education and healthcare sectors. For example, should schools for children with disabilities be run by volunteer welfare organizations or by the government as the mainstream schools are? For healthcare, should step-down care and after-care for illnesses, such as kidney dialysis, be provided by the community or by government?

The area gets greyer when the government sets up and sustains charities and capacity builders that might otherwise have been privately led. For example, the National Council of Social Service, the umbrella body for voluntary welfare organizations in Singapore, is a government body. Its counterpart in the U.K., the National Council for Voluntary Organizations is an independent community organization.[24] Similarly, the National Volunteer & Philanthropy Center in Singapore is a government body which promotes volunteerism and philanthropic giving, while in the U.S., the Hands On Network, which is the largest volunteer organization with 370 affiliates and more than 60 million volunteers, is community-led.[25] Government-sponsored charities can even be set up for advocacy. For example, with the push for more babies in Singapore, the government initiated the setting up of I Love Children, which has the tagline "Advocacy for a Singapore that is children-plenty and children-friendly."[26]

Culture and Change in the Ecosystem

Understanding the players and their roles is only the first step towards influencing change in an ecosystem. A critical aspect is the dynamic interdependence of the various elements. A small change in one part can have a ripple effect throughout the entire system. Cause and effect are sometimes too complex to map out. Thus, while the players influence one another, deliberately doing so to achieve specific outcomes is not easy.

To influence change in any ecosystem, one needs to understand its culture—the set of ideas, beliefs and customs that have evolved over time and that impact the nuances of the behaviors of the participants.

Perhaps the prevailing culture of the charity ecosystem is this notion of "doing good." The basic intent of charity is to do good for beneficiaries and to change the world for the better. Since the focus is on helping others and improving society, good feelings result for all the participants that are in this common mission together.

Contrast this with the commercial world where the culture is that of self-interest—every man for himself. The culture of deadly competition for survival of the fittest is a well-accepted one in this environment.

Competition for survival is actually an essential characteristic of any ecosystem. Yet, most people that I have met in the charity world would dismiss such a notion. After all, we are all here to do good and to work together for the common good.

Yet, the concept of collaboration among competitors for the larger interests is also part of the commercial landscape. Some companies have reached a stage where today's competitor can be tomorrow's ally, and who they choose to partner with or compete against simply changes with time and circumstances.

The notion of competing and allying with peers should therefore also be present in the charity world because it is an integral part of any ecosystem. However, it is understated, masked by the Panadol of doing good. Any notion of competition tends to skim below the surface even if the parties implicitly recognize its existence.[27] Enclosed within the cocoon of doing good and feeling good, corporate practices of good governance and organization effectiveness tend to be eschewed by charity boards and staff because such concepts come from a world with a largely different culture.

In the study of ecosystems, change, it seems, is inevitable. There will be change as the players interdependently interact with each other to reach a stage of equilibrium. Equally, disruptive factors can cause the whole ecosystem to shift towards a new level of equilibrium.

The S-Curve of Change

In the study of change in organizations and systems, the S-curve model of change has sometimes been used. In the initial stage of the change, a few early adopters respond to the change factor, such as a new technology or a new idea. Usually due to some kick factor often a disruptive one, there is an inflexion point where players take it up in sufficient numbers for the change to be empirically noticed and become more prevalent. As critical mass is reached, massive take-up occurs. When most players in the system are on board, the change is at a new equilibrium.

The charity ecosystem around the world seems to be undergoing change. These are driven by similar factors, partly because globalization is importing awareness and influence across borders. The recent S-curve of change in the Singapore charity scene, which I am familiar with, is probably steeper than in many other countries. This wave of change had slowly been making its way to our shores for several years. (See Figure 20.2.)

It started with a rising tide of corporate governance fervor in the commercial world. Many donors, especially foundations and neo-philanthropists, are now applying concepts like governance, accountability and outcomes to the charity world.

For many players, the trigger point has been the emergence of charity scandals.[28] Without a doubt, the National Kidney Foundation saga was the inflexion point of this change curve in Singapore.

The net impact of these scandals and the subsequent responses by all the players, from regulators, donors, media, to the public, has been a sea change in the thinking and mindset of all within and outside the charity sector. We are moving from an era where charity is simply about "Just Doing Good" to one where there are new demands for it to perform and prove that it is "Doing Good Well."

In this brave new world, the greatest onus falls, perhaps, on the charities. Management and boards of charities will now have to take

Figure 20.2 Charity's Tidal Wave of Change

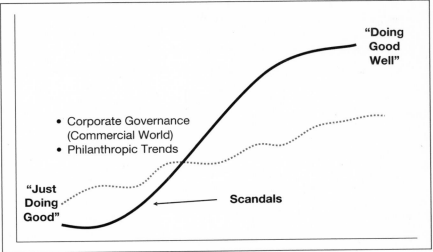

their jobs much more seriously than before. They need to demonstrate good governance. They are expected to be more professional in their work and be driven to deliver outcomes relative to their missions. In their communications and reporting, there will be a demand for greater transparency and accountability.

It is not only the charities themselves, but the entire chain of players within the ecosystem that is impacted by this wave of change.

The regulator is required to be more alert and forthcoming. Certainly, depending on whether it is the black box or glass house model that is adopted, more fortified disclosure and other rules, and investigative resources and powers will need to be rustled up.

The shortcomings of capacity builders need to be urgently addressed. There is currently a significant shortage of capacity builders of all kinds. Both government and grantmakers can help fill the gaps by creating, sponsoring and supporting analysts, watchers and providers.

The community has been much sensitized and engaged with the unraveling of the scandals. The role of the media and community leaders is to moderate the public's response to avoid overreaction and view matters from a balanced perspective. The active support of the community has never been more needed because, after all, it is the community's money, time and confidence that enables the sector to continue to function.

A New Era

The charity ecosystem framework can, therefore, be a useful starting tool for driving change in the charity sector. Only by first understanding and then influencing the role and motivations of the different players in the ecosystem can policy makers and sector leaders seek to level the sector up.

After all, the mission of any charity is to change the world for the better. In this new era of greater demands for accountability and higher performance, the charity sector has to change for the better itself—at the same time as it goes about its mission of changing the rest of the world.

Endnotes

Adapted from: "The Charity Ecosystem," *Social Space* 2008.

1   The subject of the definition of "charity" and its implications is explored in Chapter 17, "For richer or for poorer" and summarized here.

2   The subject of the mission of charities and mission creep is explored in Chapter 5, "End game: extinction."

3   Information on these two organizations can be found at: www.home.org.sg and www.migrants.org.sg. Other organizations include the Good Shepherd Center, Hopeline and Pertapis Home for Women and Girls.

4   www.twc2.org.sg. The book by John Gee and Elaine Ho, *Dignity Overdue* (Select Publishing, 2006), records the story of TWC2's experience in seeking to change attitudes and practices.

5   www.wilberforcecentral.org/wfc

6   Leong Wee Keat, "TWC2 running out of funds," *Today*, April 25, 2008; "A word from John," *TWC2 Newsletter*, July-August 2007, www.twc2.org.sg/site/newsletters/2007-july-aug.html.

7   The disconnect is described in Chapter 1, "The missing hand of Adam Smith." The position of the grantmaker to bridge this disconnect is described in Chapter 2, "The visible hand of the donor."

8   Some of the service providers cover more than the area in which they are cited. Information on the respective service providers can be found at: www.bridgespangroup.org, www.ssti.org.sg, www.compasspoint.org, www.bridgestar.org, www.boardnetusa.org, www.goodwillgallery.co.uk, www.thebp.org.uk, www.ammado.com, and www.hackersforcharity.org. Ammado is actually a recent for-profit enterprise but its goal of being the Facebook of the nonprofit world, globally connecting "nonprofits, socially responsible corporates and engaged individuals" merits mention.

9   www.computertroubleshooters.org

10   www.ncvo-vol.org.uk

11   www.instituteforphilanthropy.org.uk

12   The subject of informed giving is explored in Chapter 2, "The visible hand of the donor."

13   See Chapter 2, "The visible hand of the donor," for a more detailed description of the charity watchers. For Guidestar, go to www.guidestar.org. For Charity Navigator, go to www.charitynavigator.org. For BBB Wise Giving Alliance, go to www.give.org. For American Institute of Philanthropy, go to www.charitywatch.org. There are no equivalents of these industry watchers in Singapore.

14   The two different approaches to regulation are explored in Chapter 4, "Black box or glass house?"

15   Chapter 3, "Who governs a nonprofit, really?" describes the extreme situations, and Chapter 19, "NKF: The saga and its paradigms" further expands on the case of the NKF.

16   The points regarding the public being the ultimate level of governance, the practicality of informed giving by individual donors, and the importance of grantmaking are covered in Chapter 2, "The visible hand of the donor" and Chapter 3, "So who governs a nonprofit, really."

17   The subject of the neo-philanthropists is explored in Chapter 14, "The second philanthropic revolution."

18   The subject of corporate social responsibility is explored in Chapter 8, "Is the business of business just business?"

19   A forum "The NKF Story—News Reporting or Advocacy?" organized by the INSEAD Alumni Association in the aftermath of the NKF saga and held on August 20, 2005 drew divided responses on whether the media should get into, or sustain advocacy work.

20   Chris Greenwood. "The State of the Third Sector 2007," *nfpSynergy*, 2008, www.nfpsynergy.net.

21   Lester M. Salamon, S. Wojciech Sokolowski and Regina List, *Global Civil Society: An Overview* (Center for Civil Society Studies, Institute for Policy Studies, The Johns Hopkins University, 2003).

22   In Singapore, donations to Institutions of a Public Character receive double tax deductions in the donor's tax returns. Gift aid is tax relief on money donated to U.K. charities. See www.hmrc.gov.uk/charities/gift-aid.htm.

23   www.capacitybuilders.org.uk

24   www.ncss.org.sg and www.ncvo-vol.org.uk. NCVO is also described in the section on "Capacity Builders" of this chapter.

25   www.nvpc.org.sg and www.handsonnetwork.org

26   www.ilovechildren.org.sg

27   In the U.K. survey, *The State of the Third Sector 2007* by nfpSynergy (www.nfpsynergy.net), big charities were perceived by executives of small charities to have an overall negative effect on the charity sector.

28   See Chapter 3, "Who governs a nonprofit, really?" for a discussion of scandals causing
charity reforms in various countries. The charity scandals in Singapore include the
National Kidney Foundation, Singapore Association for the Visually Handicapped,
Youth Challenge, St. John's Home for Elderly Persons and Ren Ci Hospital and
Medicare. The NKF saga is covered in greater detail in Chapter 19, "NKF: the saga
and its paradigms."

Index